献给那些四年来因为调查台湾总统蔡英文和伦敦政经学院之间学位诈欺丑闻而遭恐吓、跟监、死亡威胁、刑事起诉、司法迫害、没收护照、通缉和坐牢的勇士们

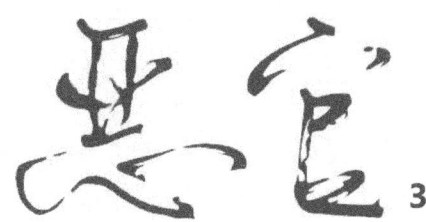

书　　名：恶官 3　Evils III
主　　编：彭文正博士
发 行 人：彭文正
初版一刷发行：2024/3/15
定　　价：USD$35
出　　版：Pegasus International Press
著作权所有・翻印必究
ISBN：978-1-7381418-2-1

捐款赞助
《政经关不了》

1. 台湾观众银行捐款➡
元大银行 806 台北分行
帐号：20032000051114　户名：政经传媒有限公司

----

2. 海外观众 PayPal 捐款➡
https://www.paypal.me/truevot

----

3. 美国：支票邮寄 Weng Jeng Peng,
409 Tennant Station #215,
Morgan Hill, CA 95037

更多捐款资讯

您的支持是我們
一直前進的動力

彭文正

作者介绍

/ 主编

彭文正 博士

台湾大学学士，美国威斯康辛大学麦迪逊校区公共政策与管理硕士、新闻学博士。

记者、主播、政论节目主持人、制作人，台湾大学新闻研究所教授、所长、多媒体研究中心主任、台湾公共广播集团董事、公共广播集团客家电视台执行长；并以社会公正人士身分担任第一届检察官评鉴委员会委员兼发言人，并于2021年因追查论文门事件而获得加拿大"正义之星奖"。

彭文正博士如今因为质疑蔡英文和伦敦政经学院合谋诈骗学位，2021年被司法设局通缉、没收台湾护照、成为滞留在美国的无国籍人球。

/ Editor-in-Chief

Dr. Dennis Peng

Bachelor from National Taiwan University, Master of Public Policy and Administration, and Doctorate in Journalism from the University of Wisconsin-Madison.

Dr. Peng's career spans roles as a reporter, news anchor, political talk show host, and producer. He was held academic positions as a Professor and the Director of the Graduate Institute of Journalism at National Taiwan University, as well as the Director of the Multimedia Research Center. His contributions extend to executive roles, including servingon the board of Taiwan Broadcasting System (TBS) and as the CEO of Hakka Television at the TBS. As an advocate for social justice, he was appointed as a member and spokesperson for the Prosecutor Evaluation Committee. In 2021, Dr. Peng received the "Star of Justice Award" from Canada for his investigative efforts in the "LSE Thesis-Gate Scandal" controversy.

Currently, Dr. Peng is notable for questioning the legitimacy of Tsai Ing-wen's degree and alleging collusion with the London School of Economics and Political Science. As a result of these allegations, he was subject to an arrest warrant in 2021, had his Taiwanese passport revoked, and now resides in the United States as a stateless person.

目次

作者介绍	3
大事记	6
英国 Tribunal Court 判决揭露：	13
– LSE 提供虚假证据给台湾的法院	
给读者的话	25
"消失"的论文：麻省理工学院学者的启示	29
办公室的紧急会议：LSE 内部建议、策略与决策	63
寻找真相：2015 年的调查者	70
风暴的起源：1985/86 学年修业规定的影本	80
LSE 与总统府间的平衡策略游戏	102
机密的指示：伦敦大学的内部角力	116
时间的迷雾：1984 年与 2011年的交错	128
LSE的模糊策略	154
真相的封锁：LSE 内部的真相与策略	174
三张证书的谜团：蔡英文学位疑云再起	180

黑皮书的谜团：台湾代表的 LSE 之旅	198
LSE 的策略：罐头答复与形象维护	207
妇女图书馆的谜团：蔡英文论文的存放之谜	234
LSE 面对质疑的策略：都是假帐号攻击！	290
《恶官Ⅰ》收藏于世界各大图书馆	332
附录	350
论文门关系人物列表	364
结语	386

大事记

2015

2015.6.19 一名麻省理工学院台湾学者投书加拿大星岛日报，标题为"蔡英文博士论文无处寻"，表示自己无论用什么方式都找不到蔡英文的论文。

2019

2019.05.04 前北美台湾人教授协会会长，北卡罗莱纳州立大学夏洛特分校商学院教授林环墙，开始对发电子邮件询问伦敦政经学院（LSE）蔡英文失踪的论文展开调查。

2019.05.20 台大法学院名誉教授贺德芬，举行记者会提出蔡英文论文在世界上图书馆都找不到的疑问，点燃了台湾社会的论文门质疑。

2019.06.10 国立台湾大学新闻研究所前所长彭文正，在脸书回应说这是他在学术界25年来碰过最怪的事。

2019.06.11 北美台湾人教授协会会长李中志，回避对论文不存在的质疑，在脸书上贴出蔡英文2015年补发的LSE毕业证书照片。

2019.06.11 台大法学荣誉教授贺德芬，在由前台大新闻所所长主持的网路节目政经关不了，首度对台湾揭露蔡英文的论文门疑云。

2019.06.28 蔡英文的论文"Unfair Trade Practices and Safeguard Actions"电子索引，首度出现在LSE电子目录，并且出现与Michael Elliott同列双作者。

2019.07.10 蔡英文访问台湾的网路媒体Dcard，将其2015年补发之"LSE博士毕业证书"以塑胶袋装，在媒体面前闪了20秒。

2019.07.19 教育部将蔡英文在台湾东吴大学和政治大学的教师聘任及升等资料以"公文附件"的方式，封锁到2049年12月31日。

2019.08.27 林环墙教授发表了50页的"蔡英文论文独立调查报告"。

2019.08.29 总统府发言人张惇涵召开记者会，宣布对林环墙和贺德芬两位教授提告。

2019.09.12 台湾大学前新闻研究所所长彭文正教授连续一星期天天声援两位学者，总统府于中秋节前夕深夜，发表新闻稿追加告诉彭文正教授。

接下页

2019

2019.09.18 英国牛津大学博士徐永泰，在亲自去看过蔡英文所谓论文后，在世界日报发表蔡英文论文观后感上中下篇，并提出伦敦政经学院妇女图书馆所展示之黑皮书并非正式论文的观点。徐永泰同时去函LSE法律系请求调查蔡英文的博士纪录，LSE系所回应没有保存任何蔡英文博士资料。

2019.09.19 蔡英文首度接受媒体访问回应自己的学位疑云，强调有学位就有论文。

2019.09.23 总统府首度召开论文门记者会，现场以白手套呈现蔡英文一页一页的论文草稿，但内容纸张明显年代不符。同一天立委管碧玲首度曝光蔡英文的第三张毕业证书，也就是2010年补发的毕业证书。蔡英文出现三张毕业证书，两张补发违反了伦敦大学的补发限一次的规定。

2019.09.24 蔡英文南下左营最后一次就论文门事件接受媒体提问。再次强调哪有一页一页，都是一整本一整本的，并表示国家图书馆已经同意收纳并公布论文。

2019.09.27 国家图书馆违反学位授予法，收录了蔡英文所谓"Unfair Trade Practices and Safeguard Actions"论文到硕博士专区。

2019.10.08 LSE官网出现一则"LSE Statement on PhD of Dr Tsai Ing-wen"的声明。

2019.10.14 立法委员陈学圣在立法院质询，询问现场48位国立大学校长有几位相信总统学位是真的，最后只有六位校长举手，连蔡英文曾经任教的政治大学校长郭明政都没有举手。

2019.10.18 彭文正教授率团到英国伦敦，在LSE校内图书馆进行第一手的调查，并录下与图书馆馆员们的访谈，证明校方各图书馆从未收藏过这本论文。当天并与林环墙教授在伦敦召开一场论文门丑闻的记者会。

2019.10.21 美国独立记者Michael Richardson以FOIA自由资讯公开法，向LSE提出公开蔡英文口试委员与口试日期的请求。LSE资讯暨纪录经理Rachel Maguire回复口试日期是1983.10.16，经查这一天是星期天，并回复说口试相关资料由伦敦大学保存。Michael Richardson转向伦敦大学发起《资讯自由法》（FOIA）请求。

2019.10.31 欧崇敬教授发现蔡英文所谓"博士论文"之六页目录错了79处。

接下頁

2019

2019.11.02 陈水扁在自己的节目上,透露蔡英文的2015毕业证书是透过前资策会副执行长黄国俊亲赴英国向英国伦敦政经学院前院长Anthony Giddens"处理"来的。

2019.11.04 在英国Whatdotheyknow网站上,揭露了一笔LSE自2008年2014年间所有捐款纪录,其中六百笔资料当中,只有一笔以匿名捐款48万英镑,并且指定给LSE台湾研究计划室共同主任施芳珑使用。

2019.11.09 网友发现现任高雄市长陈其迈2011年的脸书照片,内容有萧美琴、谢志伟、陈其迈、张小月还有蔡英文五人,出现在LSE拜会英国伦敦政经学院前院长Anthony Giddens、代理院长Ms. Dame Judith Rees以及涉及博士学历丑闻的利比亚领袖Gaddafi儿子Saif al-Islam Gaddafi之指导教授David Held。

2019.11.28 立法委员陈学圣在立法院举办"论文门公听会",政大国关中心研究员严震生提出蔡英文所谓论文有444个错字,并将蔡英文学位调查案正式纪录在台湾国会正式公文当中。

2019.12.05 彭文正教授为了避免蔡英文在总统大选后撤告,对蔡英文提出诬告以及确认论文不存在两项告诉。同时对总统府发言人张惇涵提出加重毁谤告诉。

2020

2020.01.15 台北地方法院法官张咏惠在未开庭,未阐明的情况下,突袭判决确认论文不存在之诉,彭文正败诉。

2020.01.26 对于美国独立记者Michael Richardson的FOIA申请公布蔡英文口试委员案,伦敦大学以个资法为由拒绝公布。Michael Richardson随后向英国ICO资讯办公室提出仲裁上诉。

2020.03.24 Michael Richardson收到资讯特任官办公室ICO的调查报告,告知公开口试委员会对当事人造成痛苦(distress)与伤害(damage),并告知因为疫情的关系这份报告可能会拖延许久。

接下頁

2020

2020.06.11 Michael Richardson公开蔡英文口试委员案，ICO提出仲裁结果，同意伦敦大学拒绝公开的决定。

https://ico.org.uk/media/action-weve-taken/decision-notices/2020/2617860/fs50908339.pdf

这份报告依据伦敦大学资讯保护暨法遵主管Kit Good的证词，称伦敦大学持有蔡英文论文出版记录与口试报告以及学位资料。并解释蔡英文的论文在1980-2010s年代之间，因为图书馆整修遗失或错放。Kit Good于 2021年9月无预警离职。ICO的报告进一步指出目前存放在LSE的论文，可能是草稿也可能不是草稿。
Michael Richardson随后向英国资讯法庭Tribunal Court对ICO提出上诉。

2020.07.08 ICO另外一份仲裁报告出炉，针对蔡英文2019年才送入的所谓论文，ICO做出了这是一份非经过正式评估过的论文版本之结论。

https://ico.org.uk/media/action-weve-taken/decision-notices/2020/2618008/fs50898869.pdf

2020.07.17 ICO以Michael Richardson非英国籍为由，要Tribunal Court拒绝受理其FOIA。案子暂时被冻结，待国籍争议解决。

2021

2021.02.24 英国行政法院同意资讯自由法FOIA无涉国籍、领土，只要愿意提供真实姓名与居住所，于是公开蔡英文口试委的FOIA案件解冻。

2021.03.27 ICO交付法庭答辩提出四项观点，（一）蔡英文个人隐私比公共资讯公开更为重要。（二）法庭的权力有限，ICO才是个资保护的最终裁判所。（三）1985年IALS法学索引，已经提供足够的资讯。（四）台湾的法院已经对质疑者提出法律诉讼。

2021.03.31 在台湾，彭文正教授因被蔡英文总统提告，被台北地检署依加重诽谤罪起诉，另外两名学者贺德芬与林环墙则不起诉处分。

2021.04.06 彭文正教授破天荒同时收到台北地方法检署的起诉书与不起诉书。

接下页

2021

2021.05.04 蔡英文提告学者的加重诽谤案于台北地院首度开庭，公诉检察官黄冠运以"为什么不相信蔡英文"为主要理由起诉彭文正。彭文正与其律师张静在庭外记者会痛批："台湾检察官都姓蔡"。

2021.05.26 Michael Richardson第二度对LSE发起FOIA请求，要求口试委员名单。LSE董事会秘书Louise Nadal回复Michael Richardson：学校不持有您所要求的信息。Michael Richardson上诉ICO。

2021.09.13 Michael Richardson提出的公布蔡英文口试委员FOIA案，First-tier tribunal判决出炉。法庭在审视了伦敦大学提供的不公开的文件后，认定其中有蔡英文的口试委员名单，并判决ICO胜诉，伦敦大学不需要公布蔡英文口试委员。

Michael Richardson再次向Upper Tribunal提出上诉。
https://informationrights.decisions.tribunals.gov.uk/DBFiles/Decision/i2943/032%20200921%20Richardson%20EA%202020%200212%20p.pdf

First-tier tribunal判决书。

2021.10.20 由蔡英文对学者提告的官司，台北地方法院进入准备程序，正在美国探亲的被告彭文正教授以疫情严峻和受到恐吓跟监有身家安全之虞为由，申请视讯出庭被法院不附理由拒绝，公诉检察官刘承武提出要求对彭文正教授发布通缉，要求其出庭说明是否有真实恶意。法官姚念慈也在提出"为什么彭文正未到庭"以及"为什么状子上面没有彭文正盖印"后，旋即退庭。留下现场错愕的群众。

2021.11.19 台北地院在没有附任何合法理由的情况下，对彭文正教授发布通缉十三年。

2021.11.26 Michael Richardson二度对LSE发起FOIA请求，LSE是否保有蔡英文的博士口试报告相关纪录，ICO作出仲裁结论，LSE否认持有蔡英文博士口试相关纪录。并表示从逻辑上推论，相关纪录应该由伦敦大学保存。
https://ico.org.uk/action-weve-taken/decision-notices/ic-109451-s1m2/ ICO仲裁报告。

2021.12.18 对于伦敦大学表示蔡英文的论文在1980-2010年之间，因为图书馆整修错放或遗失的说法，Tribunal Judge Hazel Oliver在审视了由彭文正教授提出的图书馆调查影片，法官判决表示论文遗失的说法不正确。

接下页

2022

2022.01.11

接任Kit Good的伦敦大学新上任的资讯保护暨法遵主管Suzie Mereweather，在Whatdotheyknow网站上回应询问，为什么LSE的纪录经理Rachael Maguire可以知道蔡英文的口试日期？是否由伦敦大学告知？

Suzie Mereweather表示学位授予的主要纪录由机构成员持有，而非伦敦大学。

https://www.whatdotheyknow.com/request/did_rachael_maguire_of_lse_get_t#incoming-1949200

同一天再回复询问蔡英文论文的出版日期时，Suzie Mereweather公开承认伦敦大学并没有出版过蔡英文的论文。推翻了Kit Good 2020年在ICO的报告。

https://www.whatdotheyknow.com/request/the_publication_date_of_tsai_ing#incoming-1949227

2022.02.02

伦敦大学在官网上发表声明University of London statement on missing thesis，表示虽然不清楚论文是否存放在大学图书馆，但蔡英文博士学位是被正确授予的。但原本声明提到的1984年2月被授予学位，被更改为1984年3月。

2022.02.10

三位学者彭文正、林环墙、贺德芬发起联合声明，正式指控伦敦大学以及伦敦政经学院包庇蔡英文博士学位诈欺。

2022.06.21

针对LSE于2021.11.26 ICO仲裁报告里，否认持有蔡英文博士口试相关纪录，Michael Richardson上诉到Tribunal Court，并提出彭文正教授在台北地检署的起诉书物证，其中LSE法务经理Kevin Haynes向台北地方法院作证，并提出两位口试委员名单。

LSE在法庭上否认Kevin Haynes向台北地检署提出的证据，表示那是偶然取得，并且无法确定是否为正确的资讯。

Tribunal Judge Alison Mckenna判决LSE必须在两个星期内重新回复Michael Richardson的FOIA请求。LSE于2022.9.1改口以这是个资保护范围提出豁免权。

https://www.bailii.org/uk/cases/UKFTT/GRC/2022/2021_0373.html

First-tier tribunal判决书。

接下页

2023

2023.03.03 ICO主委John Edwards将所有对蔡英文学位质疑的FOIA请求,全面以vexatious的理由驳回,并在Whatdotheyknow删除了一百多个提问及账号。

2023.06.21 林环墙教授以FOIA要求LSE公开其2019.10.8声明,是由校方哪个单位发出,结果遭到LSE以及ICO以vexatious驳回。一审Tribunal也同意ICO看法,认定这是无理取闹的举动。林环墙教授上诉Upper Tribunal获得胜诉,案件重新退回一审,并且法庭必须更换法官。
https://assets.publishing.service.gov.uk/media/64cd08bc9958270010c1e963/UA_2023_000363_GIA.pdf

2023.08.22 英国的调查团体Watchdog依据FOIA调阅到的LSE内部掩护蔡英文学位诈欺丑闻的1000多封串证电子邮件全部公开在网站上。

2022.10.19 台湾驻旧金山办事处在彭文正教授前往申请护照换新时没收并注销了他的有效期护照,使其至今仍成为无法上飞机的无国籍人球。

英国 Tribunal Court 判决揭露
LSE 提供虚假证据给台湾的法院

NCN

Case Reference: EA/2021/0373

FIRST-TIER TRIBUNAL
GENERAL REGULATORY CHAMBER
INFORMATION RIGHTS

Heard: By determination on the papers
Heard: On 13 June 2022
Decision Given on: 21 June 2022

MICHAEL RICHARDSON	Appellant
- and -	
THE INFORMATION COMMISSIONER	Respondent

Before:
JUDGE ALISON MCKENNA
SUSAN WOLF
DAN PALMER-DUNK

DECISION

1. The appeal is allowed.

2. Substituted Decision Notice:

A. The Tribunal finds that Decision Notice IC-109451-SIM2 dated 26 November 2021 was erroneous and that information within the scope of the information request is held by LSE;

B. LSE must within 28 days issue a fresh response to the Appellant's original information request which confirms that information within the scope of his request is held and either disclose it or claim any exemptions to disclosure on which it relies.

REASONS

Mode of Hearing

3. The parties and the Tribunal agreed that this matter was suitable for determination on the papers in accordance with rule 32 of the Chamber's Procedure Rules[1].

4. The Tribunal considered an agreed open bundle of evidence comprising pages 1 to 86. It also considered submissions from the public authority, the Council of the London School of Economics and Science ('LSE') and further evidence and submissions from the Appellant.

Background to Appeal

5. The Appellant made a request to LSE on 2 May 2021 for the names of the examiners who examined the then Miss Tsai Ing-Wen (now President of Taiwan) for her PhD and the report from her viva.

6. LSE responded on 4 May and 26 May 2021 that it did not hold the requested information because at the relevant time (1984), it was the University of London which awarded degrees to LSE students.

7. The Information Commissioner issued Decision Notice IC-109451-SIM2 on 26 November 2021. It concluded on the balance of probabilities that the requested information was not held by LSE.

8. The Appellant appealed to the Tribunal. LSE was sent the appeal papers and invited to make submissions or to apply to be joined as a party to the appeal. It chose only to make submissions, but also supplied evidence.

The Law

9. S. 1(1)(a) of the Freedom of Information Act 2000 ('FOIA') provides that a person making an information request is entitled to be informed in writing whether the public authority holds information within the scope of the request. Where information within the scope of the request is held, it must either be disclosed or an exemption claimed.

---

[1] https://www.gov.uk/government/publications/general-regulatory-chamber-tribunal-procedure-rules

10. Where there is a dispute about whether information is held, the Tribunal makes a finding of fact on the evidence before it, applying the civil standard of proof, the balance of probabilities.

11. The Upper Tribunal's Decision in *Malnick v IC and ACOBA* [2018] UKUT 72 (AAC)[2], confirmed that a public authority must pass through the 'gateway' of compliance with ss. 1, 2 and 17 FOIA before being entitled to raise a late exemption before the Tribunal. As the public authority in this case stated that it did not hold the requested information, it has not yet claimed any applicable exemptions to disclosure. This means that the Tribunal cannot in this appeal decide whether any exemptions to disclosure apply.

12. The powers of the Tribunal in determining this appeal are set out in s.58 of FOIA, as follows:

> "If on an appeal under section 57 the Tribunal considers -
>
> (a) that the notice against which the appeal is brought is not in accordance with the law, or
> (b) to the extent that the notice involved an exercise of discretion by the Commissioner, that he ought to have exercised his discretion differently,
>
> the Tribunal shall allow the appeal or substitute such other notice as could have been served by the Commissioner, and in any other case the Tribunal shall dismiss the appeal.
>
> On such an appeal, the Tribunal may review any finding of fact on which the notice in question was based."

Submissions and Evidence

13. The Appellant's Notice of Appeal dated 14 December 2021 relied on grounds that (i) the Decision Notice was erroneous in concluding on the balance of probabilities that information was not held; (ii) that President Tsai's office has provided consent to the disclosure of any personal data on her student file; and (iii) that LSE has failed to comply with its legal obligations under FOIA. He requested that the Tribunal remits the matter to the Information Commissioner and directs a more thorough investigation.

14. The Information Commissioner's Response dated 19 January 2022 resisted the appeal and maintained the analysis set out in the Decision Notice. It is also submitted that, in another case on the subject of President Tsai's PhD (in which the public authority was the University of London), the Tribunal found that the names of the examiners were exempt from disclosure under s. 40 (2) FOIA. The Information Commissioner invited the Appellant to withdraw his appeal.

---

[2] 2018_AACR_29ws.pdf (publishing.service.gov.uk)

15. The Appellant's Reply made clear that he would not be withdrawing his appeal. He submits that the Information Commissioner had not informed him that it had any concerns about the provenance of a copy email he had provided dated 16 December 2020 and had simply failed to take it into account in reaching the conclusions in the Decision Notice. So that the Tribunal would not have similar concerns, he produced a further copy exhibited to an affidavit (see below). He addressed the question of the examiners' names being their personal data.

16. In response to the Registrar's Directions of 7 March 2022, LSE declined to be joined as a party to this appeal but made submissions and provided evidence. Its submission to the Tribunal dated 14 March 2022 it stated that *"…the information we hold on file is only there accidentally… we cannot be certain that this information is accurate"*.

17. LSE confirmed to the Tribunal that it holds President Tsai's student file, comprising 278 pages. It stated that there is a letter on this file in which a person appears to self-identify as one of the Viva examiners, but that it has no official notification from University of London whether this information was correct, and it holds no information on the identity of the co-examiner. Commenting on the email of 16 December 2020 (see below), LSE states that its review found that the information provided by LSE in that email was *"likely inaccurate. This was based on a hurried view of a scanned file that cannot be key word searched. The email chain… is attached"*.

18. The Appellant made final submissions in which he asked the Tribunal to direct LSE to disclose pages from President Tsai's student file.

19. The Tribunal considered the following evidence, produced by the Appellant.

(i) An email dated 16 December 2020 in which a senior employee of LSE stated in an email that he had reviewed President Tsai's student file and *"…it appears from her student file that [XX][3] and [YY] examined President Tsai's thesis in October 1983"*.

(ii) The 16 December 2020 email was provided by the Appellant to the Information Commissioner's Office during its investigation, but it did not ask LSE about it, apparently being uncertain of its provenance. The Appellant provided the Tribunal with a further copy of the email, exhibited to an affidavit dated 24 January 2022 signed by journalist Dennis Peng, who states he obtained it via disclosure during defamation proceedings brought against him by President Tsai and that the addressee of the email is *"the inquiry of the Taiwanese Judiciary Institution"* which is investigating President Tsai's PhD.

---

[3] We have here anonymized the persons named as a precaution in view of the Tribunal's Decision referred to in paragraph 14, although we note we are not bound to take the same view. We understand that the Appellant has seen these names in full because they were provided to the Tribunal unredacted.

(iii) The Appellant also relied on evidence in the form of an email dated 12 June 2019, in which President Tsai's office gave LSE consent to the disclosure of personal data in her student file.

(iv) The Appellant produced an email dated 14 June 2019 from a member of staff at LSE to President Tsai's office in which there is a reference to "fending off" enquiries about President Tsai's PhD. The Appellant relies on this as evidence that LSE is reluctant to comply with its duties under FOIA.

20. The Tribunal considered the following evidence, provided by LSE with its submissions of 14 March 2022:

An internal email dated 31 March 2021, addressed to the member of staff who sent the 16 December 2020 email, as follows:

Looking at it again, I was wondering where in the student file you got the information that she had two internal examiners – [XX] and [YY] – and one external examiner – [ZZ].

As far as I can see the only examiners referred to in the file are:

-[ZZ], named as external examiner in a letter from Pres Tsai to …Sec of Graduate School at LSE, 5 December 1983

-[XX], who refers to 'my co-examiner and myself' in a memo … dated 16/1/1983. This also suggests there were only two examiners, [XX] and one other.

I see [YY] is mentioned in the file but couldn't find him specifically named as an examiner.

21. We have not seen the reply to that email. We note that LSE has not disputed that the email of 16 December 2020 was sent, only that it now doubts the accuracy of its contents.

Conclusion

22. The Decision Notice concluded on the balance of probabilities that LSE did not hold the requested information. The Tribunal has had the benefit of additional evidence provided by the Appellant and by LSE itself with its submissions.

23. We conclude on the basis of all the evidence before us and on the balance of probabilities that information within the scope of the request is held by LSE in President Tsai's student file. That information has been referred to in email correspondence between LSE and others (including apparently being supplied to a judicial inquiry) and is also referred to in its submission to the Tribunal. We understand that LSE doubts the accuracy of this information, but we conclude that this is not a basis for stating that information is not held under FOIA.

24. It may be that exemptions will be claimed, but we conclude that LSE must now issue a fresh response in which that issue is addressed. As we have concluded that information is held, the correct course is for LSE to issue a fresh response on the basis that information within the scope of the request is held, and at that stage either disclose the requested information (with contextual commentary, if necessary) or claim any exemptions to disclosure that it considers apply. If the Appellant disagrees with that response, he may complain to the Information Commissioner. The Tribunal may only become involved if a further Decision Notice is issued.

25. We allow this appeal on the basis of the Appellant's first ground of appeal, that the Decision Notice was erroneous in its conclusion that information was not held.

26. As to the Appellant's second ground of appeal, we note that President Tsai may only give permission to disclose her own personal data and may not override the privacy rights of third parties. In any event, this Tribunal may not determine the applicability of exemptions which have not yet been claimed and have not been considered in a Decision Notice.

27. As to the Appellant's third ground, this Tribunal's jurisdiction extends only to considering the Decision Notice. It is not our role to comment on LSE's handling of the request.

28. We now allow the appeal and make the substituted Decision Notice above.

(Signed)

JUDGE ALISON MCKENNA   DATE: **20 June 2022**

© CROWN COPYRIGHT 2022

NCN

案例编号：EA/2021/0373

第一审法庭
普通监管法
庭资讯权利

以文件裁决方式审理：

听证日期：2022年6月13日

裁决日期：2022年6月21日

上诉人 迈克尔·理察森

被上诉人 资讯专员办公室

法官 阿丽森·麦肯纳

苏珊·沃尔夫

丹·帕尔默 - 邓克

裁决

1. 上诉准许。
2. 替代裁决通知：

A. 法庭认为2021年11月26日的裁决通知IC-109451-SIM2有误，请求的资讯范围内的资讯由伦敦政经学院持有；

B. 伦敦政经学院必须在28天内对上诉人的原始资讯请求发出新回应，确认持有请求范围内的资讯，并进行披露或声称任何披露豁免。

理 由

听证方式

3. 当事双方和法庭同意，根据法庭程序规则第32条，本案件适合以文件方式裁决。

4. 法庭考虑了证据合订本第1至86页的证据。它还考虑了公共机构伦敦政治经济学院（"伦敦政经学院"）的意见书，以及上诉人的进一步证据和意见书。

上诉背景

5. 上诉人于2021年5月2日向伦敦政经学院提出请求，要求提供曾经审查过蔡英文博士论文（现任台湾总统）的审查员姓名，以及她的论文答辩报告。

6. 伦敦政经学院于2021年5月4日和5月26日回应称，它们不持有所要求的资讯，因为在相关时间（1984年），伦敦大学才是颁发伦敦政经学院学生学位的机构。

7. 资讯专员办公室于2021年11月26日作出裁决通知IC-109451-SIM2。它认为请求的资讯在可能性上并未被伦敦政经学院持有。

8. 上诉人向法庭提出上诉。伦敦政经学院收到上诉文件并被邀请提交意见书或申请加入上诉方。它选择只提交意见书，但也提供了证据。

法律

9. 2000年资讯自由法（"资讯自由法"）第1（1）（a）条规定，提出资讯请求的人有权以书面形式获知公共机构是否持有请求范围内的资讯。如果持有请求范围内的资讯，必须进行披露或声称豁免。

10. 如果对持有资讯存在争议,法庭会在其掌握的证据基础上作出事实认定,采用民事标准,以可能性大于小的方式。

11. 上级法院在 Malnick v IC and ACOBA [2018] UKUT 72（AAC）案中的裁决确认,公共机构必须先通过资讯自由法第 1、2 和 17 条门槛,才有权在法庭面前提出迟来的豁免。由于本案中的公共机构声称不持有所请求的资讯,它还没有声称任何适用的披露豁免。这意味着法庭在本次上诉中无法决定任何豁免是否适用。

12. 法庭在裁定本次上诉时的权力载于资讯自由法第 58 条,如下:

"如果上诉法庭根据第 57 条认为上诉的通知与法律不符,或在通知涉及专员酌情决定权的范围内,他本应不同方式行使酌情决定权,则上诉法庭应允许上诉或替换专员本可以发出的其他通知,在任何其他情况下,上诉法庭应驳回上诉。
在该上诉中,上诉法庭可以审查作出有关通知所依据的任何事实认定。"

意见书和证据

13. 上诉人于 2021 年 12 月 14 日的上诉通知书提出以下理由:（i）裁决通知误认在可能性上资讯未被持有;（ii）蔡英文总统办公室已同意披露她学生档案中的任何个人资料;以及（iii）伦敦政经学院未能遵守资讯自由法下的法定义务。他要求法庭将案件发回资讯专员办理处进行更全面的调查。

14. 资讯专员办公室于 2022 年 1 月 19 日的回应反对上诉,并维持裁决通知中载明的分析。它还提出,在另一起与蔡英文博士论文相关的案件中（公共机构为伦敦大学）,法庭裁定审查员姓名符合资讯自由法第 40（2）条豁免规定免于披露。资讯专员办公室邀请上诉人撤回上诉。

15. 上诉人在回复中明确表示不会撤回上诉。他认为资讯专员办公室并未告知他对他提供的 2020 年 12 月 16 日电子邮件副本的真实性有任何疑虑，而是简单地在作出裁决通知结论时未予考虑。为免法庭有类似疑虑，他另外提供了一份以宣誓方式证实的副本（见下文）。他解释了审查员姓名作为其个人资料的问题。

16. 为回应法庭于 2022 年 3 月 7 日的指示，伦敦政经学院拒绝加入本次上诉的当事方，但提交了意见书和证据。其于 2022 年 3 月 14 日提交给法庭的意见书中称"……我们持有的档案资讯仅属偶然 我们无法确定这些资讯是否准确"。

17. 伦敦政经学院向法庭确认，它持有蔡英文的学生档案，包含 278 页。它称档案中有一封信，里面一个人似乎自称是论文答辩审查员之一，但它没有伦敦大学的任何正式通知，确认这些资讯是否正确，也不持有关于共同审查员身份的任何资讯。关于 2020 年 12 月 16 日的电子邮件（见下文），伦敦政经学院称其复核发现，该电子邮件中伦敦政经学院提供的资讯"可能不准确。这基于匆忙查看无法进行关键词搜索的扫描档案。所附的电子邮件链……"。

18. 上诉人作出最终意见书，要求法庭指示伦敦政经学院披露蔡英文学生档案中的若干页面。

19. 法庭考虑了以下上诉人提供的证据。

(i) 一封日期为 2020 年 12 月 16 日的电子邮件，伦敦政经学院一位高级职员在电子邮件中称，他已检视过蔡英文的学生档案，"……她的学生档案显示 [XX] 和 [YY] 于 1983 年 10 月审查了蔡英文总统的论文"。

(ii) 上诉人在资讯专员办公室调查期间向其提供了 2020 年 12 月 16 日的电子邮件，但资讯专员办公室并未就此询问伦敦政经学院，显然对其真实性存疑。上诉人向法庭提供了该电子邮件的另一份副本，作为 2022 年 1 月 24 日记者彭文正签署的宣誓书的附件，他在宣誓书中称，他通过蔡英文总统对他提起诽谤诉讼所进行的披露获得了该电子邮件，而电子邮件收件人是"台湾司法机构对蔡英文博士论文的询问"。

(iii) 上诉人还依据 2019 年 6 月 12 日的一封电子邮件作为证据，蔡英文办公室在其中给予伦敦政经学院同意，披露她学生档案中的个人资料。

(iv) 上诉人提供了一封伦敦政经学院职员于 2019 年 6 月 14 日寄给蔡英文办公室的电子邮件，其中提到"挡下"关于蔡英文博士论文的询问。上诉人依据此主张伦敦政经学院不愿意遵守其在资讯自由法下的义务。

20. 伦敦政经学院随 2022 年 3 月 14 日意见书提供了以下证据，法庭予以考虑：

一封内部电子邮件，日期为 2021 年 3 月 31 日，收件人是 2020 年 12 月 16 日电子邮件的发件人，内容如下：

再次看似乎，我在想你从学生档案中得到的资讯是她有两个内部审查员 – [XX] 和 [YY] – 以及一个外部审查员 – [ZZ]。

据我所见，档案中提到的唯一审查员是：

-[ZZ]，在蔡英文 1983 年 12 月 5 日给伦敦政经学院研究生院秘书的信中被命名为外部审查员

-[XX]，在一份注明 1983 年 1 月 16 日的备忘录中提到"我和共同审查员"。这也表明只有两位审查员，[XX] 和另一位。

我看到 [YY] 在档案中被提及，但没有具体找到他被指定为审查员的资讯。

21. 我们未看到该电子邮件的回复。我们注意到，伦敦政经学院并未争辩其是否发送了 2020 年 12 月 16 日的电子邮件，只是现在质疑其内容的准确性。

结论

22. 裁决通知认为，在可能性上，请求的资讯未被伦敦政经学院持有。法庭获益于上诉人和伦敦政经学院本身随意见书提供的额外证据。

23. 根据法庭掌握的所有证据，在可能性大于小的基础上，我们认为请求范围内的资讯由伦敦政经学院在蔡英文的学生档案中持有。这些资讯已在伦敦政经学院与他人（包括显然提供给司法调查）的电子邮件往来中被提及，也在其提交给法庭的意见书中被提及。我们理解伦敦政经学院质疑这些资讯的准确性，但我们认为这并不能作为其在资讯自由法下声称不持有资讯的依据。

24. 可能会声称适用豁免，但我们认为伦敦政经学院现在必须在新的回应中解决这一问题。由于我们认定持有资讯，正确的做法是伦敦政经学院在持有请求范围内资讯的前提下发出新回应，并在那时要么披露所请求的资讯（必要时附上说明），要么主张其认为适用的任何豁免。如果上诉人不同意该回应，可以向资讯专员办公室投诉。只有在作出进一步裁决通知时，法庭才可能介入。

25. 我们允许本次上诉，理由是上诉人的第一个上诉理由，裁决通知误认资讯未被持有。

26. 关于上诉人的第二个上诉理由，我们注意到，蔡英文总统只能允许披露她自己的个人资料，不能凌驾第三方的隐私权。无论如何，本法庭不能裁定尚未被声称且未在裁决通知中考虑过的豁免的适用性。

27. 关于上诉人的第三个理由，本法庭的管辖权仅限于考虑裁决通知。我们的角色不是评论伦敦政经学院处理请求的方式。

28. 现在我们允许上诉，并作出上述替代裁决通知。

（签名）

法官 阿丽森·麦肯纳

日期：2022 年 6 月 20 日

© 英国皇家版权 2022

给读者的话

给读者的话

经过四年半的调查，发生在伦敦政经学院和台湾的总统府之间的奇怪现象，是否合乎学术标准和逻辑？

1. 伦敦政经学院（LSE）允许博士论文指导教授只有学士学位而且是专长完全不相关领域的人担任吗？

2. 两位博士口试委员都是伦敦大学校内教师，完全没有校外的口试委员，可能吗？

3. 指导教授担任口试委员没有违反伦敦大学规定吗？

4. LSE 博士论文从来没有被引注过，连自己都没有引注，有可能吗？

5. 论文的口试日期可能如 LSE 所说在 1983 年 10 月 16 日（星期天）吗？

6. 学生记录表中 1982 年 11 月 10 日的 WD（financial difficulties）不是 withdrawal 吗？

7. Withdrawal 的学生有可能在接下来的第二年取得博士学位吗？

8. LSE 学生 1983 年没有缴费记录，可能在 1983 年口试然后在 1984 年取得学位吗？

9. 287 页学生记录出现的绝大部分资料是由台湾总统府在 2019 年陆续送入的资料，这个可以用来证明博士学位吗？

10. 没有博士口试之前必须缴交的 entry form 有可能进行博士口试吗？

11. 一个学生 1983 年一月论文题目被认可，经过五个月后就缴交了论文口试本，可能吗？

12. 一本论文口试完之后，完全不需要修改？这在 LSE 发生过吗？

13. LSE 的论文有可能目录页错 79 处，整本论文错 444 个错字吗？

14. LSE 博士论文 Acknowledgements 有可能把指导教授名字写错吗？

15. LSE 可以允许一本博士论文出现两百多处用铅笔修改和修正液修改的论文吗？

16. LSE 可以允许一本博士论文用不同的字型打字吗？

17. LSE 1984 年博士论文注释中有可能出现 1984 年以后的文章吗？

18. LSE 可以允许一本博士论文一部分向左靠齐一部分向右靠齐一部分两边对齐吗？

19. LSE 的博士论文可以允许一字不漏地从两本中文期刊（台大法学论丛和东吴法律学报）上面直接翻译多达 200 页吗？

20. LSE 在电子邮件中证实 2015 年的补发毕业证书是假的，为何完全没有启动任何的调查？

21. 蔡英文在她的自传当中说 LSE 颁给他的是 1.5 个博士学位是真的吗？

22. LSE 会允许一个毕业 35 年的校友把自己宣称的在学资料送进学生档案吗？

23. LSE 可以接受一个毕业 35 年的校友将自己的伪造资料送给学校放入档案中，作为学历认证的根据吗？

24. LSE 可以把不知道在哪里取得的不正确资料提供给台湾的司法部门作伪证却不用负法律责任吗？

25. LSE、伦敦大学都没有保存蔡英文的口试委员相关资料，全世界图书馆都没有蔡英文的 1984 年微缩胶卷就可以替博士学位背书吗？

26. 1983 年 9 月就回台湾东吴大学任教的人，可能 1983 年 10 月 15 日从台湾出发参加 10 月 16 号在伦敦政经学院的口试吗？

27. 蔡英文在她的自传中说，她的论文写得太好，指导教授和考试委员经过详细的讨论，究竟要颁发给她一个博士学位还是两个博士学位，最后决颁给她 1.5 个博士学位（https://youtu.be/vJ8CditYjzw?si=faCocV7M7q9KGVKd），请问这是

LSE 或伦敦大学授予学位的方式吗？

28. 在伦敦政经学院担任台湾研究计划室主任的施芳珑，曾经在 2007 年 8 月 1 日至 2014 年 9 月 30 日获一笔匿名（捐款中唯一匿名）的 48 万英镑指名捐给她个人的捐款（https://www.whatdotheyknow.com/request/from_which_government_ngo_or_pri_7），在整起事件中，她扮演什么角色？为什么可以穿梭于伦敦政经学院和伦敦大学的高层之间？

本书中揭露之电子邮件是根据 FOIA（Freedom of Informtion Act）向相关单位得的，信件中涂黑的部分是资料提供方所为，需要透过司法诉讼进一步解密。

3

"消失"的论文：麻省理工学院学者的启示

"消失"的论文：麻省理工学院学者的启示

2019 年，一场关于台湾总统蔡英文学历的争议在国际学术界掀起波澜。当时，蔡英文的学历成为了选举的焦点，而这场风波也不断扩大，牵扯到了许多学术界的重量级人物。

早在 2015 年 6 月 19 日，一名麻省理工学院的台湾学者在加拿大星岛日报上发表了一篇投书，标题为"蔡英文博士论文无处寻"。他表示，无论用何种方式，都无法找到蔡英文的博士论文。这篇文章当时并没有在学术界引起震撼。

四年后的 2019 年 5 月 4 日，前北美台湾人教授协会会长，北卡罗莱纳州立大学夏洛特分校商学院教授林环墙，开始对于这篇失踪的论文展开调查。不久后，台大法学院名誉教授贺德芬也加入了这场调查，并在 5 月 20 日举行记者会，提出蔡英文的论文在全球的图书馆都找不到，这一说法立刻引起了广泛的关注和质疑。

随后，美国政治评论作家曹长青在《政经关不了》节目中质疑蔡英文的学历真实性。该节目的主持人，国立台湾大学新闻研究所前所长彭文正，在脸书上回应说，这是他在学术界 25 年来碰到最奇怪的事情。

2019 年 6 月 11 日，北美台湾人教授协会会长李中志，在脸书上贴出了蔡英文 2015 年补发的 LSE 毕业证书照片，试图以此为蔡英文辩护。然而，同一天，贺德芬教授也在《政经关不了》节目中，首度对台湾社会揭露了这场论文门的疑云。

这场风暴的中心，是一位在 LSE 咨询服务经理 Clive Wilson。Clive Wilson 曾经参与 2015 年 LSE 关于蔡英文论文的内部调查，他从一开始就意识到，这场争议不仅仅是关于一篇论文，更是涉及到学术诚信、政治选举和国家形象的大事。他决定带领团队，用"国际关系"的处理手法，对外给出一个统一的说法，以平息这场风波。起初 LSE 决定使用最简单的回复来打发外界，只提供已知的事实。就是图书馆从来没有蔡英文的论文，对学位也不做说明。

然而，事情的发展超出了他的预料。总统府主动提出要送入蔡英文的论文电子版和精装版，希望能够证明蔡英文的学历是真实的。而 LSE 台湾研究计画室共同主任的施芳珑，代表总统府与 LSE 进行接触，进一步要求学校提供口试委员名单和指导教授名单，希望能够深入了解如何合理化这起纷争。

Wilson 和施芳珑之间的交流成为了这场风波的焦点。Wilson 表示，如果总统府能够提供论文的电子版，他们可以协助将其编入图书馆，以证明其真实性。但在这之后，一封匿名信寄到了施芳珑和 Wilson 的手中，信中请求论文不要公开，并希望 LSE 能够发出声明，声援蔡总统。

面对这样的压力，Wilson 从台湾总统府取得论文的标题和致谢页，希望能够从中找到一些有关论文指导教授以及口试委员的线索。风暴不断延烧，检举信也不停地寄到校长室。在这样的情况下，Wilson 提出了一个建议：使用总统府提供的材料，来澄清这场争议。但由于疑点太多，LSE 的媒体关系经理也加入了这场风波，他希望能够统一回复，避免造成更大的困扰。而 Wilson 则提出内部讨论如何降低外界的进一步询问，而不是揭露真相。

2019 年 6 月 28 日，蔡英文的论文《不公平贸易和防卫机制》（Unfair Trade Practices and Safeguard Actions）首度出现在 LSE 的电子目录中，并且与 Michael Elliott 同列为双作者。这一发现再次引起了广泛的关注和讨论。

在这样的背景下，LSE 博士学程校务处副处长 Marcus W Cerny 认为，除了公共利益，还需要更谨慎地发布讯息。而 Wilson 则决定召开一场内部机密会议，商讨如何处理这件事，最终导致了人类史上层级最高、牵连最广的学位诈骗丑闻。

FW_ FYI - LSE PhD thesis Taiwan president

From: Wilson,Clive
Sent: 11 June 2019 12:35
To: Bell,M; Bhullar,J; Challis,D; Collings,R; Dawson,H; Fry,AE; Gomes,S; Graham1,N; Hayward,S; Horsler,PN; Hussain,R; Murphy,GE; Orson,R; Payne1,D; Reid,MJ; Towlson,A; Wilkinson,E; Wilson,Clive; Zajasensky,L; Benton,A; Rodriguez; Poulose,S; Donnelly,S; Wilson1,K; Griffiths,CB
Cc: Lsethesesonline
Subject: LSE PhD thesis - Taiwan president

Hi All

sorry to send this so widely, but I'm trying to cover all bases. Please forward if you think I've missed anyone.

There are presidential primaries in Taiwan this week to decide who the candidate for the DPP will be. One is the current president and LSE alumna Ing-wen Tsai.

Ing-wen Tsai received her PhD from LSE in 1984: Unfair trade practices and safeguard actions.

We have had three queries in the last two weeks about it.

There was also great interest in it when she first stood for election and we had to do a lot of digging. LSE Library has never had a copy and Senate House could not find their copy. We tried IALS as some law theses went there but they didn't have it either. The student record was checked and LSE is satisfied that the PhD was awarded correctly.

The standard response to any query about the thesis is as follows:

> Thank you for expressing an interest in this thesis. Unfortunately, LSE Library has never had a copy of this thesis. All PhDs from that period were awarded under the University of London banner and would have been sent first to Senate House Library. As you can appreciate there has been a lot of interest in Dr Tsai's thesis, we have been in correspondence with the University of London about it and extensive checks have been made. Unfortunately Senate House are unable to find their copy.
>
> I am sorry we cannot help further.

But please copy any queries to both me and lsethesesonline@lse.ac.uk

thanks

Clive

寄件者： Wilson，Clive
日期： 2019 年 6 月 11 日 12：35
收件者： Bell，M； Bhullar，I； Challis，D； Collings，R； Dawson，H； Fry，AE； Gomes，S； Graham1，N； Hayward，S； Horsler，PN； Hussain，R； Murphy，GE； Orson，R； Payne1，D； Reid，MI； Towlson，A； Wilkinson，E； Wilson，Clive； Zajasensky，L； Benton，A； Rodriguez； Poulose，S； Donnelly，S； Wilson1，K； Griffiths，CB
副本： Lsethesesonline   主旨： LSE 博士论文 - 台湾总统

大家好，

很抱歉这么广泛地传阅，但我试图说明并涵盖所有的可能性。如果您认为我遗漏了任何人，请帮我转寄。

本周台湾将举行总统初选，以决定民进党的候选人。其中一位是现任总统和 LSE 校友蔡英文。

蔡英文于 1984 年从 LSE 获得博士学位：不公平贸易和防卫机制。

最近两周我们收到了三次有关它的查询。

当她首次参选时，这也引起了很大的兴趣，我们不得不进行大量的挖掘。LSE 图书馆从未有过纸本论文，总图书馆也找不到他们的纸本论文。我们尝试在 IALS 内找寻，因为一些法律类论文被送到那里，但他们也没有。学生记录被检查，并确认 LSE 正确授予了博士学位。

对于任何有关论文的查询，标准回应如下：

感谢您对这篇论文的兴趣。不幸的是，LSE 图书馆从未有过这篇论文的纸本论文。那段时间的所有博士学位都在伦敦大学的名义下授予，并首先被送到伦敦大学总图书馆。正如您所理解的，对于蔡博士的论文，我们收到很多兴趣，我们已与伦敦大学就此事进行通信，并广泛的检查。不幸的是，总图书馆找不到他们的纸本。

很抱歉我们无法提供更多帮助。

并且请将任何查询的内容转寄给我和 lsethesesonline@lse.ac.uk。

谢谢，
Clive

From: Wright,NC
Sent: 11 June 2019 15:54
To: Pressoffice <Pressoffice@lse.ac.uk>
Cc: Nadal,L <L.Nadal@lse.ac.uk>; Hix,S <S.Hix@lse.ac.uk>; Thomson,MT <M.T.Thomson@lse.ac.uk>
Subject: FYI - LSE PhD thesis - Taiwan president

Dear all,

Just a quick alert that the Library has been receiving queries about this alum and the PhD. This happened a few years ago and Simeon Underwood at that time investigated and established these details. We are responding as per the below text. This could be high profile during the election period in Taiwan.

Best wishes,
Nicola

寄件者： Wright，NC
日期： 2019 年 6 月 11 日 15：54
收件者： Pressoffice <Pressoffice @lse.ac.uk>
副本： Nadal，L <L.Nadal@lse.ac.uk>； Hix，S <S.Hix@lse.ac.uk>； Thomson，MT <M.T.Thomson@lse.ac.uk>
主旨： FYI - LSE 博士论文 - 台湾总统

各位，

只是快速提醒，图书馆最近收到有关此校友及其博士学位的查询。几年前也发生过这种情况，当时 Simeon Underwood 进行了调查并确定了这些细节。我们按照以下文字回应。在台湾的选举期间，这可能会成为高度关注的议题。

祝好，

Nicola

FW_-Greetings-from-the-Presidential-office-of-Tsai

From: █████████
Date: Wednesday, 12 June 2019 at 09:08
To: "Wilson,Clive" <CLIVE.Wilson@lse.ac.uk>
Cc: "Shih,F" <F.Shih@lse.ac.uk>
Subject: Greetings from the Presidential office of Taiwan

Dear Mr. Clive Wilson,

I extend my cordial greetings to you.

As you might already be aware of the recent argument with respect to the admission of Taiwan President Tsai, Ing-Wen's PhD degree awarded by LSE in 1983. We note that LSE has taken actions to identify related documentation in this regard. On behalf of President Tsai, I would like to give consent to the disclosure of personal information in her PhD thesis, "Unfair Trade Practice and Safeguard Actions."

Further, we are able to provide both the electronic and hardbound editions of the subject thesis for the library collection upon your request. Please kindly let us know if this is feasible at your convenience.

Thank you for your assistance on this matter.

Sincerely yours,
█████████
Spokesperson of the President
Office of the President, ROC(Taiwan)
No.122, Sec.1,Chingqing S.Rd, Taipei City, Taiwan

寄件者： ▇▇▇▇
日期： 2019年6月12日，星期三，上午09：08
收件者： "Wilson，Clive" CLIVE.Wilson@lse.ac.uk
副本： "Shih，F" F.Shih@lse.ac.uk
主旨： 来自台湾总统办公室的问候

亲爱的 Clive Wilson 先生，

我向您致以亲切的问候。

如您可能已经知道，最近关于台湾总统蔡英文于 1983 年由 LSE 授予的博士学位的争论。

我们注意到 LSE 已采取行动查找相关文档。我代表蔡总统想公开她的博士论文"不公平贸易和防卫机制"中的个人资讯。此外，若您希望，我们可以为图书馆提供这本博士论文的电子版和精装版。请告诉我们这是否方便。

感谢您在此事上的协助。

此致，
▇▇▇▇
总统府发言人
中华民国（台湾）总统府
台北市中正区重庆南路一段 122 号

From: Shih,F
Sent: 12 June 2019 09:47
To: Wilson,Clive
Cc: ▮
Subject: Re: Greetings from the Presidential office of Taiwan

Dear Clive,

As suggested, President Tsai Ing-wen has now given her consent for the school to the disclosure of personal information related to her PhD thesis, entitled "Unfair Trade Practice and Safeguard Actions." Please see below the permission message.

As such, please add these information in the school letter: (1)

the names of her supervisor and viva examiners; (2) upon request, the electronic and hardbound editions of her PhD thesis will arrive at the LSE library.

As such, please give the address and the name where and who to receive this thesis. Many thanks!

Dear ▮,

When will the electronic and hardbound editions of her PhD thesis be posted?

How long will it take from Taiwan to the LSE?

Many thanks!
Fang-long

Dr Fang-long Shih
Co-Director, Taiwan Research Programme
London School of Economics and Political Science
Houghton Street
London WC2A 2AE
United Kingdom

LSE Taiwan Research Programme
http://www.lse.ac.uk/researchAndExpertise/units/TaiwanProgramme/Home.aspx

Journal *Taiwan in Comparative Perspective*
http://www.lse.ac.uk/researchAndExpertise/units/TaiwanProgramme/Journal/Home.aspx

寄件者：Shih，F
日期：2019年6月12日 09：47
收件者：Wilson，Clive
主旨：回复：来自台湾总统办公室的问候

亲爱的 Clive，
如建议，蔡英文总统现已同意学校公开有关她的博士论文"不公平贸易和防卫机制"的个人资讯。请参见下面的许可消息。因此，请在学校信中添加以下资讯：

（1）她的指导教授和口试委员的名字；（2）应要求，她的博士论文的电子和精装版本将抵达 LSE 图书馆。

因此，请提供地址和名称，以及谁来接收这篇论文。非常感谢！

亲爱的 ▮▮▮▮▮
请问她的博士论文电子版和精装版何时会公开？从台湾寄到伦敦政经学院需要多久时间？非常感谢！

芳珑
施芳珑博士
台湾研究计划室共同主任
伦敦政经学院
霍顿街
伦敦 WC2A 2AE
英国
伦敦政经学院台湾研究计划室
http://www.lse.ac.uk/researchAndExpertise/units/TaiwanProgramme/Home.aspx
《台湾比较视野期刊》
http://www.lse.ac.uk/researchAndExpertise/units/TaiwanProgramme/Journal/Home.aspx

From: Wilson,Clive
Sent: 12 June 2019 09:56
To: Shih,F
Cc: ▬▬▬▬▬▬▬
Subject: RE: Greetings from the Presidential office of Taiwan

Dear Both

If there is an electronic copy, we can almost certainly catalogue it from that and make it available if it is a decent copy.

A hardbound copy can be sent to me at

Clive Wilson
Enquiry Services Manager (Academic Services)
London School of Economics
10 Portugal Street
London WC2A 2HD

It might not be a quick thing to retrieve President Tsai's student record and make the information available but I have asked if that is possible

Fang-long – are you still coming here at 10?

Clive

寄件者： Wilson，Clive
日期： 2019 年 6 月 12 日 09：56
收件者： Shih，F
副本： ▇▇▇▇
主旨： 回复：来自台湾总统府的问候

亲爱的二位，

如果有电子版论文，我们几乎可以确定从那里着手进行编目并使其可用，如果它是一个好的电子版论文。精装纸本论文可以寄给我。

Clive Wilson
咨询服务部经理（学术服务）
伦敦政经学院
电话：020 7955 7475
葡萄牙街 10 号
伦敦 WC2A 2HD

可能不容易取得并提供蔡总统的学生记录，但我已经问过是否可能。

芳珑，你还会在 10 点来这里吗？

Clive

From: ▓▓▓▓▓▓▓▓▓▓▓▓▓▓▓▓
Sent: 12 June 2019 11:34
To: Shih, F
Cc: Wilson, Clive
Subject: RE: Greetings from the Presidential office of Taiwan

Dear Both,

Thank you so much for your kind assistance and understanding.

We are sending the hardbound editions of the subject thesis tomorrow and I believe it will arrive by next week. As for the electronic copy, we will email it to you by Friday. Please only use it for the LSE internal check not for the public release at this stage as it is indeed likely going to invite more irrational speculations.

LSE is one of the leading academic institutions in the world, and any statement issued by LSE certainly carries weight by itself. We truly appreciate your assistance and help us defend President Tsai's academic credential.

Sincerely,

▓▓▓

寄件者： ▇▇▇▇
日期： 2019 年 6 月 12 日 11：34
收件者： Shih，F
副本： Wilson，Clive
主旨： 回复：来自台湾总统府的问候

亲爱的二位，

非常感谢您们的亲切协助和理解。

我们将于明天寄送论文的精装版本，我相信它将于下周到达。至于电子版，我们将于周五通过电子邮件将其发送给您。请仅将其用于 LSE 的内部检查，此阶段不要公开发布，因为这确实可能引起更多不合理的猜测。

LSE 是世界上领先的学术机构之一，LSE 发布的任何声明本身肯定具有分量。我们真心感谢您的协助，并帮助我们捍卫蔡总统的学术资格。

诚挚的，
▇▇▇▇

Sent: Wednesday, June 12, 2019 6:12 PM
To: Wilson,Clive <CLIVE.Wilson@lse.ac.uk>
Cc:
Subject: Re: Greetings from the Presidential office of Taiwan

Dear Clive,

Thank you. It is possible to get the electronic copy of the thesis today.

However, unfortunately, to make the electronic copy available at http://etheses.lse.ac.uk/ with other LSE theses will not end the speculation but invite many more 'irrational' speculations from anti-Tsai's camp.

As such, is it OK only to mention the arrival of the hardbound copy of the thesis.

However, the Presidential Office is ok to send you the electronic copy now, but please only use it for the LSE internal check not for the public release. I hope you could understand the fragile situation under the irrational attack now.

Many thanks,
Fang-long

寄件者：Shih，F [mailto：F.Shih@lse.ac.uk]
日期：2019 年 6 月 12 日 18：12
收件者：Wilson，Clive
副本：█████████
主旨： 回复：来自台湾总统府的问候

亲爱的 Clive，

谢谢您。今天可以取得论文的电子纸本论文。

但不幸的是，将电子纸本论文放在 http://etheses.lse.ac.uk/ 与其他 LSE 论文一起不会结束这些猜测，反而会引起更多反蔡营的"非理性"猜测。

因此，是否只提及论文的精装纸本论文已经到达？
无论如何，总统府同意现在发送电子纸本论文给您，但请只用于 LSE 的内部检查，不要公开发布。希望您能理解目前在非理性攻击下的脆弱情况。 非常感谢，

施芳珑

From: Wilson,Clive
Sent: 17 June 2019 11:18
To: Cerny,MW; O'Connor,D; Graham1,N; Kelloway,C
Subject: FW: Greetings from the Presidential office of Taiwan

Dear All

we have been sent the title and acknowledgement page (attached) of the thesis from President Tsai's office with the promise we will receive a complete copy later this week. .

Not sure how much these help at the moment although it clearly confirms who her supervisor was. Michael J Elliott passed away in 2016.

https://www.weforum.org/people/michael-j-elliott
https://en.wikipedia.org/wiki/Michael_J._Elliott

Also thanked:

Brian Hindley (LSE) passed away in 2012:
http://www.lse.ac.uk/newsletters/pressAndInformation/staffNews/2012/20120614.htm

██

However, the Michael Elliott links show he left LSE for the Economist in 1984. This fits with what ███████ from UL sent us (copied again below) that Mr Elliott left both copies with LSE asking LSE to return them to Senate House. It's only circumstantial evidence but one could easily see them being left in his office and that being cleared out ...

I also wonder whether it's worth contacting ███████████ to let him know of the interest. Even if we only ever make the print copy available through the archives reading room, his name is still likely to 'get out there'

Clive

Clive Wilson
Enquiry Services Manager (Academic Services)
London School of Economics   Tel.:   020 7955 7475
10 Portugal Street   Fax.:   020 7955 7454
London WC2A 2HD   Email: Datalibrary@lse.ac.uk
                                        clive.wilson@lse.ac.uk

寄件者：Wilson，Clive
日期：2019年6月17日 11：18
收件者：Cerny，MW；O'Connor，D；Grahaml，N；Kelloway，C
主旨：转发：来自台湾总统办公室的问候

亲爱的大家，
我们已经从蔡总统的办公室收到了论文的标题和致谢页（附件），并承诺我们将在本周晚些时候收到完整副本。

我不确定这些目前有多大帮助，尽管它清楚地确认了她的指导教授是谁。Michael J Elliott 在 2016 年过世。

https://www.weforum.org/people/michael-j-elliott
https://en.wikipedia.org/wiki/Michael_J._Elliott

也感谢：
Brian Hindley（LSE）于 2012 年过世：
https://www.lse.ac.uk/newsletters/pressAndInformation/staffNews/2012/20120614.htm

然而，Michael Elliott 的连结显示他在 1984 年离开 LSE 去了《经济学人》。这符合█████ 从伦敦大学发给我们的内容（下面再次复制），即 Elliott 先生在口试后将他的副本留在了他的办公室，并要求 LSE 将它们退回给伦敦大学总图书馆。这只是间接证据，但人们可以轻易地看到它们被留在了他的办公室中…

我也在想是否值得联系█████，让他知道这个兴趣。即使我们只是透过档案阅览室提供论文的印刷副本，他的名字仍然可能会"传出去"。
Clive

    Clive Wilson
    咨询服务部经理（学术服务）
    伦敦政经学院　电话：020 7955 7475
    葡萄牙街 10 号 伦敦 WC2A 2HD 传真：020 79557454
    电子邮件 Datalibrary@lse.ac.uk、clive.wilson@lse.ac.uk

From: Wilson,Clive
Sent: 17 June 2019 16:16
To: Cerny,MW; O'Connor,D; Graham1,N; Kelloway,C
Subject: RE: Greetings from the Presidential office of Taiwan
Sensitivity: Confidential

Hi everyone

sorry – me again!

After discussion with Rachel Maguire, Sue Donnelly sent me a copy of Tsai Ing-Wen's student file but with the caveat I can't even share it internally without Dr Tsai's further permission.

I have copied two pages from it though and, as I have permission from her office, I think these could be released if it was thought they would be helpful.

Clive

寄件者：Wilson，Clive
日期：2019 年 6 月 17 日 16：16
收件者：Cerny，MW； O'Connor，D； Grahaml，N； Kelloway，C
主旨：回复：来自台湾总统府的问候
敏感度：机密

大家好，很抱歉——又是我！
在与 Rachel Maguire 讨论后，Sue Donnelly 寄给我一份蔡英文博士学生档案的副本，但附带了一个警告，即我不能在没有蔡博士进一步许可的情况下与内部分享。

不过，我从中复制了两页，并且由于我得到了她办公室的许可，我认为如果认为这些会有帮助的话，这些可以被发布。

Clive

From: Cerny,MW
Sent: 17 June 2019 16:51
To: Kelloway,C; Wilson,Clive; O'Connor,D; Graham1,N
Cc: Metcalfe,F
Subject: RE: Greetings from the Presidential office of Taiwan
Sensitivity: Confidential

Dear Charlotte,

We have just received another query seeking the thesis in the PhD Academy but I am intending to simply reply with the standard response. I am assuming that we are not needing to refer these on for response from a single point but please could you confirm.

I have asked for all queries either here or in the Law department to be forwarded to me but I expect that the Library is the standard point of contact for external enquirers requesting a thesis.

Regards,
Marcus

Marcus Cerny
Deputy Director, PhD Academy
London School of Economics and Political Science
Houghton Street
London WC2A 2AE

Please consider the environment and do not print this email unless absolutely necessary.
Please access the attached hyperlink for an important electronic communications disclaimer:
http://lse.ac.uk/emailDisclaimer

寄件者：Cerny，MW
日期：2019 年 6 月 17 日 16：51
收件者：Kelloway，C；Wilson，Clive；O'Connor，D；Grahaml，N
副本：Metcalfe，F
主旨：回复：来自台湾总统府的问候
敏感度：机密

亲爱的 Charlotte，

我们刚刚收到另一个寻找博士生学院论文的询问，但我打算简单地用标准回应来回复。我假设我们不需要将这些转发并请你确认。

我已要求所有在这里或法务部门的查询都转发给我，但我预计图书馆是外部查询者索求论文的标准联系据点。

问候，
Marcus

Marcus Cerny
博士生学院副主任
伦敦政经学院
Houghton Street
伦敦 WC2A 2AE

为了环保，除非绝对必要，否则请不要列印此电邮。请访问附加的超连结，以获取一个重要的电子通讯免责声明：https://lse.ac.uk/emailDisclaimer

From: Wilson, Clive
Sent: 21 June 2019 10:38
To: Cerny,MW; Kelloway,C; O'Connor,D; Graham1,N; Thomson,MT
Cc: Metcalfe,F
Subject: RE: Greetings from the Presidential office of Taiwan
Sensitivity: Confidential

Thanks Marcus

I feel this is one of those times it would be easier for us all to get together!

I understand the need for caution but she did win her party nomination and the elections are in January so this could run for a bit yet. ▮▮

▮▮▮▮▮▮▮▮▮▮▮▮▮▮▮▮▮▮▮▮▮▮▮▮▮▮▮▮▮▮▮▮▮▮▮▮▮▮ I was introduced to her office by Fang-long and already have permission from her office to release her information as appropriate. If an amended release would be helpful – both to us and to her – we could therefore seek specific permission on that statement. (And I asked Info Sec to confirm that it was her office.)

I would completely agree that I'm not the person to decide what we might release or to whom. I hope it was clear mine was just a suggestion 😊 . I am hoping that if we do receive the promised copy that will kill most of the speculation but then Mike Elliott's name as well as Brian Hindley and ▮▮▮▮▮▮▮▮ ▮▮▮▮▮▮▮▮▮▮ will get out there anyway.

Clive

寄件者：Wilson，Clive
日期：2019 年 6 月 21 日 10：38
收件者：Cerny，MW； Kelloway，C； O'Connor，D； Grahaml，N； Thomson，MT
副本：Metcalfe，F
主旨：回复：来自台湾总统府的问候
敏感度：机密

感谢 Marcus，
我觉得这是我们大家更应该聚在一起讨论的时刻！

我理解我们需要谨慎，但她确实赢得了她的政党提名，选举也在进行中。███

███我是由施芳珑介绍到她的办公室的，并且已经得到她办公室的许可，适当地发布她的资讯。如果一个修改过的声明对我们和她都有帮助，我们因此可以寻求在该声明上的特定许可。（而且我已要求资讯安全部门确认那是她的办公室。）

我完全同意，我不是决定我们可能发布什么或发布给谁的决策者。希望我提供的只是一个建议 。希望如果我们收到承诺的纸本论文，将终结大多数的臆测，但然后 Mike Elliott 的名字以及 Brian Hindley 和███之于众。

Clive

From: Cerny,MW
Sent: 20 June 2019 16:50
To: Wilson,Clive; Kelloway,C; O'Connor,D; Graham1,N; Thomson,MT
Cc: Metcalfe,F
Subject: RE: Greetings from the Presidential office of Taiwan
Sensitivity: Confidential

Dear Clive,

Thanks for this.

I am a bit concerned about providing details about a registration, examination and processes to third parties. I would not release information for any candidates without their approval and even then it would be limited to registration dates and award details.

I understand that this case needs additional consideration because of the public interest aspect but I still feel the need for caution about what we should and shouldn't release. Other than what is in the public domain I would not discuss information with a third party about any current student or a graduate. I believe that these would be matters for them to respond to and would be of the opinion that a review of the file was undertaken by Simeon as the Academic Registrar in 2015 which concluded that he was satisfied that there was not an issue of the registration or award being in any way questionable. I am not sure it is appropriate to enter into discussion about this other than to confirm the award and that LSE is satisfied with this.

I've copied to Mark Thomson as his predecessor was the last person to review the file formally. It may be that either he or I should review this to make sure that any dates we are discussing are definitively correct. What we might release and to whom is a separate discussion but I would be more comfortable discussing this knowing we definitely had the correct timeline.

My main question now is who decides what we release and to whom?

Thanks,
Marcus

Marcus Cerny
Deputy Director, PhD Academy
London School of Economics and Political Science
Houghton Street
London WC2A 2AE

Please consider the environment and do not print this email unless absolutely necessary.
Please access the attached hyperlink for an important electronic communications disclaimer:
http://lse.ac.uk/emailDisclaimer

寄件者：Cerny，MW
日期：2019 年 6 月 20 日 16：50
收件者：Wilson, Clive；Kelloway, C；O'Connor, D；Grahaml, N；Thomson, MT
副本：Metcalfe, F
主旨：回复：来自台湾总统府的问候
敏感度：机密

亲爱的 Clive,
感谢您的讯息。
我对于向第三方提供有关注册、考试和流程的详细资讯感到有些担忧。我不会在没有他们的批准的情况下发布任何博士候选人的资讯，即便有批准，也仅限于公布学生注册日期和学位详情。

我理解这个个案由于公众利益方面，需有额外的考虑，但我仍然觉得我们需要谨慎对待我们应该和不应该发布的资讯。除了公共领域中的讯息，我不会与第三方讨论任何现有学生或毕业生的讯息。我认为这些应该由他们来回应，并且我认为教务长 Simeon 在 2015 年进行的文件审查得出的结论是，他对注册学程或学位没有任何疑问。我不确定进入这个讨论是否适当，除了确认学位并且 LSE 对此感到满意。

我已将这份邮件传给 Mark Thomson，因为他职位的前任是最后一个正式审查这份文件的人。也许他或我应该审查这个，以确保我们讨论的任何日期都是绝对正确的。我们可能发布些什么以及发布给谁是一个单独的讨论，但我会更自在地讨论这个议题，知道我们确定有正确的时间表。
我现在的主要问题是，谁决定我们发布什么以及对谁发布？ 谢谢，Marcus

Marcus Cerny
博士生学院副主任
伦敦政经学院
Houghton Street
伦敦 WC2A 2AE

为了环保，除非绝对必要，否则请不要列印此电邮。请访问附加的超连结，以获取一个重要的电子通讯免责声明：https://lse.ac.uk/emailDisclaimer

From: Wilson, Clive
Sent: 24 June 2019 09:38
To: Adeyemi, R
Subject: RE: Greetings from the Presidential office of Taiwan
Sensitivity: Confidential

HI Remi

as follows – I've also attached a summary of Ing-Wen Tsai's students record.

Clive

On the 4th June (2019) a junior colleague sent our standard text to a US professor. He shared the text with some of his colleagues and suddenly it makes the Taiwanese news – with our member of staff's name attached. After several representations (about a week), her name was removed.

We have since had at least 22 requests that I am aware of: most of have come directly to the Library as it's a thesis (but to several departments here), but they have also gone to registry, the PhD Academy, Minouche …

We have been replying with:

> Thank you for your email. We have checked our records and both the London School of Economics and Political Science and the University of London confirm that Tsai Ing-Wen was awarded a PhD in Law 1984.
>
> However, all PhDs from that period were awarded under the University of London banner and would have been sent first to their Senate House Library. We have been in correspondence with the University of London about the thesis and extensive checks have been made. Unfortunately, Senate House are presently unable to find their copy.

Most of the people have come back with further questions.

寄件者： Wilson，Clive
日期： 2019年6月24日 09：38
收件者： Adeyemi, R
主旨： 回复：来自台湾总统府的问候
敏感度： 机密

嗨 Remi，

如下 - 我还附上了蔡英文的学生记录摘要。

Clive

在6月4日（2019年），一位初阶同事将我们的标准回复发送给一位美国教授。他与一些同事分享了这段文字，突然间它出现在台湾的新闻上—我们的员工名字也被附上。经过几次沟通（大约一周），她的名字才被删除。

自那时以来，我知道我们至少收到了22个请求：大多数直接询问图书馆，因为它是一篇论文（发到图书馆的几个部门），但这些请求也发到了注册处、博士生学院、我们LSE校长Minouche那里……

我们一直在回复：

感谢您的电子邮件。我们已经查找过我们的记录，伦敦政经学院和伦敦大学确认蔡英文于1984年正确获得法学博士学位。

然而，那个时期的所有博士学位都是在伦敦大学的名下授予的，并且首先会被发送到他们的总图书馆。我们已经与伦敦大学就论文进行了对话，并进行了广泛的查核。不幸的是，总图书馆目前找不到他们的副本。

大多数人又对我们进一步提出了问题。

The issue of course is that we were never able to find a copy of her thesis. When she first stood for office in 2015, it blew over fairly quickly. Now she has stood for (and won) her party's nomination to run again with the elections in January it seems to have become much more of a story.

 at UL confirmed in 2015 that 3 copies were submitted. Senate House and IALS lost one copy between them, but not before it was catalogued and so it is listed in all the places you would expect to see a thesis listed. The external examiner left his copy with the supervisor (Michael Elliott). Michael Elliott appears to have been away from LSE in the last year of her PhD (sabbatical?) and subsequently left LSE in 1984 to join the Economist having left instructions to pass them on. Clearly this never happened.

Fang-long Shih in t e Taiwan Research Programme put me in touch with President Tsai's office and she sent copies of her title page and the acknowledgments page. We have been promised a full copy.

Our current reply confirms that the degree was awarded in 1984 but the non-existence of the thesis invites further questions. Her supervisor being the main one - Michael Elliott passed away in 2016.

The question - to me - is whether we continue to straight bat further queries which will hopefully go away if we receive a copy and make it available like all other print theses, or whether we release additional information to answer some of the questions people are asking.

当然，问题是我们从未能找到她的纸本论文。当她在 2015 年首次竞选时，这个事件很快就淡化了。现在她赢得了她所属的政党提名，再次参加 1 月的选举，这似乎已经成为一个更大的故事。

在 2015 年，伦敦大学的 ▓▓▓▓ 确认提交了 3 份纸本论文。

伦敦大学总图书馆和 IALS 之间丢失了一份纸本论文，但在被编目前并没有丢失，所以它被列在你期望看到论文的所有地方。口试委员将蔡英文的纸本论文留给了指导教授（Michael Elliott）。Michael Elliott 似乎在她博士学位的最后一年离开了 LSE（休假？），并在 1984 年离开 LSE 加入了《经济学人》，留下了传递它们的指示。显然，这从未发生过。

▓▓▓▓▓▓▓▓▓▓▓▓▓▓▓▓▓▓▓▓▓▓▓▓▓▓▓▓▓▓▓▓

台湾研究计划室的施芳珑将我与蔡总统的办公室联系起来，她发送了她的标题页和致谢页纸本。我们被承诺会收到一份完整的纸本论文。

我们目前的回复确认该学位于 1984 年授予，但论文不存在引起了进一步的问题。她主要的指导教授是 Michael Elliott，他于 2016 年过世。

在我看来，问题在于我们是继续直接面对更多的质疑，如果我们收到一份副本并像所有其他印刷论文一样提供给读者，希望这些质疑就会消失，还是发布更多资讯来回答人们提出的一些问题。

From: ▓▓▓▓▓▓▓▓▓▓▓▓▓▓▓▓▓▓▓
Sent: 29 June 2015 15:13
To: ▓▓▓▓▓▓
Cc: Wilson,Clive; Lsethesesonline
Subject: RE: PhD LSE Law Thesis 1984
Importance: High

Dear ▓▓▓▓

My colleague has now retrieved the file on this student from our Archive Storage. From this I can see the history of chasing for copies of the thesis both by the Research Degrees Examinations office at Senate House and enquiries from Senate House Library too. In 2011 the SHL confirmed that it sent a copy of the thesis to the Institute for Advanced Legal Studies. At that time, ▓▓▓▓▓▓▓▓▓▓▓▓▓▓▓▓▓▓▓▓▓▓▓▓▓▓ established that IALS no longer had a copy of the said thesis.

The Research Degrees Examinations office had also chased both examiners (appointed for the PD examination) and the supervisor (Mr M J Elliott) for the return of the copies of the thesis. Apparently, the Internal Examiner left his copy of the PhD thesis with Mr Elliott post-viva. Mr Elliott left both copies with the LSE asking the LSE to return these to Senate House. These were never received.

The copy referred to above which went over to IALS would have been the spare third copy submitted to the Research Degrees Examinations office for examination on 15 June 1983.

I am sorry I cannot be more helpful.

With best wishes,

Lorraine

寄件者： ▇▇▇▇
日期： 2015 年 6 月 29 日 15：13
收件者： ▇▇▇▇
副本： Wilson，Clive； Lsethesesonline
主旨： 回复：1984 年 LSE 法学博士论文
重要性： 高

亲爱的 ▇▇▇▇，

我的同事现在已从我们的档案储存中取出了这位学生的档案。从中我可以看到伦敦大学总图书馆的研究学位考试办公室和伦敦大学总图书馆追踪纸本论文的历史。在 2011 年，伦敦大学总图书馆确认它将论文的一份纸本发送到了高等法律研究所。当时，▇▇▇▇ 确认 IALS 不再拥有该论文的副本。

研究生学位考试办公室也追踪了两位口试委员（为博士论文考试指定的）和指导教授（M J Elliott 先生）以取回纸本论文。显然，内部口试委员在口试后将她的纸本论文留给了 Elliott 先生。Elliott 先生将两份纸本留在了 LSE，要求 LSE 将其退回到伦敦大学总图书馆。但这些论文从未被总图书馆收到。

上述提到的纸本论文是 1983 年 6 月 15 日被提交给研究生学位考试办公室作为考试用的第三份纸本论文。

很抱歉我不能提供更多的帮助。

祝好，
Lorraine

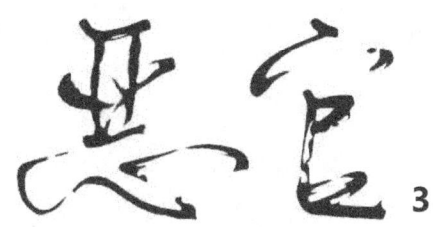

办公室的紧急会议:
LSE 内部建议、策略与决策

办公室的紧急会议：LSE 内部建议、策略与决策

伦敦政经学院（LSE），咨询服务经理 Clive Wilson 紧急地草拟了一份统一的对外回复不久，LSE 博士学程校务处副处长 Marcus W Cerny 收到了 Wilson 的草拟回复。他认为，回复中必须强调蔡英文已经获得学位，并且得到了伦敦大学和 LSE 的确认。这是一个关键的信息，可以为学院辩护，也可以平息外界的质疑。

在经过多次的讨论和修改后，LSE 终于统一了对外的回复。他们新增了一个重要的信息：确定蔡英文已经获得学位。这一信息，无疑是对外界最有力的回击。

然而，这场风波还没有结束。Wilson 决定向 LSE 媒体关系部门负责人 Daniel O'Connor 教学，用大英图书馆的索引来诱导外界认为蔡英文的论文从以前就存在。他希望这样可以为学院争取更多的时间，也可以避免更多的质疑。

但是，有人提出了一个尖锐的问题：论文如果未被接受，如何授予学位？这一问题，让 LSE 陷入了困境。经过内部的讨论，LSE 决定不对这一问题给予回应。

此时，LSE 秘书部门档案管理员 Sue Donnelly 从蔡英文的学生纪录的 43-46 页中找到一份 1987 年由中央登记处教务处职员 P.C. Kennedy 所签发的文件。她认为，LSE 和伦敦大学可以公布这份文件，以此为学院辩护。

但这份所谓 278 页的蔡英文学生纪录，来源始终不明。LSE 在 2022 年 6 月 21 日 Tribunal Court Judge Alison Mckenna 的一场判决当中，坦承资料不精准，内容更是偶然取得的。

然而，风波还没有结束。LSE 院长再次接到了一封检举信。这一次，他知道，这场学术争议将会更加激烈。

在这场风暴的背后，是一场关于真相和权力的斗争。LSE 必须面对的，不仅仅是外界的质疑，更是学术界的道德标准和学院的声誉。而在这场斗争中，每一个决策，都将影响到学院的未来。

FW_-Greetings-from-the-Presidential-office-of-Tsai

From: O'Connor,D
To: Metcalfe,F
Subject: FW: Ing-Wen Tsai's PhD thesis
Date: 11 June 2019 14:06:00

FYI

From: Cerny,MW
Sent: 11 June 2019 14:03
To: Graham1,N <N.Graham1@lse.ac.uk>; Orson,R <R.Orson@lse.ac.uk>
Cc: O'Connor,D <D.O'Connor@lse.ac.uk>; Wilson,Clive <CLIVE.Wilson@lse.ac.uk>; Lsethesesonline <Lsethesesonline@lse.ac.uk>
Subject: RE: Ing-Wen Tsai's PhD thesis

Hi Nancy,

The examination went through the University of London procedures and we had the award confirmed from them with a March 1984 award date. It was recorded in the 1985/86 Calendar and is recorded in both on LSE and U of L records.

Thanks,
Marcus

Marcus Cerny
Deputy Director, PhD Academy
London School of Economics and Political Science
Houghton Street
London WC2A 2AE

Please consider the environment and do not print this email unless absolutely necessary.
Please access the attached hyperlink for an important electronic communications disclaimer:
http://lse.ac.uk/emailDisclaimer

From: Graham1,N
Sent: 11 June 2019 13:58
To: Cerny,MW; Orson,R
Cc: O'Connor,D; Wilson,Clive; Lsethesesonline
Subject: RE: Ing-Wen Tsai's PhD thesis

Hi all

My colleague Clive Wilson has sent out some advice on this very issue today. He's drafted the following text for anyone to use if they receive a query. Clive has asked that if you do receive a query and reply, to copy both him and LSE Theses Online in – lsethesesonline@lse.ac.uk

> Thank you for expressing an interest in this thesis. Unfortunately, LSE Library has never had a copy of this thesis. All PhDs from that period were awarded under the University of London banner and would have been sent first to Senate House Library. As you can appreciate there has been a lot of interest in Dr Tsai's thesis, we have been in correspondence with the University of London about it and extensive checks have been made. Unfortunately Senate House are unable to find their copy.

寄件者：O'Connor，D
收件者：Metcalfe，F
主旨：蔡英文的博士论文
日期：2019年6月11日 14：06：00

供您参考
寄件者：Cerny，MW
日期：2019年6月11日 14：03
收件者：Graham1，N；Orson，R
副本：O'Connor，D；Wilson，Clive；Lsethesesonline
主旨：蔡英文的博士论文

嗨，Nancy，
考试是透过伦敦大学的程序进行的，我们已经从他们那里确认了学位授予，授予日期为1984年3月。它被记录在1985/86的行事历中，并在LSE和伦敦大学的记录中都有记录。
谢谢，Marcus

Marcus Cerny
博士生学院副主任
伦敦政经学院
Houghton Street
伦敦 WC2A 2AE
为了环保，除非绝对必要，否则请不要列印此电邮。请访问附加的超连结，以获取一个重要的电子通讯免责声明：https://lse.ac.uk/emailDisclaimer

----

寄件者：Graham1，N
日期：2019年6月11日 13：58
收件者：Cerny，MW；Orson，R
副本：O'Connor，D；Wilson，Clive；Lsethesesonline
主旨：蔡英文的博士论文

嗨，大家
我的同事 Clive Wilson 今天已经就这个问题发出了一些建议。他为收到查询的人草拟了以下文本。Clive 要求，如果您收到查询并回复，请抄送他和 LSE 网路论文—lsethesesonline@lse.ac.uk
感谢您对这篇论文的关心。不幸的是，LSE 图书馆从未有过这篇论文的纸本论文。那段时间的所有博士学位都是在伦敦大学的名义下授予的，并首先被发送到伦敦大学总图书馆。正如您所理解的，对蔡博士的论文有很大的兴趣，我们已经与伦敦大学就此事进行了通信，并进行了广泛的检查。不幸的是，总图书馆找不到他们的纸本论文。

From: Griffiths,CB
Sent: 13 June 2019 14:07
To: Kelloway,C
Cc: Orson,R; Metcalfe,F; Clarkl,B; Wilson,Clive; O'Connor,D
Subject: RE: Ing-Wen Tsai's PhDthesis
Importance: High

Dear Charlotte,

I believe the press statement has been released which is good news- however Ruth's name is still appearing on the People's News web page. (https://www.peoplenews.tw/news/4l075ad6-3253-4db4-a689-38d8ea3eIe)f)

Can you please let Ruth (and I) know where we are in relation to getting it removed? And can this be followed up if they do have not taken it down today?

Thanks,
Camilla

From: Kelloway,C
Sent: 12 June 2019 14:05
To: Wilson,Clive
Cc: Griffiths,CB; O'Connor,D; Metcalfe,F
Subject: RE: Ing-Wen Tsai's PhDthesis

Hi Clive,

We've adapted the reply to members of the public who are getting in touch. Please see below. Happy for you to send this out this out in reply to any general enquires, although do let us know if you would prefer this to come from us.

General response:

Thank you for your email. We have checked our records and both the London School of Economics and Political Science and the University of London confirm that Tsai Ing-Wen was awarded a PhD in Law 1984.

However, all PhDs from that period were awarded under the University of London banner and would have been sent first to their Senate House Librruy. We have been in correspondence with the University of London about the thesis and extensive checks have been made. Unfo11unately, Senate House are presently unable to find their copy.

Kinds regards,

寄件者：Griffiths，CB
日期：2019 年 6 月 13 日 14：07
收件者：Kelloway，C
副本：Orson，R；Metcalfe，F；Clark1，B；Wilson，Clive；O'Connor，D
主旨：回复：关于蔡英文的博士论文
重要性：高

亲爱的 Charlotte，

我相信新闻声明已经发布，这是个好消息—然而 Ruth 的名字仍然出现在《民报》的网页上。（https://www.peoplenews.tw/news/41075ad6-3253-4db4-a689-38d8ea3e1e1f）可以请你告诉Ruth（和我）我们在删除相关报导吗？如果他们今天没有把它拿下来，这能继续跟进吗？

谢谢，Camilla

_____

寄件者：Kelloway，C
日期：2019 年 6 月 12 日 14：05
收件者：Wilson，Clive
副本：Griffiths，CB；O'Connor，D；Metcalfe，F
主旨：回复：关于蔡英文的博士论文

嗨，Clive，

我们已经调整了回复给联系我们的公众的答复。请见下文。你可以发送这个回复给任何一般的查询，尽管如果你希望这来自我们，请让我们知道。

一般回应：
感谢您的电子邮件。我们已经检查了我们的记录，伦敦政经学院和伦敦大学都确认蔡英文于 1984 年获得了法学博士学位。

然而，那个时期的所有博士学位都是在伦敦大学的名下颁发的，并且首先会被发送到他们的总图书馆。我们已经与伦敦大学就论文进行了通信，并且已经进行了广泛的检查。不幸的是，总图书馆目前找不到他们的论文。

亲切的问候，

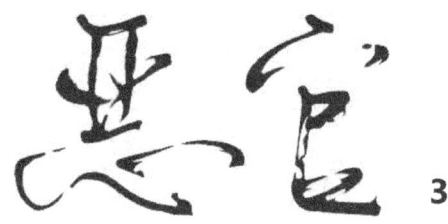

寻找真相：2015 年的调查者

寻找真相：2015 年的调查者

伦敦政经学院（LSE）的媒体关系部门负责人 Daniel O'Connor 正在确定学院对外的统一发言。然而，这场风波的核心，是蔡英文指导教授的身份。LSE 咨询服务经理 Clive Wilson 知道个资法不保护亡者的资讯。但他仍然拒绝公布蔡指导教授的名字。他认为，这是学院的一个原则，也是对学术的尊重。但实情却是，这份资料来源是由台湾总统府提供，Clive Wilson 在还没确定实情之前，并不想贸然响应。

LSE 台湾研究计画室共同主任施芳珑对此表示不满。她希望 LSE 在第一版本的声明上，抹去没有收到论文的说法。她认为，这是对蔡英文的不公平对待。她还指示 LSE，应该补充声明，以《个资法》为由，拒绝答复外界的质疑。

LSE 的高层决定去询问 2015 年的调查者 Simeon Underwood。Simeon Underwood 表示，他所看到的文件是完整的。但他不确定其中是否有任何的"运作"，甚至可能被伪造。

Simeon Underwood 会这样说的原因很简单，因为他所看到的都是影本，而不是原始文件。这场风波，让 LSE 陷入了前所未有的困境。

To: ▇
Date: 12 June 2019 17:08:17
Attachments: image002.png
image003.png
image005.png

Dear ▇,

Thank you for your correspondence, I have been asked to respond with some more information.

Further to your remarks, the records of both the London School of Economics and Political Science and the University of London confirm that Tsai Ing-Wen was awarded a PhD in Law 1984. For your interest, I have attached a scan of a relevant entry in the 'LSE Calendar' of 1985/86, which is an official public record of awards and degrees given to LSE students for the previous year.

The student record shows that the thesis was submitted but the supervisor copy that should have come to LSE Library (the British Library of Political and Economic Science) never did.

As previously circulated, all PhDs from that period were awarded under the University of London banner and would have been sent first to their Senate House Library. They clearly received their copy because otherwise it could not have been catalogued and appear on their catalogue – and from there to the British Library catalogue.

We have been in correspondence with the University of London about the thesis and extensive checks have been made. Senate House are presently unable to find their copy.

I am in touch with colleagues regarding the other pieces of information requested. However, some of them may be restricted by UK data protection laws.

Daniel O'Connor
Head of Media Relations | Communications Division
The London School of Economics and Political Science
Houghton Street, London WC2A 2AE
t: +44 (0)20 7955 7417
e: oconnord@lse.ac.uk
lse.ac.uk

LSE is ranked #1 in Europe for social sciences
(QS World University Ranking 2018)

寄件人：▇▇▇

日期：2019 年 6 月 12 日 17：08：17

附件：image002.png image003.png image005.png

亲爱的 ▇▇▇

感谢您的来信，我被要求提供一些更多的资讯回复您。

关于您的评论，伦敦政经学院和伦敦大学的记录都确认蔡英文于 1984 年获得法学博士学位。为了您的参考，我附上了一张 1985/86 年度"LSE 行事历"的相关条目扫描影本，这是上一学年授予 LSE 学生学位和学位的官方公开记录。

学生记录显示论文已经提交，但应该由指导教授送到 LSE 图书馆（英国政治经济图书馆）的纸本论文从未到达。

如之前所说，那个时期的所有博士学位都在伦敦大学的名下授予，并且首先会被送到他们的总图书馆。他们显然收到了他们的纸本论文，否则它不可能被编目并出现在他们的目录上——从那里再出现在大英图书馆的目录上。

我们已经与伦敦大学就论文进行了通信，并进行了广泛的检查。总图书馆目前无法找到他们的纸本。

我正在与同事联系，讨论其他要求的资讯。然而，其中一些可能受到英国数据保护法的限制。

Daniel O'Connor
媒体关系主管 | 传播部门
伦敦政经学院
霍顿街，伦敦 WC2A 2AE
电话：+44（0）20 7955 7417
电邮：oconnord@lse.ac.uk
网站：lse.ac.uk

LSE 在社会科学领域中在欧洲排名第一
（QS 世界大学排名 2018）

RE_For your modification re my draft

To: Wilson,Clive; Kelloway,C
Cc: Metcalfe,F
Subject: RE: For your modification re my draft
Date: 12 June 2019 16:32:48

From: Shih,F
Sent: 12 June 2019 15:16
To: Wilson,Clive <CLIVE.Wilson@lse.ac.uk>; Kelloway,C <C.Kelloway@lse.ac.uk>
Cc: O'Connor,D <D.O'Connor@lse.ac.uk>; Metcalfe,F <F.Metcalfe@lse.ac.uk>
Subject: For your modification re my draft

Dear Clive and Charlotte,

Thank you very much for all your efforts in preparing this LSE press release.

This is very important for alumna President Tsai Ing-wen and the school's reputation as they have been under the irrational attack by anti-Tsai camp during the nomination election in her own political party – DDP.

To be brief, the anti-Tsai's camp includes:

(1)   Taiwanese nationalists (who is against Tsai's policy beyond Chinese and Taiwanese nationalisms toward democracy);

(2)   Taiwanese Independence fundamentalists (who is against Tsai's policy in maintaining the status quo with China);

(3)   Church members (who is against Tsai's government which has recently passed same-sex marriage law)

It is hoped you and the school could understand the current fragile situation and support our alumna and her lead of Taiwan's democracy to the next step as well as to redress the

寄件者：Wilson，Clive； Kelloway，C
副本：Metcalfe，F
主旨：回复：关于我的草稿，请您修改
日期：2019 年 6 月 12 日 16：32：48

寄件者： Shih，F
日期：2019 年 6 月 12 日 15：16
收件者： Wilson，Clive CLIVE.Wilson@lse.ac.uk； Kelloway，C C.Kelloway@lse.ac.uk
副本： O'Connor，D D.O'Connor@lse.ac.uk； Metcalfe，F F.Metcalfe@lse.ac.uk
主旨： 关于我的草稿，请您修改

亲爱的 Clive 和 Charlotte，

非常感谢你们在准备这份 LSE 新闻稿方面所做的所有努力。

这对于校友蔡英文总统和学校的声誉非常重要，因为在她自己的政党——民进党的提名选举中，她们一直受到反蔡阵营的非理性攻击。

简单来说，反蔡的阵营包括：

1. 台湾民族主义者（反对蔡英文超越中国和台湾民族主义，走向民主的政策）；

2. 台湾独立基本教义派（反对蔡英文维持与中国现状的政策）；

3. 教会成员（反对蔡政府，该政府最近通过了同性婚姻法）。

希望您和学校能理解目前的脆弱情况，并支持我们的校友及她领导台湾民主迈向下一步，以及纠正反蔡阵营对蔡总统和 LSE 造成的损害。

damages to President Tsai and the LSE done by anti-Tsai camp.

The draft letter is fine but is it possible to cut it shorter and add a response to the question of her supervisor and viva examiners?

If this sentence -- "Unfortunately, the LSE Library has never held a copy of Tsai Ing-wen's thesis"- has appeared again, the anti-Tsai camp will continue to attack Tsai, saying she has never submitted her thesis, no matter how many reasons in explaining this. As such, the rest of the sentences regarding her thesis is better not to repeat again (already said in Ruth Orson's 2 emails which have invited the conspiracy to accuse her deceiving of her doctoral degree).

As such, it is hoped you will agree this modified version and please see below:

If not, we also understand the school's concern. Many thanks!

An LSE spokesperson said:

"University of London and LSE records confirm Tsai Ing-wen was awarded a PhD in Law in 1984. The LSE has all information, such as the names of Tsai's supervisor and viva examiners. But due to the private data protection, the LSE is unable to release this information without the consent of the individuals. Nevertheless, it is not an unusual case as the supervisor name wasn't always included in the thesis in those days."

All the very best,
Fang-long

对于反蔡阵营对蔡英文总统和 LSE 所造成的损害。

草稿信件很好，但是否可以将其缩短，并加入关于她的指导教授和口试委员的回答？

如果这句话—"不幸的是，LSE 图书馆从未持有蔡英文的论文纸本论文"—再次出现，反蔡阵营将继续攻击蔡英文，说她从未提交过她的论文，无论解释这一点有多少理由。因此，关于她的论文的其余句子最好不要再重复（Ruth Orson 的 2 封电子邮件已经提到，这引起了阴谋论者指控她欺骗她的博士学位）。

因此，希望您能同意这个修改版本，请参见下方
如果不行，我们也理解学校的担忧。非常感谢！

LSE 发言人说，
"伦敦大学和 LSE 的记录证实蔡英文于 1984 年获得法学博士学位。LSE 拥有所有资讯，例如蔡英文的指导教授和口试委员的名字。但由于私人资料保护，LSE 无法在未经个人同意的情况下公开这些资讯。然而，这不是一个不寻常的情况，因为在那些日子里，指导教授的名字并不总是包含在论文中"。

祝一切顺
利，

施芳珑

RE_ In confidence

From: Thomson,MT
To: "Simeon Underwood"
Subject: RE: In confidence
Date: 25 June 2019 09:11:53
Attachments: image002.png
image003.png
image005.png
image006.png
Sensitivity: Confidential

Thanks Simeon, that all tallies with what I can make out. I have no doubt that the award was made in line with UoL requirements at the time; and I think there is enough to show that the thesis made its way to Senate House (i.e. because there is a record of it being catalogued), but seems to have been lost when they forwarded it to the Institute for Advanced Legal Studies.

Lots of noise and heat around this one, re: influential LSE alumna, Taiwanese election, political opponents, etc. The play here is to follow regulations and not make any allowances we wouldn't make for any of our graduates.

You may get back to your retirement now.

All best,

MTT

From: Simeon Underwood [mailto:simeon.underwood@outlook.com]
Sent: 25 June 2019 09:05
To: Thomson,MT <M.T.Thomson@lse.ac.uk>
Subject: Re: In confidence
Sensitivity: Confidential

Mark

I have a vague memory of this. My recollection is that it was no big deal. I got the student file from the archive, and then liaised with Senate House (I am not sure whether Susan Johnson had left by that time). All the paperwork was in order -- by contrast to some files I had seen, notably the senior New Zealand civil servant whose claim to have a PhD turned out to be unprovable and possibly fraudulent. I am not sure there are any "workings". If you are in need of anything further, though, I can have a go at looking further, but without much expectation of finding anything. On the missing thesis, I suspect that this is down to Senate House, the Library or both.

Does that help ?

Simeon

寄件者： Thomson，MT
收件者： "Simeon Underwood"
主旨： 回复：机密事项
日期： 2019 年 6 月 25 日 09：11：53
附件： image002.png、image003.png、image005.png、image006.png
敏感度：机密

感谢 Simeon，这与我所知的一切都相符。我确信这项学位是根据当时的伦敦大学要求授予的；我认为有足够的证据显示论文已经送到总图书馆（即因为有其被编目的记录），但似乎在他们将其转发到高等法律研究所时丢失了。

这一事件引起了很多关注，涉及有影响力的 LSE 校友、台湾选举、政治对手等。我们的策略是遵循规定，不为我们的毕业生提供任何特殊待遇。

你现在可以回到你的退休生活了。

祝好，
MTT

寄件者： Simeon Underwood [mailto：simeon.underwood@outlook.com]
日期： 2019 年 6 月 25 日 09：05
收件者： Thomson，MT M.T.Thomson@lse.ac.uk
主旨： 回复：机密事项
敏感度：机密

Mark，

我对此只剩模糊的记忆。我的记忆是这不是什么大问题。我从档案中取得了学生档案，然后与总图书馆联系（我不确定 Susan Johnson 那时是否已离职）。所有的文件都是完整的，与我看过的一些文件相比，尤其是一位资深的纽西兰公务员，他声称拥有博士学位，但这是无法证明且可能是伪造的。我不确定是否有任何"运作"。但如果你需要更多的东西，我可以试着再查找，但不太期望能找到什么。关于丢失的论文，我怀疑这是总图书馆、LSE 图书馆或两者的问题。

这有帮助吗？

Simeon

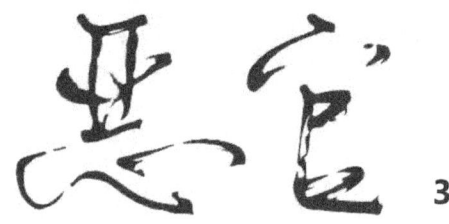

3

风暴的起源：1985/86 学年修业规定的影本

风暴的起源：1985/86 学年修业规定的影本

伦敦政经学院（LSE）学术争议的风暴焦点是一份被称为 1985 年与 1986 学年修业规定的影本。这份文件，对于外界来说，似乎是证明某位学者学位正确授予的唯一证据。但对于学院内部，这份文件背后的故事远比表面上看起来要复杂得多。

LSE 媒体关系部门负责人 Daniel O'Connor 一直在寻找能够证明学位正确授予的实质证据。但他面对的，却是一个困境。2015 年，学院曾表示，口试委员和指导老师的名单，因为涉及到学者的隐私，没有其允许不能对外公开。但现在，这份 85/86 学年修业规定的影本，似乎成为了他唯一能够拿出来的证据。尽管他自己也承认，这份文件没有办法作为实质的证据，但他还是一再以此对外声明。

LSE 博士学程校务处副处长 Marcus W Cerny 则有着不同的看法。他认为，学院应该舍弃这场争议，站在这位校友的一边。他一再拿出 2015 年的调查结果，试图搪塞外界的质疑。尽管他明知这份调查结果存在诸多疑点，但他仍然不愿意进一步调查。他甚至建议，可以拿 1985 年与 1986 学年修业规定的影本作为佐证，证实这位学者确实拥有学位。

LSE 台湾研究计画室共同主任施芳珑对此表示不满。她决定与 Wilson 和学院的一名高级官员约见面。但在见面前，她突然不再回应任何邮件。这次的见面，似乎成为了揭开这场学术争议真相的关键。

Re_Ing-Wen Tsai's PhD thesis（4）

From: Orson,R
To: Wilson,Clive; O'Connor,D
Cc: Cerny,MW; Metcalfe,F; Kelloway,C
Subject: Re: Ing-Wen Tsai's PhD thesis
Date: 11 June 2019 22:08:25

I will not be in the office tomorrow but I would like to know what Nicola and Martin's response to this situation is as soon as possible tomorrow morning.

Ruth Orson
Library Assistant, Research Support Services | LSE Research Online
London School of Economics and Political Science
10 Portugal Street, London WC2A 2HD
tel: 020 7955 3528 | email: R.Orson@lse.ac.uk

From: Wilson,Clive
Sent: 11 June 2019 20:04:42
To: O'Connor,D
Cc: Cerny,MW; Metcalfe,F; Kelloway,C; Graham1,N; Orson,R; Lsethesesonline
Subject: Re: Ing-Wen Tsai's PhD thesis

I've just sent two very polite holding replies although Professor ▓▓▓ chasing is bordering on the rude - although I do appreciate how important the issue is.

Dr Shih is going to come in to see me in the morning at 10. I'll leave a proper reply to the emails until I have spoken to her - but of course happy for anyone to join us.

Clive

From: O'Connor,D
Sent: 11 June 2019 19:54
To: Wilson,Clive
Cc: Cerny,MW; Metcalfe,F; Kelloway,C; Graham1,N; Orson,R; Lsethesesonline
Subject: Re: Ing-Wen Tsai's PhD thesis

Thanks for this, Clive. Useful to know.

Ruth do forward on any further letters and we can collate and reply from central LSE accounts

Danny

On 11 Jun 2019, at 17:39, Wilson,Clive <CLIVE.Wilson@lse.ac.uk> wrote:

> Hi All
>
> just had a chat with Dr Fang-Long Shih in the LSE Taiwan Research Programme who is a supporter of Dr Tsai.
>
> Apparently the Taiwan press and the opposition party are trying to relate this to the incident over Saif gaddafi and the Libyan donation.

寄件者：Orson，R
收件者：Wilson, Clive；O"Connor, D
副本：Cerny, MW；Metcalfe, F；Kelloway, C
主旨：关于蔡英文的博士论文
日期：2019年6月11日 22：08：25

我明天不会在办公室，但我希望能在明天早上尽快知道 Nicola 和 Martin 对此情况的回应。
Ruth Orson
研究支援服务助理，LSE 研究在线 | 伦敦政治经济学院
10 Portugal Street，London WC2A 2HD
电话：020 7955 3528 | 电子邮件：R.Orson@lse.ac.uk

寄件者：Wilson, Clive
日期：2019年6月11日 20：04：42
收件者：O'Connor, D
副本：Cerny, MW；Metcalfe, F；Kelloway, C；Graham1, N；Orson, R；Lsethesesonline
主旨：关于蔡英文的博士论文

我刚刚发送了两封非常有礼貌的回复，■■■■教授的追问已经有点无礼了 - 但我确实理解这个问题的重要性。
明天早上 10 点，施芳珑博士将会来见我。在和她谈话之前，我不会正式回复那些电子邮件 - 但当然欢迎任何人加入我们的讨论。
Clive

寄件者：O'Connor, D
日期：2019年6月11日 19：54
收件者：Wilson, Clive
副本：Cerny, MW；Metcalfe, F；Kelloway, C；Graham1, N；Orson, R；Lsethesesonline
主旨：关于蔡英文的博士论文

感谢您的资讯，Clive。很有帮助。

Ruth，如果有任何进一步的信件，请转发给我们，我们可以从 LSE 的中央帐户汇整并回复。
Danny
2019年6月11日，17：39，Wilson, Clive CLIVE.Wilson@lse.ac.uk 写道：
大家好，
我刚与 LSE 台湾研究计划的施芳珑博士进行了交谈，她是蔡博士的支持者。
据悉，台湾媒体和反对党正试图将此事与赛义夫·格达费和利比亚捐款事件相关联。

Supporters of Dr Tsai are therefore very keen to be able to prove that the degree was awarded correctly/successfully and may be able to get permission from Dr Tsai to release more information from her record as appropriate.

And the Calendar is a public document that anyone from outside LSE can request to view through our archives so there is no DP/GDPR issue.

Clive

From: Cerny,MW
Sent: 11 June 2019 17:15
To: O'Connor,D; Metcalfe,F; Kelloway,C; Wilson,Clive; Graham1,N; Orson,R
Cc: Lsethesesonline
Subject: RE: Ing-Wen Tsai's PhD thesis

My opinion is we should leave it in. We should look like we're pretending to have had nothing to do with this and she is an LSE alumnus (we trumpeted as much ourselves when she got elected).

Thanks,
Marcus

Marcus Cerny
Deputy Director, PhD Academy
London School of Economics and Political Science
Houghton Street
London WC2A 2AE

Please consider the environment and do not print this email unless absolutely necessary.
Please access the attached hyperlink for an important electronic communications disclaimer:
http://lse.ac.uk/emailDisclaimer

From: O'Connor,D
Sent: 11 June 2019 17:09
To: Metcalfe,F; Kelloway,C; Wilson,Clive; Graham1,N; Cerny,MW; Orson,R
Cc: Lsethesesonline
Subject: RE: Ing-Wen Tsai's PhD thesis

Thanks. As we're sharing one of LSE's records (the Calendar) I think we should probably leave it in.

(Can switch it around to 'UoL and LSE' though).

D

From: Metcalfe,F
Sent: 11 June 2019 17:07
To: Kelloway,C <C.Kelloway@lse.ac.uk>; O'Connor,D <D.O'Connor@lse.ac.uk>; Wilson,Clive <CLIVE.Wilson@lse.ac.uk>; Graham1,N <N.Graham1@lse.ac.uk>; Cerny,MW

因此，蔡博士的支持者非常希望能够证明该学位是正确/成功授予的，并可能能够获得蔡博士的许可，从她的记录中释放更多的资讯。

行事历是一份公开文件，LSE 外部的任何人都可以通过我们的档案要求查看，所以没有 DP/GDPR 问题。
Clive

寄件者：Cerny，MW
日期：2019 年 6 月 11 日 17：15
收件者：O'Connor，D；Metcalfe，F；Kelloway，C；Wilson，Clive；Graham1，N；Orson，R
副本：Lsethesesonline
主旨：关于蔡英文的博士论文

我认为我们应该跟它耗着。我们应该摆出一副事不关己的样子，况且她本来就是 LSE 的校友（当她当选时，我们还自吹自擂了一番）。

感谢，Marcus
Marcus Cerny
博士生学院副主任
伦敦政经学院
Houghton Street
伦敦 WC2A 2AE

为了环保，除非绝对必要，否则请不要列印此电邮。请访问附加的超连结，以获取一个重要的电子通讯免责声明：https://lse.ac.uk/emailDisclaimer

----

寄件者：O'Connor，D
日期：2019 年 6 月 11 日 17：09
收件者：Metcalfe，F；Kelloway，C；Wilson，Clive；Graham1，N；Cerny，MW；Orson，R
副本：Lsethesesonline
主旨：关于蔡英文的博士论文

谢谢。由于我们正在分享 LSE 的记录（行事历），我认为我们应该保留它。（可以将其更改为"伦敦大学和LSE"）。
D

寄件者：Metcalfe，F
日期：2019 年 6 月 11 日 17：07
收件者：Kelloway，C C.Kelloway@lse.ac.uk； O'Connor，D D.O'Connor@lse.ac.uk； Wilson，Clive CLIVE.Wilson@lse.ac.uk； Graham1，N N.Graham1@lse.ac.uk； Cerny，MW M.W.Cerny@lse.ac.uk； Orson，R R.Orson@lse.ac.uk

<M.W.Cerny@lse.ac.uk>; Orson,R <R.Orson@lse.ac.uk>
Cc: Lsethesesonline <Lsethesesonline@lse.ac.uk>
Subject: Re: Ing-Wen Tsai's PhD thesis

Looks good to me. You could lose LSE from the first line putting the ownership firmly in UoL court but is that overkill?

Get Outlook for iOS

From: Kelloway,C <c.kelloway@lse.ac.uk>
Sent: Tuesday, June 11, 2019 4:49 PM
To: O'Connor,D; Wilson,Clive; Graham1,N; Cerny,MW; Orson,R
Cc: Lsethesesonline; Metcalfe,F
Subject: RE: Ing-Wen Tsai's PhD thesis

Hi all,

We have put together a reply to Hwan and a media statement for any press requests we get about this. Please find these below.

We can send the reply to ▇▇▇▇ (with the library copied in) as it seems this story is starting to spread into the media from sources such as Hwan.

Just one question on the scan of the calendar – does anyone know if sharing this document with external parties will raise any data protection/GDPR issues?

Letter:
Dear ▇▇▇▇,

Thank you for your correspondence, I have been asked to respond with some more information.

Further to your remarks, the records of both the London School of Economics and Political Science and the University of London confirm that Tsai Ing-Wen was awarded a PhD in Law 1984. For your interest, I have attached a scan of a relevant entry in the 'LSE Calendar' of 1985/86, which is an official public record of awards and degrees given to LSE students for the previous year.

Unfortunately, the LSE Library has never held a copy of Tsai Ing-wen's thesis. All PhDs from that period were awarded under the University of London banner and would have been sent first to their Senate House Library.

We have been in correspondence with the University of London about the thesis and extensive checks have been made. Senate House are presently unable to find their copy.

[Given these circumstances, it may be worth contacting Dr Tsai's office for detail of the thesis, if she still has a copy]. [optional?]

Kind regards

副本：Lsethesesonline Lsethesesonline@lse.ac.uk
主旨：关于蔡英文的博士论文

看起来对我来说很好。您可以从第一行中删除 LSE，将所有权确定在伦敦大学法庭上，但这是否过分？

从 iOS 的 Outlook 获取

寄件者：Kelloway, C c.kelloway@lse.ac.uk
日期：2019 年 6 月 11 日 16：49
收件者：O'Connor, D；Wilson, Clive；Graham1, N；Cerny, MW；Orson, R
副本：Lsethesesonline； Metcalfe，F
主旨：关于蔡英文的博士论文

大家好，
我们已经为林环墙和任何关于此事的媒体请求准备了回复和媒体声明。请在下面找到这些。

我们可以将回复发送给 ▓▓▓▓ （并抄送给图书馆），因为这个故事似乎开始从林环墙等来源传播到媒体中。

只有一个问题是关于行事历的扫描 - 有人知道与外部方分享此文档是否会引起任何数据保护 /GDPR 问题？

信件：亲爱的 ▓▓▓▓ ，

感谢您的来信，我被要求回复一些更多的资讯。

根据您的评论，伦敦政经学院和伦敦大学的记录都确认蔡英文于 1984 年获得法学博士学位。为了您的兴趣，我附上了 1985/86 年"LSE 行事历"的相关条目的扫描，这是 LSE 学生在前一年获得的奖项和学位的官方公开记录。

不幸的是，LSE 图书馆从未持有蔡英文的纸本论文。那段时期的所有博士学位都是透过伦敦大学授予的，并且首先会发送到他们的总图书馆。

我们已与伦敦大学就论文进行了通信，并进行了广泛的检查。总目前找不到他们的副本。

[鉴于这些情况，联系蔡博士的办公室以获得论文的详细资讯可能是值得的，如果她还有纸本论文]。[可选的？]
此致，

Media Statement:

An LSE spokesperson said:

"LSE and University of London records confirm Tsai Ing-wen was awarded a PhD in Law in 1984.

"Unfortunately, the LSE Library has never held a copy of Tsai Ing-wen's thesis. All PhDs from that period were awarded via the University of London and would have been sent first to their Senate House Library.

"We have corresponded with the University of London about the thesis and extensive checks have been made. Senate House Library are presently unable to find their copy."

/END

As background

I have attached a scan of the relevant entry in the LSE Calendar of 1985/86, which acts an official record of awards and degrees given to LSE students in 1984.

Many thanks,
Charlotte

Charlotte Kelloway
Media Relations Officer | Communications Division
The London School of Economics and Political Science
Houghton Street, London WC2A 2AE
t: +44 (0)20 7955 6558
e: c.kelloway@lse.ac.uk
lse.ac.uk

<image001.jpg>

<image002.png><image003.png><image004.jpg><image005.png><image006.jpg>

LSE is ranked #2 in the world for social science and management.
(QS World University Ranking 2018)

From: O'Connor,D
Sent: 11 June 2019 15:20
To: Wilson,Clive; Graham1,N; Cerny,MW; Orson,R
Cc: Lsethesesonline; Metcalfe,F; Kelloway,C
Subject: RE: Ing-Wen Tsai's PhD thesis

媒体声明：

LSE 发言人说：

"LSE 和伦敦大学的记录确认蔡英文于 1984 年获得法学博士学位。

"不幸的是，LSE 图书馆从未持有蔡英文的论文副本。那段时期的所有博士学位都是通过伦敦大学授予的，并且首先会发送到他们的总图书馆。

"我们已与伦敦大学就论文进行了通信，并进行了广泛的检查。总目前找不到他们的副本。"

/ 结束

背景资料
我附上了 1985/86 年 LSE 行事历的相关条目的扫描，该行事历作为 1984 年给予 LSE 学生的学位官方记录。

非常感谢，Charlotte

Charlotte Kelloway
媒体关系官 | 传播部门
伦敦政经学院
Houghton Street，
伦敦 WC2A 2AE
电话：+44 （0）20 7955 6558
电子邮件：c.kelloway@lse.ac.uk
lse.ac.uk

<image001.jpg>
<image002.png><image003.png><image004.jpg><image005.png><image006.jpg>

LSE 在社会科学和管理方面在全球排名第二。
（QS 世界大学排名 2018）

———————————————————

寄件者：O'Connor，D
日期：2019 年 6 月 11 日 15：20
收件者：Wilson, Clive； Graham1, N； Cerny, MW； Orson, R
副本：Lsethesesonline； Metcalfe, F； Kelloway, C
主旨：关于蔡英文的博士论文

人类史上最大学位诈骗案　89

Thanks for this Clive.

We're just putting together a version of the response for press/ other external parties.

Separately, we will also retrieve a scan of the relevant 1985/86 calendar page. It's not exactly a smoking gun but might be useful if we start getting more hassle for proof.

I'll ask the School Secretary's office in the first instance...as I imagine they have them to hand.

Thanks,

Danny

From: Wilson,Clive
Sent: 11 June 2019 15:11
To: Graham1,N <N.Graham1@lse.ac.uk>; Cerny,MW <M.W.Cerny@lse.ac.uk>; Orson,R <R.Orson@lse.ac.uk>
Cc: O'Connor,D <D.O'Connor@lse.ac.uk>; Lsethesesonline <Lsethesesonline@lse.ac.uk>
Subject: RE: Ing-Wen Tsai's PhD thesis

Hi All

yes, I dealt with this for the Library first time around.

Simeon Underwood who was Academic Registrar at the time had the student record retrieved and stated he was satisfied that the degree was correctly awarded (copied below)

It was also decided that all information relating to supervisor, thesis committee and the oral defense committee, etc could not be released without Dr Tsai's permission.

Nancy's copied our standard reply below, which I have already tweaked slightly to make current. Simeon's instruction also was that anyone pursuing further should be referred to Lorraine. I believe Mark Thomson was also happy with this approach (as he took over directly from Simeon)

happy to try to answer any further questions about what we did if I can.

Clive

Clive Wilson
Enquiry Services Manager (Academic Services)
London School of Economics   Tel.:   020 7955 7475
10 Portugal Street   Fax.:   020 7955 7454
London WC2A 2HD   Email: Datalibrary@lse.ac.uk
                                        clive.wilson@lse.ac.uk

谢谢你，Clive。

我们正在为新闻 / 其他外部方准备一个版本的回复。

另外，我们还将检索 1985/86 行事历页的扫描。这不完全是一把烟枪，但如果我们开始获得更多的证据，这可能会很有用。

我将首先问学校秘书办公室 ... 因为我想象他们手边有。

谢谢，
Danny

———————————————————————

寄件者：Wilson，Clive
日期：2019 年 6 月 11 日 15：11
收件者：Graham1，N N.Graham1@lse.ac.uk； Cerny，MW M.W.Cerny@lse.ac.uk；Orson，R R.Orson@lse.ac.uk
副本：O'Connor，D D.O'Connor@lse.ac.uk； Lsethesesonline Lsethesesonline@lse.ac.uk
主旨：关于蔡英文的博士论文

大家好，
是的，我第一次为图书馆处理这个问题。
当时的学术教务长 Simeon Underwood 取回了学生记录，并表示他确信学位是正确授予的（如下所示）。

还决定，未经蔡博士的许可，不能释放有关导师、论文委员会和口头答辩委员会等的所有资讯。

Nancy 已经复制了我们的标准回复，我已经稍微调整了一下以使其保持最新。Simeon 的指示还是，任何进一步追求的人都应该被转介给 Lorraine。我相信 Mark Thomson 也对这种方法感到满意（因为他直接从 Simeon 接手）

如果我能的话，我很乐意尝试回答我们所做的任何进一步的问题。
Clive
Clive Wilson
查询服务经理（学术服务）
伦敦政经学院
10 Portugal Street
电话：020 7955 7475
传真：020 7955 7454
电子邮件：Datalibrary@lse.ac.uk clive.wilson@lse.ac.uk

RE_-Ing-Wen-Tsais-PhD-thesis

From: O'Connor,D
Sent: 11 June 2019 15:20
To: Wilson,Clive; Graham1,N; Cerny,MW; Orson,R
Cc: Lsethesesonline; Metcalfe,F; Kelloway,C
Subject: RE: Ing-Wen Tsai's PhD thesis

Thanks for this Clive.

We're just putting together a version of the response for press/ other external parties.

Separately, we will also retrieve a scan of the relevant 1985/86 calendar page. It's not exactly a smoking gun but might be useful if we start getting more hassle for proof.

I'll ask the School Secretary's office in the first instance...as I imagine they have them to hand.

Thanks,

Danny

From: Wilson,Clive
Sent: 11 June 2019 15:11
To: Graham1,N <N.Graham1@lse.ac.uk>; Cerny,MW <M.W.Cerny@lse.ac.uk>; Orson,R <R.Orson@lse.ac.uk>
Cc: O'Connor,D <D.O'Connor@lse.ac.uk>; Lsethesesonline <Lsethesesonline@lse.ac.uk>
Subject: RE: Ing-Wen Tsai's PhD thesis

Hi All

yes, I dealt with this for the Library first time around.

Simeon Underwood who was Academic Registrar at the time had the student record retrieved and stated he was satisfied that the degree was correctly awarded (copied below)

It was also decided that all information relating to supervisor, thesis committee and the ora defense committee, etc could not be released without Dr Tsai's permission.

Nancy's copied our standard reply below, which I have already tweaked slightly to make current. Simeon's instruction also was that anyone pursuing further should be referred to Lorraine. I believe Mark Thomson was also happy with this approach (as he took over directly from Simeon)

寄件者：O'Connor，D
日期：2019 年 6 月 11 日 15：20
收件者：Wilson，Clive；Graham1，N；Cerny，MW；Orson，R
副本：Lsethesesonline；Metcalfe，F；Kelloway，C
主旨：回复：蔡英文的博士论文

感谢你的回复，Clive。
我们正在为新闻媒体/其他外部单位整理回应的版本。
另外，我们也将取得 1985/86 年历的相关页面的扫描副本。虽然这不完全是确凿的证据，但如果我们开始受到更多的证明要求，这可能会很有用。
我会首先询问学校秘书办公室...因为我想象他们手边有这些资料。

感谢，Danny

寄件者：Wilson，Clive
日期：2019 年 6 月 11 日 15：11
收件者：Graham1，N N.Graham1@lse.ac.uk； Cerny，MW M.W.Cerny@lse.ac.uk；Orson，R R.Orson@lse.ac.uk
副本：O'Connor，D D.O'Connor@lse.ac.uk； Lsethesesonline Lsethesesonline@lse.ac.uk
主旨：回复：蔡英文的博士论文

大家好，
是的，我第一次为图书馆处理这件事。
当时的学术教务长 Simeon Underwood 取得了学生的记录，并表示他确信该学位是正确授予的（如下所示）。
还决定了所有与指导教授、论文委员会和口头答辩委员会等相关的资讯，未经蔡博士的许可不能被公开。
Nancy 在下面复制了我们的标准回复，我已经稍微修改了它以使其更为流畅。Simeon 的指示同样是任何进一步探寻的人都应该被转介给 Lorraine。我相信 Mark Thomson 也对这种方法感到满意（因为他直接接替了 Simeon）。
如果我能的话，我很乐意尝试回答我们所做的任何进一步的问题。
Clive
Clive Wilson
查询服务经理（学术服务）
伦敦政经学院
10 Portugal Street
London WC2A 2HD
电话：020 7955 7475
传真：020 7955 7454
电邮：Datalibrary@lse.ac.uk clive.wilson@lse.ac.uk

From: Cerny,MW
Sent: 11 June 2019 17:15
To: O'Connor,D; Metcalfe,F; Kelloway,C; Wilson,Clive; Graham1,N; Orson,R
Cc: Lsethesesonline
Subject: RE: Ing-Wen Tsai's PhD thesis

My opinion is we should leave it in. We should look like we're pretending to have had nothing to do with this and she is an LSE alumnus (we trumpeted as much ourselves when she got elected).

Thanks,
Marcus

Marcus Cerny
Deputy Director, PhD Academy

London School of Economics and Political Science
Houghton Street
London WC2A 2AE

Please consider the environment and do not print this email unless absolutely necessary.
Please access the attached hyperlink for an important electronic communications disclaimer: http://lse.ac.uk/emailDisclaimer

寄件者：Cerny，MW
日期：2019年6月11日 17：15
收件者：O'Connor, D； Metcalfe, F； Kelloway, C； Wilson, Clive； Graham1, N； Orson, R
副本：Lsethesesonline
主旨：回复：蔡英文的博士论文

我认为我们应该保留它。我们应该看起来像是与此无关，而她是LSE的校友（当她当选时，我们自己也这么宣称过）。

谢谢，Marcus

Marcus Cerny
博士生学院副主任
伦敦政经学院 Houghton Street
London WC2A 2AE

为了环保，除非绝对必要，否则请不要列印此电邮。请访问附加的超连结，以获取一个重要的电子通讯免责声明：https://lse.ac.uk/emailDisclaimer

From: O'Connor,D
Sent: 11 June 2019 19:54
To: Wilson,Clive
Cc: Cerny,MW; Metcalfe,F; Kelloway,C; Graham1,N; Orson,R; Lsethesesonline
Subject: Re: Ing-Wen Tsai's PhD thesis

Thanks for this, Clive. Useful to know.

Ruth do forward on any further letters and we can collate and reply from central LSE accounts

Danny

On 11 Jun 2019, at 17:39, Wilson,Clive <CLIVE.Wilson@lse.ac.uk> wrote:

> Hi All
>
> just had a chat with Dr Fang-Long Shih in the LSE Taiwan Research Programme who is a supporter of Dr Tsai.
>
> Apparently the Taiwan press and the opposition party are trying to relate this to the incident over Saif gaddafi and the Libyan donation.

Supporters of Dr Tsai are therefore very keen to be able to prove that the degree was awarded correctly/successfully and may be able to get permission from Dr Tsai to release more information from her record as appropriate.

And the Calendar is a public document that anyone from outside LSE can request to view through our archives so there is no DP/GDPR issue.

Clive

寄件者：O'Connor，D
日期：2019年6月11日19：54
收件者：Wilson，Clive
副本：Cerny，MW； Metcalfe，F； Kelloway，C； Graham1，N； Orson，R； Lsethesesonline
主旨：回复：蔡英文的博士论文

Clive，谢谢你的资讯，很有帮助。

Ruth，如果还有其他的信件，请转发给我们，我们可以从LSE的主帐号汇整并回复。
Danny

2019年6月11日，17：39，Wilson，Clive CLIVE.Wilson@lse.ac.uk 写道：

大家好，

我刚和LSE的台湾研究计划中的施芳珑博士聊过，她是蔡博士的支持者。

据说台湾的新闻媒体和反对党正试图将此事与赛夫·格达费和利比亚捐款的事件相关联。

因此，蔡博士的支持者非常希望能够证明该学位是正确/成功授予的，并且可能能够从蔡博士那里获得更多适当的记录资讯的许可。

而且，该行事历是一份公开文件，LSE以外的任何人都可以通过我们的档案要求查看，所以没有DP/GDPR的问题。

Clive

RE_ FOI query - thesis supervisor

From: O"Connor,D
To: Wilson,Clive; Maguire,RE
Subject: RE: FOI query - thesis supervisor
Date: 27 June 2019 14:23:00

I'm happy that we can say something like, "following data protection guidelines we do not, as standard, release the names of PhD supervisors."

It is our default policy, after all.

Danny

From: Wilson,Clive
Sent: 27 June 2019 14:12
To: Maguire,RE <R.E.Maguire@lse.ac.uk>
Cc: O'Connor,D <D.O'Connor@lse.ac.uk>
Subject: RE: FOI query - thesis supervisor

Thanks Rachael, much appreciated.

I can't help think this journalist will just find it very convenient that the supervisor has died. But although we could release it – we don't have to. It's only really chance that I know that he passed away. Danny – your call on that one ☺

thanks again

Clive

From: Maguire,RE
Sent: 27 June 2019 14:04
To: Wilson,Clive
Cc: O'Connor,D
Subject: RE: FOI query - thesis supervisor

Hello Clive,

This is not true as this is third party personal information which is being requested. Section 40 of the Freedom of Information Act requires that we consider whether the data protection principles will be breached if we release personal data. The personal data in this case is:

- The degree granted
- The supervisor's name.

The main data protection principle is the first, relating to fairness. We have to consider if it will be fair to release personal data relating to another individual. Regarding the degree, this is fair to release as it is usually in the student's interests to confirm they received the degree they are saying they received. There will be negative consequences for them if we don't. Regarding the supervisor's name, this would not normally be fair because the School does not release the names of teaching staff on a regular basis and there would be an expectation from staff that their names were not released. However, as the supervisor is dead, data protection no longer

寄件者： O'Connor, D
收件者： Wilson, Clive；Maguire, RE
主旨： 回复：资讯自由查询—论文指导教授
日期： 2019 年 6 月 27 日 14：23：00

我很满意我们可以这么说，"根据资料保护指引，我们通常不公开博士指导教授的名字"。毕竟，这是我们的预设政策。
Danny

寄件者： Wilson, Clive
日期： 2019 年 6 月 27 日 14：12
收件者： Maguire, RE R.E.Maguire@lse.ac.uk
副本： O'Connor, D D.O'Connor@lse.ac.uk
主旨： 回复：资讯自由查询—论文指导教授

谢谢 Rachael，非常感谢。
我不禁想，这位记者会发现指导教授已经去世是非常容易的。但是，尽管我们可以公开它，我们不必这么做。我知道他去世只是偶然的。Danny，这个决定由你来做。
再次感谢，
Clive

寄件者： Maguire，RE
日期： 2019 年 6 月 27 日 14：04
收件者： Wilson，Clive
副本： O'Connor，D
主旨： 回复：资讯自由查询—论文指导教授

你好，Clive，
这不是真的，因为这是第三方的个人资讯。根据《资讯自由法》的第 40 节，我们必须考虑是否会违反资料保护原则，如果我们公开个人资料。在这种情况下，个人资料是：
　　授予的学位
　　指导教授的名字。
主要的资料保护原则是第一条，涉及公平性。我们必须考虑公开与另一个人相关的个人资料是否公平。关于学位，这是公平的，因为这常见于学生的权益中，去确认他们获得了他们所说的学位。如果我们不这么做，他们会受到负面影响。关于指导教授的名字，这通常是不公平的，因为学校不定期地公开教学人员的名字，教职员工会期望他们的名字不被公开。但是，由于指导教授已经去世，资料保护不再适用。所以在这种情况下，可以公开指导教授的名字。

applies. You have to be a living individual. So the supervisor's name in this instance could be released.

FoI is not a complete right to information anyway, there are exemptions and other reasons we can refuse e.g. vexatious requests. I suggest linking to the ICO's website for more information www.ico.org.uk as a further resource.

Regards,
Rachael

From: Wilson,Clive
Sent: 27 June 2019 13:52
To: Maguire,RE <R.E.Maguire@lse.ac.uk>
Cc: O'Connor,D <D.O'Connor@lse.ac.uk>
Subject: FOI query - thesis supervisor

Hi Rachel

sorry, more on the Ing-Wen Tsai thesis.

A Chinese journalist has been writing on the disappearance of Ing-Wen Tsai's thesis. I had initially replied to him with our standard response and told him that releasing the supervisor's name was not allowed under UK data protection rules – as Simeon Underwood had stated 4 years ago.

The journalist has come back with

I consulted a British writer and checked with The Freedom of Information Act of UK, it came to my knowledge that as a public figure, a government official, and let alone a sitting president of a democratic country, any information regarding Ms.Tsai's degree, her thesis, her supervisor, etc. should be public information and LSE is responsible to provide whatever they have.

(I haven't included the long non-LSE related bumpf)

The supervisor passed away in 2016 and hadn't been at LSE since 1984. I feel as though, if he were alive, we would need his permission to release his name. But as Ing-Wen Tsai is the current president of Taiwan do we need to release this?

(I also see there is an international relations exclusion but that's probably a stretch)

Many thanks

Clive

Clive Wilson
Enquiry Services Manager (Academic Services)
London School of Economics   Tel.:   020 7955 7475

FoI 不是一个完整的资讯权利，还有例外和其他我们可以拒绝的原因，例如恼人的请求。我建议链接到 ICO 的网站 www.ico.org.uk 以获得更多资讯。

问候，

Rachael

寄件者： Wilson，Clive
日期： 2019 年 6 月 27 日 13：52
收件者： Maguire，RE R.E.Maguire@lse.ac.uk
副本： O'Connor，D D.O'Connor@lse.ac.uk
主旨： 资讯自由查询—论文指导教授

嗨，Rachel， 对不起，关于蔡英文的论文还有更多。 一位中文媒体写了关于蔡英文论文失踪的文章。我最初用我们的标准回答回复了他，并告诉他根据英国的资料保护规定，不允许公开指导教授的名字，正如 Simeon Underwood 四年前所说的那样。记者的回应是

我咨询了一位英国作家，并查阅了英国的《资讯自由法》，我了解到，作为公众人物、政府官员，更何况是民主国家的现任总统，有关蔡女士的学位、论文、导师等资讯都应该是公开资讯。有关蔡女士的学位、论文、导师等任何资讯都应是公开资讯，伦敦政经学院有责任提供他们所掌握的任何资讯。他们有责任提供任何资讯。

（我没有把与伦敦政经学院无关的冗长废话包括在内）

导师于 2016 年去世，自 1984 年起就不在 LSE 工作了。我觉得，如果他还活着，我们应该征得他的同意才能公布他的名字。 但由于蔡英文是现任台湾总统，我们有必要公布吗？

（我还看到有国际关系排除在外，但这可能有点牵强）。

非常感谢，Clive

Clive Wilson

咨询服务部经理（学术服务）

伦敦政经学院

电话：020 7955 7475

LSE 与总统府间的平衡策略游戏

LSE 与总统府间的平衡策略游戏

伦敦政经学院（LSE）咨询服务经理 Clive Wilson 翻开了从总统府寄来的两份纸本论文。他决定与蔡英文团队进行协商，希望能够找到一个双赢的解决方案。

LSE 媒体关系部门负责人 Daniel O'Connor 也对这份论文感到担忧。因为这份论文在 2019 年才出版，这将引起更多的质疑和争议。他试图找到一个能够平息外界质疑的方法。

LSE 博士学程校务处副处长 Marcus W Cerny 则有着更加明确的看法。他认为，学院应该承认当年的授予学位程序，但对于这份论文是否是当年的合格论文，学院应该保持中立，既不承认也不否认。他认为，这样可以保护学院的名誉，同时也不会得罪总统府。

Wilson 听完 Cerny 的建议后，"如果我们的图书馆没有这份论文的目录，但作者的家人送来了一本副本，我会咬掉他们的手"。

经过一系列的调查和讨论，学院终于决定了对外的第三个版本声明。这份声明试图平衡学院的名誉和总统府的要求，但是否能够平息外界的质疑，还是一个未知数。

RE_ More on the PhD Thesis by Ing-Wen Tsai

From: O'Connor,D
Sent: 28 June 2019 13:27
To: Wilson,Clive; Thomson,MT; Kelloway,C; Cerny,MW; Metcalfe,F
Subject: RE: More on the PhD Thesis by Ing-Wen Tsai ...

Hi Clive,

In normal circumstances, this all sounds very sensible.

However, as Marcus highlighted at the meeting, would we do the same if it were from a run-of-the-mill PhD graduate from the 1980s?

Also, I have a feeling announcing that we now have a facsimile copy might lead to a more confused message and a run of questions, such as : 'can you say it's genuine?' 'If not, are you *refusing* to endorse it?' "It says 2019, are you saying she only just wrote this?" etc. Answerable but may get us in the weeds.

Not saying we shouldn't go with the suggestion, it sounds like a good compromise, but just want to make sure our messaging is in order.

Hope that makes sense. Thanks very much,

Danny

From: Wilson,Clive
Sent: 28 June 2019 12:11
To: Thomson,MT <M.T.Thomson@lse.ac.uk>; Kelloway,C <C.Kelloway@lse.ac.uk>; O'Connor,D <D.O'Connor@lse.ac.uk>; Cerny,MW <M.W.Cerny@lse.ac.uk>; Metcalfe,F <F.Metcalfe@lse.ac.uk>
Subject: More on the PhD Thesis by Ing-Wen Tsai ...

Hi everyone

I received two copies of the thesis from Taiwan late yesterday. One soft bound and one hard bound. But both photocopies.

There are two draft chapters and an outline on the student record and – in my humble opinion - there is enough of those in the thesis to suggest it is good. And besides, even with the whole wheel of government behind you, it would still be a rather neat trick to fake or rewrite a thesis as if it was done in 1983 and in the same font as the draft chapters. ☺ However, as Marcus said on Monday, we still can't really prove that this is what she actually submitted in 1983.

寄件者： O'Connor，D
日期： 2019 年 6 月 28 日 13：27
收件者： Wilson，Clive；Thomson，MT；Kelloway，C；Cerny，MW；Metcalfe，F
主旨： 回复：关于蔡英文的博士论文…

嗨，Clive，
在正常情况下，这一切听起来都很有道理。
然而，正如 Marcus 在会议上所强调的，如果这是来自 1980 年代的一位普通博士毕业生，我们会这样做吗？

此外，我有一种感觉，宣布我们现在有一份影印本可能会导致更加混淆的讯息和一连串的问题，例如："你能说这是真的吗？""如果不是，你拒绝支持它吗？""上面写着 2019 年，你是说她只是刚写完这篇论文吗？"等等。这些问题都可以回答，但可能会让我们陷入困境。

我不是说我们不应该按照这些建议，这听起来像是一个很好的妥协，但只是想确保我们的讯息是有秩序的。

希望这有意义。非常感谢，
Danny

寄件者： Wilson，Clive
日期： 2019 年 6 月 28 日 12：11
收件者： Thomson，MT；Kelloway，C；O'Connor，D；Cerny，MW；Metcalfe，F
主旨： 关于蔡英文的博士论文…

大家好，
我昨天晚上从台湾收到了两份论文的纸本。一份是软封面的，另一份是硬封面的。但两者都是影印的。

学生记录上有两个草稿章节和一个大纲，而在我的卑微的意见中，这些在论文中足够证明它是好的。而且，即使有整个政府的支持，伪造或重写一篇像是在 1983 年完成的论文还是一个相当巧妙的技巧。然而，正如 Marcus 星期一所说，我们仍然不能真正证明这是她在 1983 年实际提交的。

One of my cataloguing colleagues has said we can probably catalogue it as a facsimile. For example:

Tsai, Ing-Wen. Unfair trade practices and safeguard actions: a facsimile copy of her 1983 PhD thesis presented to LSE Library by President Ing-Wen Tsai of Taiwan. 2019

This makes it clear it's a copy and was presented to us by her – so some deniability on our part if necessary.
By saying it was presented (again) and addressing her as President - it shows we are proud and still claiming brownie points for her as an LSE alumna.
The date shows as 2019 because that's when the copy was made – so again, not claiming it is the actual thesis.

To me, that sounds like a win-win for us and for her team. But happy to take it under advisement.

And then, as previously, we don't have permission to digitise it so it would only be available in the special collections reading room where we have two people at all times who can monitor any copying or defacing. And I would suggest we only give out the soft copy.

How does that sound?

Clive

Marcus in the PhD Academy is concerned that, although it almost certainly is valid, we can't prove that this is what she submitted in 1983. There are two draft chapters and an outline on the student record and there is enough of those in the copy to suggest it is good. And besides, even with the whole wheel of government behind you, it would be a rather neat trick to fake or rewrite a thesis as if it was done in 1983.

Clare said she needed to check but we could catalogue it as a facsimile. Marcus will (probably) be happy provided we make it clear (or ambiguous even) that we are not claiming it's the actual thesis.

So I am thinking something like:

Tsai, Ing-Wen. Unfair trade practices and safeguard actions: a facsimile copy of her 1983 PhD thesis presented to LSE Library by President Ing-Wen Tsai of Taiwan. 2019

If we make it available it would have to be reading room only. Can we restrict copying? Would we still hold it with the print theses? Would we add it to Theses Online even if it isn't digitised?

我的一位编目同事说我们可能可以将其编目为影印本。例如：

蔡英文。不公平贸易和防卫机制：她的 1983 年博士论文的影印本，由台湾的蔡英文总统呈现给 LSE 图书馆。2019 年

这清楚地表明它是一份副本，并且是由她呈现给我们的，所以如果需要，我们有一些否认的空间。
透过说它是呈现的（再次）并称呼她为总统，它显示我们很自豪，并且仍然为她作为 LSE 的校友而自豪。
日期显示为 2019 年，因为那是纸本制作的时候，所以再次，不声称它是实际的论文。

对我来说，这听起来对我们和她的团队都是双赢的。但我很乐意接受建议。

然后，正如之前所说，我们没有获得电子档的许可，所以它只能在特殊收藏阅览室中提供，那里我们一直有两个人可以监控任何复制或玷污。而且，我建议我们只提供软封面的纸本。

这听起来怎么样？
Clive

Marcus 在博士学院表示担心，尽管它几乎肯定是有效的，但我们不能证明这是她在 1983 年提交的。学生记录上有两个草稿章节，其中足够的部分在副本中，这表明它是好的。而且，即使有整个政府的支持，伪造或重写一篇像是在 1983 年完成的论文还是一个相当巧妙的技巧。

Clare 说她需要检查，但我们可以将其编目为影印本。Marcus 将（可能）很高兴，只要我们清楚地表明（或甚至模糊）我们不声称它是实际的论文。

所以我在想象这样的东西：

蔡英文。不公平贸易和防卫机制：她的 1983 年博士论文的影印本，由台湾的蔡英文总统呈现给 LSE 图书馆。2019 年

如果我们使其可用，它将只能在阅览室中。我们可以限制复制吗？我们还会将其与印刷论文一起保存吗？即使它没有被数位化，我们会将其添加到线上论文吗？

From: Cerny,MW
Sent: 28 June 2019 14:09
To: O'Connor,D; Wilson,Clive; Thomson,MT; Kelloway,C; Metcalfe,F
Subject: RE: More on the PhD Thesis by Ing-Wen Tsai ...

I am happy with this being available in the library. I can see that it as we have it, and it is of interest, it should be available where possible and my view is also that it is up to the Library to decide whether to accept materials and whether to store and make them available within whatever rules/conditions apply.

However, my decision from a regulatory standpoint, is that this has to be on the basis that this is a document provided to the Library in 2019 and be clear that we are not storing this as a formal record of the thesis examined or awarded.

What wording on the catalogue that might cover this and pre-empt questions is debatable but I think Clive's formulation is a reasonable one. Even if we got the question about it being genuine or whether we endorse it can we not simply fall back on the agreed statement? Noting again that we are satisfied that the thesis was correctly awarded in line with the relevant procedures, that Senate House sent a copy to IALS, that neither Senate House nor IALS can locate a copy, and that Dr Tsai's office provided this version in 2019.

One final note on my position on this. It is not just a question as to whether we can prove that this is the thesis or whether we believe it to be. It is also a question that we would not accept a copy at this late remove in these circumstances for any other candidate and then record it as the examined or awarded thesis. Given this, for purposes of consistency, I do not think we should do so because of an individual graduates status. For the record, I am actually satisfied that this is an accurate version of the thesis examined (but I obviously could not prove it).

Thanks,
Marcus

Marcus Cerny
Deputy Director, PhD Academy
London School of Economics and Political Science
Houghton Street

London WC2A 2AE

Please consider the environment and do not print this email unless absolutely necessary.
Please access the attached hyperlink for an important electronic communications disclaimer:
http://lse.ac.uk/emailDisclaimer

寄件者：Cerny, MW
日期：2019年6月28日 14：09
收件者：O'Connor, D；Wilson, Clive；Thomson, MT；Kelloway, C；Metcalfe, F
主旨：回复：关于蔡英文的博士论文 ...

我很满意这份文件可以在图书馆中提供。我认为，由于我们有它，且它具有一定的关注，它应该在可能的情况下提供，而我也认为图书馆应该决定是否接受材料，以及是否在适用的规则/条件下存储和提供它们。

然而，从法规的角度看，我的决定是，这必须基于这是一份在2019年提供给图书馆的文件，并明确表示我们不是将其存储为被审查或授予的正式论文记录。

在目录上可能涵盖这一点并预先回答问题的措词是有争议的，但我认为Clive的表述是合理的。即使我们得到了关于它是否真实或我们是否支持它的问题，我们不能简单地回到已经同意的声明吗？再次指出，我们满意地认为论文是根据相关程序正确授予的，伦敦大学总图书馆将一份副本发送给IALS，伦敦大学总图书馆和IALS都找不到副本，并且蔡博士的办公室在2019年提供了这个版本。

关于我的立场的最后一点。这不仅仅是一个问题，关于我们是否可以证明这是论文或我们是否相信它。这也是一个问题，我们在这种情况下不会接受任何其他候选人隔了这么晚的副本，并且将其记录为被审查或授予的论文。鉴于此，为了保持一致性，我认为我们不应该这样做，因为某个毕业生的地位。就记录而言，我实际上确信这是被审查的论文的准确版本（但我显然无法证明它）。

谢谢，Marcus
Marcus Cerny
博士生学院副主任
伦敦政经学院
Houghton Street
伦敦 WC2A 2AE

为了环保，除非绝对必要，否则请不要列印此电邮。请访问附加的超连结，以获取一个重要的电子通讯免责声明：https://lse.ac.uk/emailDisclaimer

From:	Wilson,Clive
To:	Cerny,MW; O"Connor,D; Thomson,MT; Kelloway,C; Metcalfe,F
Subject:	RE: More on the PhD Thesis by Ing-Wen Tsai ...
Date:	28 June 2019 16:12:03
Attachments:	

Thanks Marcus

As a librarian I know my view is slightly coloured ☺ . But we can add notes to the record as well as purely bibliographic info, so I will see if I can come up with better wording to make it clearer.

And I know I told Marcus this already but this might also be helpful - I've copied here an email from three of our accounting faculty.

Some LSE Master's dissertations in the first half of last century were done by research. As a result they went to Senate House like the PhDs did.

When PhD theses were repatriated to LSE, the lists did not include the Master's dissertations. As a result most of those dissertations have been scrapped but the Senate House catalogue points to us.

Some of those dissertations are very heavily cited – so from a purely academic perspective are far more important - but if we did not have a duplicate they are lost. I find this heartbreaking. We get five or six enquiries a year about these. I would suspect all of those authors are dead now, but if a family member was doing some research and said, it's not on your catalogue but I have a copy – I'd bite their hand off!!

Clive

寄件者：Wilson，Clive
收件者：Cerny，MW； O'Connor，D； Thomson，MT； Kelloway，C； Metcalfe，F
主旨：关于蔡英文的博士论文 …
日期：2019 年 6 月 28 日 16：12：03

感谢 Marcus，
作为一名图书馆员，我知道我的观点可能有些偏颇。但我们可以在记录中添加注释以及纯粹的书目资讯，所以我会看看我能否找到更好的措辞来使其更清晰。
我知道我已经告诉过 Marcus 这件事，但以下的资讯可能也会有帮助—我在这里复制了我们会计学院的三位教员的电子邮件。
在上世纪的前半部分，一些 LSE 的硕士论文是通过研究完成的。因此，它们像博士论文一样被送到了总图书馆大楼。
当博士论文被遣返回 LSE 时，清单中并未包括硕士论文。
结果，大部分的这些论文已被丢弃，但总图书馆大楼的目录指向了我们。
其中一些论文被引用得非常频繁—所以从纯学术的角度看，它们更为重要 - 但如果我们没有副本，它们就会丢失。我觉得这很令人心碎。
我们每年收到五到六次关于这些的询问。我猜所有的作者现在都已去世，但如果一个团体成员正在做一些研究，并说，它不在你们的目录上，但我有一份纸本—我会非常渴望得到它！
Clive

From: Kelloway,C
Sent: 28 June 2019 16:37
To: Wilson,Clive; Cerny,MW; O'Connor,D; Thomson,MT; Metcalfe,F
Subject: RE: More on the PhD Thesis by Ing-Wen Tsai ...

Hi all,

I have added a line to the statement to reflect this new development. Let me know if you would like to make any edits.

I've tried to make it clear that the document was only recently provided to us and that we are not storing it as a formal record of the thesis but let me know if you think this isn't clear enough.

LSE spokesperson:

"The records of the University of London and London School of Economics and Political Science confirm Tsai Ing-Wen was correctly awarded a PhD in Law in 1984.

"All PhDs from that period were awarded via the University of London and would have been sent first to their Senate House Library. It is clear from Senate House Library records that a copy was received. Senate House have confirmed they sent their copy of the thesis to the Institute for Advanced Legal Studies (IALS).

"We have corresponded with the University of London about the thesis and extensive checks have been made. Neither Senate House nor IALS are able to locate a copy of the thesis.

"President Tsai Ing-wen's office recently provided the LSE Library with a facsimile copy of the thesis, *Unfair trade practices and safeguard actions*. This is available to view in the library's

寄件者： Kelloway，C
日期： 2019 年 6 月 28 日 16：37
收件者： Wilson，Clive； Cerny，MW； O'Connor，D； Thomson，MT； Metcalfe，F
主旨： 回复：关于蔡英文的博士论文 …

大家好，
我已经在声明中加入了一行，以反应这一新的发展。如果你们希望进行任何修改，请告诉我。

我试图明确表示这份文件是最近才提供给我们的，并且我们不将其存储为论文的正式记录，但如果你们认为这还不够清楚，请告诉我。

LSE 发言人：

"伦敦大学和伦敦政经学院的记录确认蔡英文于 1984 年正确地获得了法学博士学位。"

"那段时期的所有博士学位都是通过伦敦大学授予的，并且首先会被发送到他们的伦敦大学总图书馆。从总图书馆的记录中可以清楚地看到，他们收到了一份纸本。总图书馆已经确认他们将纸本论文发送到了高等法律研究所（IALS）。"

"我们已与伦敦大学就论文进行了通信，并进行了广泛的检查。总图书馆和 IALS 都无法找到纸本的论文"。

"然而，蔡英文的总统府最近向 LSE 图书馆提供了论文《不公平贸易和防卫机制》的复印本。这可以在图书馆的阅览室中查看"。

reading room."

/END

As background

I have attached a scan of the relevant entry in the LSE Calendar of 1985/86, which acts an official record of awards and degrees given to LSE students in 1984. This confirms Dr Tsai's PhD award at the time.

General response:

Thank you for your email. We have checked our records and both the London School of Economics and Political Science and the University of London confirm that Tsai Ing-Wen was correctly awarded a PhD in Law 1984.

However, all PhDs from that period were awarded via the University of London and would have been sent first to their Senate House Library. It is clear from Senate House Library records that a copy was received. Senate House have confirmed they sent their copy of the thesis to the Institute for Advanced Legal Studies (IALS).

We have corresponded with the University of London about the thesis and extensive checks have been made. Neither Senate House nor IALS are able to locate a copy of the thesis,

However, President Tsai Ing-wen's office recently provided the LSE Library with a facsimile copy of the thesis, *Unfair trade practices and safeguard actions*. This is available to view in the library's reading room.

Many thanks,
Charlotte

/ 结束

作为背景
我附上了 1985/86 年 LSE 行事历的相关条目的纸本扫描，该行事历是 1984 年授予 LSE 学位的官方记录。这确认了当时蔡博士的博士学位。

一般回应：
感谢您的电子邮件。我们已经检查了我们的记录，伦敦政经学院和伦敦大学都确认蔡英文于 1984 年正确地获得了法学博士学位。

但是，那段时期的所有博士学位都是通过伦敦大学授予的，并且首先会被发送到他们的伦敦大学总图书馆。从总图书馆的记录中可以清楚地看到，他们收到了一份纸本。总图书馆已经确认他们将论文的纸本发送到了高等法律研究所（IALS）。

我们已与伦敦大学就论文进行了通信，并进行了广泛的检查。总图书馆和 IALS 都无法找到纸本的论文。

然而，蔡英文的总统府最近向 LSE 图书馆提供了论文《不公平贸易和防卫机制》的复印本。这可以在图书馆的阅览室中查看。

非常感谢，
Charlotte

恶官 3

机密的指示：伦敦大学的内部角力

机密的指示：伦敦大学的内部角力

伦敦政经学院（LSE）学院内部的文件和纪录中，关于某位学生的口试委员名字似乎消失了，即使是指导教授的名称，也成了一个谜。这位学生，正是后来的台湾总统蔡英文。

2015 年，当蔡英文的学历争议在台湾媒体上愈演愈烈时，LSE 内部已经有人开始行动。一名不愿透露姓名的伦敦大学内部人士，已经开始下达指示，告诉学院如何回应这场争议。这一切都被高度机密地处理，只有少数人知道真相。

LSE 学术注册主管兼学术总监 Simeon Underwood 用谎言应付了许多查询者。他知道，这场争议的背后，涉及的不仅仅是学术真相，还有政治的角力。而在他的背后，还有 LSE 学术注册部门职员 Mark Thomson 和 Clive Wilson，两名 2015 年就已经涉入这场争议的核心人物。

LSE 咨询服务经理 Clive Wilson 知道，学院内部始终没有蔡英文的论文。但他也知道，这场争议的背后，有着太多的政治利益和角力。2016 年，当有人再次挖掘蔡英文的论文问题时，Clive Wilson 决定不再介入。他认为，蔡英文已经当选台湾总统，这场争议已经烧不起来了。

但真相，始终是真相。在学术的殿堂里，是否应该为了政治利益而掩盖真相？这是一个问题，也是一个挑战。

RE_-Need-to-find-a-1984-Ph.D.-dissertation-in-y

Cc: Foster,NK
Subject: RE: Need to find a 1984 Ph.D. dissertation in your department

Dear Simeon,

Please do pass any enquiries regarding this PhD examination on to me. I can help with some of questions below if you forward me his email address. As for the actual copies of the thesis itself I am sorry I am unable to shed any light on this. Both examiners' copies of the thesis were left at the LSE following examination. It seems the third copy of the thesis was sent to the IALS, and then the trail goes cold.

We have retrieved Dr Tsai's file from our Archives and I can send you through a scanned copy if that would be useful.

With best wishes,

University of London is an exempt charity in England and Wales.
We are committed to achieving a 20% cut in emissions from University buildings by 2015. Please think before you print.

寄件者： ▓▓▓▓▓▓
日期： 2015 年 7 月 3 日 25：34
收件者： Underwood，S；
副本： Foster，NK
主旨： 回复：需要找到你们部门 1984 年的博士论文

亲爱的 Simeon，

如果有关于这次博士考试的任何询问，请转交给我。如果你能提供他的电子邮件地址，我可以帮忙解释以下的一些误解。至于论文本身的实际纸本，很抱歉，我无法提供任何资讯。两份评审的论文副本在考试后都留在了 LSE。似乎第三份纸本论文被送到了 IALS，然后就没有下文了。

我们已从我们的档案中取回了蔡博士的档案，如果需要，我可以寄送一份扫描纸本给你。

祝好，

From: Underwood,S
Sent: 03 July 2015 15:44
To: Green,LJ; Yarham,R; Bannister,HR; Foster,NK; Wright,NC; Reid,MJ; Wilson,Clive; Donnelly,S; Thomas4,A; O'Connor,D
Subject: FW: Need to find a 1984 Ph.D. dissertation in your department

Colleagues

Herewith correspondence with Senate House about Dr Tsai's PhD examination and thesis. The upshot is that any future correspondence should go to Lorraine at Senate House. But please send them with a copy to me until 20 July and a copy to Louisa Green thereafter, in case there are any issues which are specific to the School.

Many thanks

simeon

From: Underwood,S
Sent: 03 July 2015 15:40
To: ▇▇▇▇
Cc: Foster,NK
Subject: RE: Need to find a 1984 Ph.D. dissertation in your department

▇▇▇

Thanks for this.

The line I have taken is that we can't give ▇▇▇ the answers to his questions for reasons to do with data protection. I wrote to him on Monday; and he hasn't got back to me as yet. I suggest that we let this lie unless he gets back to us. But if you think differently please say.

Thanks for the kind offer, but I will manage with a copy of Dr Tsai's university file, for now at least.

All the best

simeon

寄件者：Underwood，S
日期：2015年7月3日 15：44
收件者：Green, LJ; Yarham, R; Bannister, HR; Foster, NK; Wright, NC; Reid, MJ; Wilson, Clive; Donnelly, S; Thomas4, A; O'Connor, D
主旨：转寄：需要找到你们部门1984年的博士论文

同仁们，

以下是与伦敦大学总图书馆关于蔡博士的博士考试和论文的通信。结果是，任何未来的通信都应该发送给总图书馆的Lorraine。但请在7月20日之前将它们的纸本发送给我，并在此后将纸本发送给Louisa Green，以防有任何与学校特定的问题。

非常感谢，

simeon

寄件者：Underwood，S
日期：2015年7月3日 15：40
收件者：▮▮▮▮▮
副本：Foster, NK
主旨：回复：需要找到你们部门1984年的博士论文

▮▮▮▮▮

感谢您的回复。

我采取的立场是，由于与资料保护相关的原因，我们不能回答他的问题。我在星期一给他写了信；他到目前为止还没有回复我。我建议我们让这件事暂时搁置，除非他再次回复我们。但如果您有不同的看法，请告诉我。

感谢您的好意，但至少目前我只需要蔡博士的大学档案的纸本。

祝好，
Simeon

Sent: 10 November 2015 13:32
To: Green,LJ; Thomson,MT
Cc: Flanagan,D; Reid,MJ
Subject: RE: Need to find a 1984 Ph.D. dissertation in your department

Dear Mark

I'm not sure if you are aware of this particular issue or not so my apologies if much of this is known to you.

In brief, one of our alumna Ing-Wen Tsai is her party's candidate in the upcoming Taiwan elections. As the email trail below shows there appears to be no available copy of her PhD thesis although Simeon Underwood was satisfied that the record showed the award was valid.

We have had a number of requests for this thesis since the candidacy was announced and have given a standard response and referred to ████████████ at Senate House as Simeon requested.

I mention it now because it appears to have made the Chinese press in Canada and mentioned on twitter: ████████████████████████████████████

It's all fairly low level so far but I thought you should be aware

Best wishes

Clive

Clive Wilson
Enquiry Services Manager (Academic Services)
London School of Economics Tel.: 020 7955 7475
10 Portugal Street Fax.: 020 7955 7454
London WC2A 2HD Email: Datalibrary@lse.ac.uk
clive.wilson@lse.ac.uk

寄件者：Wilson，Clive
日期：2015 年 11 月 10 日 13：32
收件者：Green，LJ； Thomson，MT
副本：Flanagan，D； Reid，MJ
主旨：回复：需要找到你们部门 1984 年的博士论文

亲爱的 Mark，

我不确定您是否知道这个特定的问题，所以如果您已经知道这些，我深感抱歉。

简而言之，我们的校友蔡英文是即将到来的台湾选举中她所属政党的候选人。如下面的电子邮件记录所示，似乎没有她的博士论文的可用副本，尽管 Simeon Underwood 确信记录显示该学位授予是有效的。

自从宣布候选人身份以来，我们收到了许多关于这篇论文的请求，并给予了标准的回应，同时按照 Simeon 的要求说明是 ▇▇▇ 转介给总图书馆的。

我现在提到它，是因为它似乎已经出现在加拿大的中文媒体和 Twitter 上：

到目前为止，这都相对低调，但我认为你应该知道。

祝好，
Clive

Clive Wilson
查询服务经理（学术服务）
伦敦政经学院
电话：020 7955 7475
10 Portugal Street
伦敦 WC2A 2HD
传真：020 7955 7454
电子邮件：Datalibrary@lse.ac.uk
dive.wilson@lse.ac.uk

Cc: Flanagan,D; Reid,MJ; Yarham,R
Subject: Re: Need to find a 1984 Ph.D. dissertation in your department

Dear Mark

Sue Donnelly would be able to provide a copy of Dr Tsai's LSE student file - I have copied her in.

Simeon said in one email that:
My understanding is that the position seems to be that two copies were left with LSE from the supervisor and the internal examiner but that these were never passed on to SHL and that one copy went from Senate House Library to IALS but can no longer be found.

I am sure this was based on notes in the relevant LSE and UL records

Rachel Yarham in Law - -also copied now - was asked about it at one point but I believe the department had nothing to add.

It all became a series of unfortunate deadends with no trace of a physical copy anywhere.

Clive

From: Thomson,MT
Sent: 12 November 2015 16:34
To: Wilson,Clive; Green,LJ
Cc: Flanagan,D; Reid,MJ
Subject: RE: Need to find a 1984 Ph.D. dissertation in your department

Clive, greetings

Thank you for this note — apologies for the delayed response, but I made the mistake of being away at a conference early in the week and have paid a heavy price in terms of the state of my inbox.

I was not aware of this matter. A couple of questions:

-Does the PhD Academy have a copy of Dr Tsai's student file? If so, may I see it?

-Do we know the basis on which ▇▇▇▇▇▇▇▇▇▇, in her email of 3 July 2015, makes the statement that "Both examiners' copies of the thesis were left at the LSE following examination"?

-Do we know who Dr Tsai's supervisor was, and whether she/he is still at the School and might have a copy of the thesis? Have we tried the department?

All best,

MTT

寄件者：Wilson，Clive
日期：2015 年 11 月 13 日 15：18
收件者：Thomson，MT；Green，U
副本：Flanagan，D；Reid，MJ；Yarham，R
主旨：回复：需要找到你们部门 1984 年的博士论文

亲爱的 Mark，
Sue Donnelly 可以提供蔡博士的 LSE 学生档案的纸本—我已经把她加入寄件副本。

Simeon 在一封电子邮件中说：
我的理解是，情况似乎是，两份纸本论文从指导教授和内部考官那里留给了 LSE，但这些从未传递给 SHL，而一份纸本从伦敦大学总图书馆传递给 IALS，但现在已经找不到了。

我确信这是基于相关的 LSE 和伦敦大学记录中的笔记。
法律系的 Rachel Yarham—现在也加入寄件副本—曾经被问及此事，但我相信该部门没有其他补充。
这都成为了一系列不幸的死胡同，找不到任何实体副本。
Clive

寄件者：Thomson，MT
日期：2015 年 11 月 12 日 16：34
收件者：Wilson，Clive；Green，LJ
副本：Flanagan，D；Reid，MJ
主旨：回复：需要找到你们部门 1984 年的博士论文

Clive，你好，
感谢您的通知—对于延迟的回应表示歉意，但我在本周初参加了一场会议，并为我的收件箱的状态付出了沉重的代价。
我之前不知道这件事。我有几个问题：
- 博士学院是否有蔡博士学生档案的副本？如果有，我可以看看吗？
- 我们知道在 2015 年 7 月 3 日的电子邮件中，她说，"两位口试委员所持有的纸本论文在考试后都留在了 LSE"，这一说法有依据吗？
- 我们知道蔡博士的指导教授是谁吗？他/她是否仍然在学校，并可能有纸本论文？我们试过该部门了吗？
祝好，MTT

From: Wilson,Clive
Sent: 22 March 2016 16:51
To: Thomson,MT; Yarham,R; Green,LJ
Cc: Flanagan,D; Reid,MJ
Subject: RE: Need to find a 1984 Ph.D. dissertation in your department

Dear Mark

Rachel rang me a short while ago to say that a U.S. research student had been digging around at Senate House for more information on Dr Tsai's thesis. As there is nothing further to be uncovered at LSE I suspect that will be it, but again thought I should let you know in case they end up getting through to your office.

We don't appear to have had any further interest via the Library despite Dr Tsai winning the election.

Best wishes

Clive

寄件者： Wilson，Clive
日期： 2016 年 3 月 22 日 16：51
收件者： Thomson，MT； Yarham，R； Green，U
副本： Flanagan，D； Reid，MJ
主旨： 回复：需要找到你们部门 1984 年的博士论文

亲爱的 Mark，
Rachel 不久前打电话给我，告诉我一名美国研究生在伦敦大学总图书馆深入调查蔡博士的论文。由于 LSE 没有进一步的资讯可以揭露，我怀疑这就是全貌，但我还是认为我应该让你知道，以防他们最终联系到你的办公室。

尽管蔡博士赢得了选举，但我们似乎没有透过图书馆收到任何进一步的兴趣。

祝好，
Clive

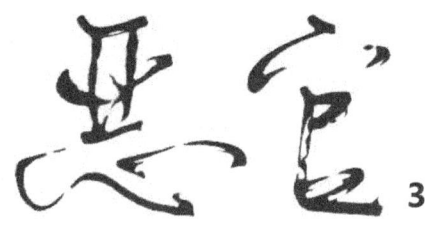

时间的迷雾：1984 年与 2011 年的交错

时间的迷雾：1984年与2011年的交错

伦敦政经学院（LSE）博士学程校务处副处长 Marcus W Cerny 面对着一个棘手的问题：蔡英文的博士论文，为何不在学院的图书馆？LSE 学术注册部门职员 Mark Thomson 表示他已经和 2015 年的调查官，即 LSE 时任教务长 Simeon Underwood 确认过了。但 Underwood 的回应却模棱两可，他说他无法确定是否有"运作"，这让整个问题更加复杂。

LSE 媒体关系部门负责人 Daniel O'Connor 打算用一种模糊的说法来回应外界：论文曾经被送到伦敦大学总图书馆。但 Cerny 知道，这其实是 2011 年的事情，而不是 1984 年。他心中挣扎，不知道是否应该坦白。

学院的图书馆员也表示疑惑，他们不知道该如何处理这个问题，于是求助于上级。Cerny 他不知道是否应该上报这个问题，担心学院的声誉会受到影响。

Rita，学院的另一名员工，则在电邮中表示她认为蔡英文没有学位，并建议通知 2015 年的调查专员。而 LSE 媒体关系部门负责人 Daniel O'Connor 则对此表示不满，他认为这是一场政治斗争，并酸言酸语地说来函询问的林环墙教授是中共的同路人。

Cerny 决定向学院的董事会报告这个问题，他担心 LSE 会为伦敦大学背黑锅。他知道，这场争议的背后，涉及的不仅仅是学术真相，还有政治的角力。最后，Cerny 决定模糊时间点的问题，让人误以为论文是 1984 年送入的。而 O'Connor 则决定用谎言回应外界，他知道这会推翻 LSE 咨询服务经理 Clive Wilson 一开始的说法，但他认为这是为了保护学院的声誉。

真相和谎言交织，政治和学术的界线变得模糊。

RE_-Need-to-find-a-1984-Ph.D.-dissertation-in-y

From: Cerny,MW
Sent: Friday, June 7, 2019 3:37:24 PM
To: Metcalfe,F
Subject: FW: PhD Thesis by Ing-Wen Tsai

Dear Fiona,

Could you or a member of your team advise on this? I would expect that there may have been queries in other parts of the School following Tsai's election as President of Republic of China and we may get more queries on this.

I am unable to answer as to why the thesis is unavailable and if the thesis is not held in either Senate House or LSE Libraries I cannot see any chance of there being any other version of it elsewhere.

The email trail between the Library and the enquirer is attached.

Thanks,
Marcus

Marcus Cerny
Deputy Director, PhD Academy
London School of Economics and Political Science
Houghton Street
London WC2A 2AE

Please consider the environment and do not print this email unless absolutely necessary.
Please access the attached hyperlink for an important electronic communications disclaimer.
http://lse.ac.uk/emailDisclaimer

寄件者：Cerny，MW
日期：2019年6月7日，星期五 3：37：24 PM
收件者：Metcalfe，F
主旨：转寄：蔡英文的博士论文

亲爱的 Fiona,
你或你的团队成员能对此提供建议吗？我预期在蔡女士当选中华民国总统后，学校的其他部分可能已经有了查询，我们可能会收到更多的查询。
我无法回答为什么论文无法取得，如果论文既不在伦敦大学总图书馆也不在 LSE 图书馆，我看不出它在其他地方还有任何其他版本的可能性。
图书馆和查询者之间的电子邮件对话已附上。
谢谢，

Marcus

Marcus Cerny
博士生学院副主任
伦敦政经学院
霍顿街
伦敦 WC2A 2AE

为了环保，除非绝对必要，否则请不要列印此电邮。请访问附加的超连结，以获取一个重要的电子通讯免责声明：https://lse.ac.uk/emailDisclaimer

From: Thomson,MT
Sent: 25 June 2019 19:38
To: Wilson,Clive; Kelloway,C; O'Connor,D; Cerny,MW; Metcalfe,F
Subject: RE: PhD Thesis by Ing-Wen Tsai

Colleagues, greetings

Further to our discussion yesterday, I got in touch with my predecessor – Simeon Underwood – who conducted the review of the file a few years ago that established that the award was made properly.

He had some memory of the case. His review amounted to looking carefully at the archived file. He concluded that all of the paperwork was in order that indicated that the award was made. He didn't have much more to add.

All best,

MTT

寄件者：Thomson，MT
日期：2019 年 6 月 25 日 19：38
收件者：Wilson，Clive；Kelloway，C；O'Connor，D；Cerny，MW；Metcalfe，F
主旨：回复：蔡英文的博士论文

同事们，你好

根据我们昨天的讨论，我联系了我的前任—Simeon Underwood—几年前他审查了该档案，确定了这个颁授是正确授予的。

他对这个案例有一些记忆。他的审查主要是仔细查看存档的档案。他得出的结论是，所有的文书都是有条理的，这表明这个学位是被授予的。他没有更多要补充的。

祝好，
MTT

_____

寄件者：O'Connor，D
日期：2019 年 6 月 24 日 15：46
收件者：Kelloway，C；Wilson，Clive；Thomson，MT；Cerny，MW；Metcalfe，F
主旨：回复：蔡英文的博士论文

我们是否可以只说：
"从总图书馆的记录中可以清楚地看到收到了一份纸本论文"。
这样可以吗？

RE_ Response on PhD Thesis by Ing-Wen Tsai

From: Cerny,MW
Sent: 27 June 2019 13:20
To: O'Connor,D <D.O.Connor@lse.ac.uk>; Wilson,Clive <CLIVE.Wilson@lse.ac.uk>
Cc: Metcalfe,F <F.Metcalfe@lse.ac.uk>; Kelloway,C <C.Kelloway@lse.ac.uk>
Subject: RE: Response on PhD Thesis by Ing-Wen Tsai

If I recall, the thesis was actually sent to IALS in 2011. This makes sense to me because it will have been around the time that the Research Degrees Office shut at UofL and remaining responsibilities were devolved to individual institutions (though LSE had already assumed these). I imagine they will have been clearing up a number of things outstanding around that time.

I would keep the date out of it and just say that Senate House Library confirmed they sent it to IALS. If anybody wants to ask them for details as to what happened and when, then that is for UoL to respond to (or not) as they see fit.

Thanks,
Marcus

Marcus Cerny
Deputy Director, PhD Academy
London School of Economics and Political Science
Houghton Street
London WC2A 2AE

Please consider the environment and do not print this email unless absolutely necessary.
Please access the attached hyperlink for an important electronic communications disclaimer: http://lse.ac.uk/emailDisclaimer

---

From: O'Connor,D
Sent: 27 June 2019 13:11
To: Wilson,Clive
Cc: Cerny,MW; Metcalfe,F; Kelloway,C
Subject: Response on PhD Thesis by Ing-Wen Tsai

Hi Clive,

I'm not dead-set on responding to ▓ but, if I were to respond, it might be along the lines below.

I realise he's clinging on to the initial response from you and Ruth, which suggested that LSE and UoL 'never received' a copy. I can indicate that this was an error but do say if you feel this misrepresents you.

(I'm not addressing all the other conspiracy bumf).

Danny

-CC- ing Marcus and colleagues for any other comments

Draft response

Dear ▓▓▓▓▓,

The response I gave still stands. All our records indicate the PhD was correctly awarded and in line with relevant procedures.

Unfortunately the thesis (which was only available as a hard copy in 1984) cannot be found by the University of London or the IALS but records do indicate it was received and processed at the time.

You state that Clive Wilson and his colleague said the 'PhD thesis has never been received in 1984 by Senate House Library and IALS library' in their initial response. This information does not appear to be correct, apologies for the confusion.

寄件者：Cerny，MW　　日期：2019 年 6 月 27 日 13：20
收件者：O'Connor，D D.O'Connor@lse.ac.uk；　Wilson，Clive CLIVE.Wilson@lse.ac.uk
副本：Metcalfe，F F.Metcalfe@lse.ac.uk；　Kelloway，C C.Kelloway@lse.ac.uk
主旨：关于蔡英文博士论文的回应

如果我记得没错，论文实际上是在 2011 年送到 IALS 的。这对我来说是有道理的，因为那是伦敦大学的研究学位办公室关闭的时候，剩下的职责被转交给各个机构（尽管 LSE 已经接手了）。我想他们那时候可能正在清理一些未完成的事情。

我会把日期留出来，只说伦敦大学总图书馆确认他们把它送到 IALS 了。如果有人想问他们详细情况和时间，那就由伦敦大学回应（或不回应）。

谢谢，Marcus

Marcus Cerny
博士生学院副主任
伦敦政经学院
Houghton 街
伦敦 WC2A 2AE

寄件者：O'Connor，D
日期：2019 年 6 月 27 日 13：11
收件者：Wilson，Clive
副本：Cerny，MW； Metcalfe，F； Kelloway，C
主旨：关于蔡英文博士论文的回应

嗨 Clive，我不是很坚持回应，但如果我要回应，可能会是以下的内容。我知道他抓住了你和 Ruth 最初建议 LSE 和伦敦大学"从未收到"副本的回应。我可以指出这是一个错误，但如果你觉得这误导了你，请告诉我。（我没有回应所有其他的阴谋论）。

Danny
-CC- 给 Marcus 和同事，看是否有其他意见
草拟回应

亲爱的，我提出的回应仍然有效。我们所有的记录都表明博士学位是正确授予的，并且符合相关程序。不幸的是，论文（1984 年只有纸本拷贝）既不能由伦敦大学也不能由 IALS 找到，但记录确实表明当时已收到并处理。您指称 Clive Wilson 和他的同事在他们初步回应中说"博士论文在 1984 年从未被伦敦大学总图书馆和 IALS 图书馆收到"。这些资讯似乎不正确，对于混淆表示歉意。

From: Kelloway,C
To: Wilson,Clive
Cc: Cerny,MW
Subject: RE: President Tsai
Date: 10 July 2019 14:40:03
Attachments: image002.png
image003.png
image005.png

Although this news story has just gone online with President Tsai holding the certificate signed by Adrian Smith...

https://www.taiwannews.com.tw/en/news/3742447

From: Kelloway,C
Sent: 10 July 2019 14:30
To: Wilson,Clive
Cc: Cerny,MW
Subject: RE: President Tsai

Thanks for the detective work on this, Clive – this is good to know!

We'll point them to University of London for questions about degree certificates but, as an aside, will also ask the origins of these certificates.

Many thanks,
Charlotte

From: Wilson,Clive
Sent: 10 July 2019 13:27
To: Cerny,MW; Kelloway,C
Subject: RE: President Tsai

I love being a librarian!!!

https://en.wikipedia.org/wiki/List_of_Vice-Chancellors_of_the_University_of_London

It looks to me like that is Adrian Smith's signature on both, University of London VP from 2012 – 2018.

But it was a different signature on the one I sent a few weeks ago ... (attached)   Randolph Quirk was VP in 1984

And UCL have also awarded their own degrees since 2008 and should be on UCL paper and signed by current president and provost Professor Michael Arthur??   And the date isn't straight ...

So the certificate for Ing-Wen Tsai is clearly a fake.   And the UCL one is almost certainly a fake.

寄件者：Kelloway，C
收件者：Wilson，Clive　　副本：Cerny，MW
主旨：回复：蔡英文总统
日期：2019年7月10日 14：40：03
附件：image002.png image003.png image005.png
虽然这则新闻故事刚在线上发布，蔡英文总统手持由 Adrian Smith 签名的证书 ...
https://www.taiwannews.com.tw/en/news/3742447

寄件者：Kelloway，C　　日期：2019年7月10日 14：30
收件者：Wilson，Clive
副本：Cerny，MW
主旨：回复：蔡英文总统
感谢你在这上面的侦查工作，Clive - 很高兴知道了这件事！
我们会将他们指向伦敦大学，询问有关学位证书的问题，但另外，我们也会询问这些证书的来源。
非常感谢，Charlotte

寄件者：Wilson，Clive
日期：2019年7月10日 13：27
收件者：Cerny，MW；　Kelloway，C
主旨：回复：蔡英文总统
我爱当图书馆员!!!
https://en.wikipedia.org/wiki/List_of_Vice-Chancellors_of_the_University_of_London
在我看来，那是 Adrian Smith 的签名，他于 2012 年至 2018 年间担任伦敦大学的副校长。
但在我几周前发送的那一份上有一个不同的签名 ...（附件）Randolph Quirk 在 1984 年是副校长。
而且伦敦大学学院自 2008 年以来也颁发了他们自己的学位，应该是伦敦大学学院的文件，并由现任校长和教务长 Michael Arthur 教授签名？而且日期不是直的 ...

所以蔡英文的证书明显是伪造的。而伦敦大学学院的那一份几乎肯定是伪造的。

Clive

From: Cerny,MW
Sent: 10 July 2019 11:58
To: Kelloway,C
Cc: Wilson,Clive
Subject: RE: President Tsai

Thanks Charlotte,

Definitely for UofL that one. I suspect that they have the signatures on file and use the one that was responsible for verifying the award at the time it was made but I don't know that for sure.

Thanks,
Marcus

Marcus Cerny
Deputy Director, PhD Academy
London School of Economics and Political Science
Houghton Street
London WC2A 2AE

Please consider the environment and do not print this email unless absolutely necessary.
Please access the attached hyperlink for an important electronic communications disclaimer:
http://lse.ac.uk/emailDisclaimer

From: Kelloway,C
Sent: 10 July 2019 11:38
To: Cerny,MW
Cc: Wilson,Clive
Subject: FW: President Tsai

Hi Marcus,

I hope you're well.

We've had the below enquiry from a journalist about President Tsai's PhD. We plan to send the response we have prepared with a note that the thesis will be available to view in the library imminently.

However, she also provides a recent University of London degree certificate and an apparent copy of President Tsai's degree certificate and questions why the Vice Chancellor's signature is the same on both despite the 34 year time difference.

We plan to say this is a question for the University of London but internally wanted to explore why this is the case and were wondering if you had any insight?

Clive

寄件者： Cerny，MW
日期： 2019 年 7 月 10 日 11：58
收件者： Kelloway，C
副本： Wilson，Clive
主旨： 回复：蔡英文总统

谢谢 Charlotte，

那绝对是伦敦大学的问题。我猜想他们拥有档案上的签名，并使用当时负责验证学位的人的签名，但我不能确定。

谢谢，Marcus

Marcus Cerny

博士生学院副主任

伦敦政经学院

霍顿街

伦敦 WC2A 2AE

为了环保，除非绝对必要，否则请不要列印此电邮。请访问附加的超连结，以获取一个重要的电子通讯免责声明：https://lse.ac.uk/emailDisclaimer

---

寄件者： Kelloway，C
日期： 2019 年 7 月 10 日 11：38
收件者： Cerny，MW
副本： Wilson，Clive
主旨： 转寄：蔡英文总统

嗨 Marcus，希望你一切都好。

我们收到了一位记者关于蔡英文总统的博士学位的以下查询。我们计划发送我们已经准备好的回应，并附带说明论文将在不久的将来在图书馆内提供查阅。

然而，她还提供了一份最近的伦敦大学学位证书和蔡英文总统学位证书的貌似真实的副本，并质疑为什么两者之间有 34 年的时间差异，但校长的签名是相同的。

我们计划说这是伦敦大学的问题，但内部想探索为什么会这样，不知道你有什么见解吗？

We're not sure of the origin of either of the photos.

Many thanks,

Charlotte

Charlotte Kelloway
Media Relations Officer | Communications Division
The London School of Economics and Political Science
Houghton Street, London WC2A 2AE
t: +44 (0)20 7955 6558
e: c.kelloway@lse.ac.uk
lse.ac.uk

[LSE] THE LONDON SCHOOL OF ECONOMICS AND POLITICAL SCIENCE

LSE is ranked #2 in the world for social science and management. (QS World University Ranking 2018)

From: ▇▇▇▇ ▇▇▇▇▇▇▇▇▇▇▇▇
Sent: 10 July 2019 06:39
To: Events
Subject: I would like to check some information from LSE

Here is

There is an issue in Taiwan , it's about President Tsai who got PHD from LSE in 1984. There are some media and people said it's a fake degree, because it couldn't find her Doctoral dissertation.

And each one of host who posted two certification to doubt why President Tsai graduated in 1984, another certification graduated in 2018, but Vise chancellor is same.

Could you please help me to figure out this issue? I'm curious the truth.

I'm apologize to bother you, and looking forward your help and reply.

Best Regard.

我们不确定这些照片的来源。
非常感谢，
Charlotte

Charlotte Kelloway
媒体关系官员 | 传播部门
伦敦政经学院
霍顿街， 伦敦 WC2A 2AE
电话：+44（0）20 7955 6558
电子邮件：c.kelloway@lse.ac.uk
lse.ac.uk

LSE 在社会科学和管理领域中的全球排名为第二。
（QS 世界大学排名 2018）

寄件者：████████
日期：2019 年 7 月 10 日 06：39
收件者：Events
主旨：我想从 LSE 核实一些资讯

这里是 ████████
在台湾有一个问题，关于蔡英文总统在 1984 年从 LSE 获得的博士学位。有一些媒体和人们说这是一个伪造的学位，因为找不到她的博士论文。

还有一些主持人发布了两份证书，质疑为什么蔡英文总统在 1984 年毕业，另一份证书在 2018 年毕业，但副校长是相同的。
你能帮我搞清楚这个问题吗？我很好奇真相。对于打扰你，我深感抱歉，并期待你的帮助和回复。最好的祝福。

████████

Note for SMC on Tsai thesis

From:	O"Connor,D
To:	Withers,JE
Cc:	Metcalfe,F
Subject:	Note for SMC on Tsai thesis
Date:	19 July 2019 11:12:00
Attachments:	image002.png
	image003.png
	image005.png

Hi,

Laura Ross has asked for a brief note on the Tsai PhD issue to inform SMC.

I've provided a two pager...but probably better this than too little.

Are you ok for me to send?

Thanks,

Danny

[CONFIDENTIAL]
Issues relating to President Tsai LSE PhD thesis

Background
At the time of her election in 2016, LSE received enquiries about the 1984 PhD in Law awarded to President Tsai Ing-wen. Upon review, it was established that neither the LSE library nor the University of London had a copy of the thesis. It appeared the University of London had lost the copy which LSE would have sent to them as standard.

Former Academic Registrar, Simeon Underwood, reviewed her student file at the time and found it to be in order. There was no reason to question the awarding of the thesis. He also indicated that the School should not share detailed information about the thesis, given data protection restrictions.

In 2019, the issue re-emerged as the Taiwan Presidential elections approach. Some activists and opponents of President Tsai, both pro-Beijing and also within her Democratic Party, are questioning the validity of the PhD, given that it cannot be found.

Further enquiries from the LSE Library in 2019 confirmed that the University of London had a record of cataloguing her thesis and sending it to Institute of Advanced Legal Studies, though they also were unable to find a copy.

The current availability of the thesis
Following a number of enquiries and some public discussion in Taiwan, the LSE Library was contacted by President Tsai's office who offered to send a copy of her PhD to the Library, to be available to view upon request.

Following discussion between representatives from the media relations office, PhD Academy, Library and Registry it was agreed the thesis could be catalogued as a 'facsimile copy provided by Tsai Ing-wen'. (Although there was no reason to believe the thesis would be different to the

寄件者：O"Connor，D
收件者：Withers，IF　**副本**：Metcalfe，F
主旨：关于蔡英文论文的 SMC 备忘录　**日期**：2019 年 7 月 19 日 11：12：00
附件：image002.png image003.png image005.png

嗨，

Laura Ross 要求提供一份关于蔡英文博士问题的简短备忘录以供 SMC 参考。我已提供了一份两页的文件 ... 但这可能比太少的资讯更好。

你觉得我可以发送吗？

谢谢，

Danny

[机密]

关于蔡英文总统 LSE 博士论文的问题

背景

在她于 2016 年当选时，LSE 收到了关于蔡英文总统于 1984 年获得的法学博士学位的查询。经过审查，确定 LSE 图书馆和伦敦大学都没有论文的副本。看起来伦敦大学已经遗失了 LSE 按标准程序发送给他们的副本。

前学术注册主任 Simeon Underwood 当时查看了她的学生档案，发现一切都是正常的。没有理由质疑论文的授予。他还表示，学校不应该分享关于论文的详细资讯，因为有数据保护的限制。

到 2019 年，由于台湾总统选举临近，这个问题再次浮现。蔡英文总统的一些积极份子与反对者，无论是亲北京还是她的民进党内部，都因为找不到论文而质疑博士学位的有效性。

LSE 图书馆在 2019 年的进一步查询确认，伦敦大学有记录将她的论文编目并发送给高等法律研究所，尽管他们也无法找到纸本。

论文的目前可用性

在收到了多次查询和台湾的一些公开讨论后，蔡英文总统的办公室联系 LSE 图书馆，他们提议将她的博士论文副本发送给图书馆，以供应要求查看。

在媒体关系办公室、博士生学院、图书馆和注册处的代表之间进行讨论后，同意可以将论文登记为"由蔡英文提供的影印本"。（尽管没有理由相信论文会与原始的 1984 年提交的版本有所不同，但由于我们没有原始副本进行比较，所以不能完全确定它是相同的）。

original 1984 submission we cannot for absolute certain it is the same, as we do not have an original copy to compare).

The thesis has been received and has, as of the week commencing 15 July, been catalogued and made available to view in the library, on request.

Media and public enquiries

The LSE Library and others have received a number of enquiries, primarily from members of the public but also from a few Taiwanese journalists.

Initial responses in June 2019 indicated that both the University of London and LSE can confirm the PhD was correctly awarded but that the University of London unfortunately no longer has a copy. A photocopy of the relevant LSE Calendar entry confirming her PhD graduation was attached as further evidence.

Following receipt of the thesis and more information becoming available, the media statement and information for public text has now been updated, as below.

LSE Statement:

'The records of the University of London and London School of Economics and Political Science confirm Tsai Ing-Wen was correctly awarded a PhD in Law in 1984

"All PhDs from that period were awarded via the University of London and would have been sent first to their Senate House Library. It is clear from Senate House Library records that a copy was received. Senate House have confirmed they sent their copy of the thesis to the Institute for Advanced Legal Studies (IALS).

"We have corresponded with the University of London about the thesis and extensive checks have been made. Neither Senate House nor IALS are able to locate a copy of the original thesis.

"Dr Tsai Ing-wen recently provided the LSE Library with a facsimile copy of the thesis, 'Unfair trade practices and safeguard actions'. This is now available to view in the library's reading room."

/END

To note, the library has confirmed LSE would catalogue facsimile copies of any missing thesis where there was substantial interest or numerous requests to view. This is not special treatment because she is President of Taiwan.

Certificate issue

Additional questions have been asked regarding the physical certificate President Tsai has been displaying in public meetings. Many critics pointed out that it bears the signature of the *current* Vice Chancellor rather than the VC from 1984 when it would have been awarded.

After consulting the LSE media relations office, The University of London have drafted a statement, to indicate that it is a legitimate certificate (it was re-issued to Tsai Ing-wen in 2015). Their re-issue policy is if that if the individual graduated under 20 years ago the signature of the VC at the time would be on the certificate. If over 20 years ago it would contain the signature of the VC at the time of re-issue.

Their statement is to be signed off imminently. Once this has been confirmed LSE will add it

论文已被接收，并在 7 月 15 日开始的那周被登记，同时在图书馆内提供查阅。

媒体和公众查询
LSE 图书馆和其他部门已收到了多次查询，主要来自公众，但也有一些台湾记者的查询。
2019 年 6 月的初步回应指出，伦敦大学和 LSE 都可以确认博士学位是正确授予的，但伦敦大学不幸地不再拥有副本。作为进一步的证据，附上了确认她的博士毕业的相关 LSE 行事历条目影印本。

在收到论文和更多资讯可用后，媒体声明和公众文字现已更新，如下所示。

LSE 声明：

"伦敦大学和伦敦政经学院的记录确认蔡英文于 1984 年正确地被授予法学博士学位"。
"那段时期的所有博士学位都是透过伦敦大学授予的，并且首先会被发送到他们的伦敦大学总图书馆。从总图书馆的记录中可以清楚地看到已经收到了一份纸本。总图书馆已确认他们将论文的副本发送给了高等法律研究所（IALS）"。
"我们已与伦敦大学就论文进行了通信，并进行了广泛的检查。总图书馆和 IALS 都无法找到原始纸本论文"。
"蔡英文博士最近向 LSE 图书馆提供了论文的影印本，名为'不公平贸易和防卫机制'。这现在可以在图书馆的阅览室内查看"。
/ 结束
值得注意的是，图书馆已确认，LSE 将会记录任何失踪论文的影印本，如果这些论文有大量的关注或多次要求查看，。这不是因为她是台湾总统而得到的特殊待遇。

证书问题
还有一些问题是关于蔡英文总统在公开会议中展示的实体证书。许多批评者指出，它带有当前副校长的签名，而不是 1984 年授予时的副校长的签名。

在咨询了 LSE 媒体关系办公室后，伦敦大学起草了一份声明，指出这是一份合法的证书（它于 2015 年重新发给蔡英文）。他们的重新发行政策是，如果该个人在 20 年前毕业，证书上将带有当时的副校长的签名。如果超过 20 年，则将包含重新发行时的副校长的签名。

alongside own statement, where relevant, with the following text:

"Questions regarding the PhD certificate itself are a matter for the University of London. They have provided the following statement on this matter:

Draft statement by University of London (TBC):
"The University of London can confirm that the diploma certificate re-issued to Dr Tsai Ing-wen is genuine and is signed by the Vice-Chancellor in post at the time of the diploma certificate being reissued.

"Any replacement diploma for an academic award that was originally made 20 or more years ago, will carry the signature of the University of London's Vice-Chancellor, who is in post at the time of the certificate being re-issued."

Next steps and ongoing coverage.
This issue is primarily being led by political opponents of President Tsai and anti-Tsai online activists. It is relatively limited to anti-Tsai media in Taiwan. Given LSE and University of London's firm stance that the PhD was legitimate- and additional evidence, such as the availability of the thesis copy – it is unlikely to break into any mainstream media.

It is likely there will be ongoing enquiries from resolute opponents, who may find any explanation hard to accept. Our recommendation is we stick to agreed statement including, where relevant, an offer for the individual to view the thesis and the statement by the University of London regarding the certificate itself.

Daniel O'Connor
Head of Media Relations | Communications Division
The London School of Economics and Political Science
Houghton Street, London WC2A 2AE
t: +44 (0)20 7955 7417
e: oconnord@lse.ac.uk
lse.ac.uk

LSE is ranked #1 in Europe for social sciences
(QS World University Ranking 2018)

他们的声明即将获得确认。一旦这已被确认，LSE 将在相关的地方加入自己的声明，以下面的文字：

"关于博士学位证书本身的问题是伦敦大学的事情。他们就此事提供了以下声明："

伦敦大学的草案声明（待确认）：
"伦敦大学可以确认，重新发给蔡英文博士的文凭证书是真实的，并由重新发给文凭证书时的副校长签名"。
"原本在 20 年或更早之前获得的学术奖项的任何替代文凭都将带有伦敦大学副校长的签名，该副校长在证书重新发行时担任职务"。

下一步和持续的报导
这个问题主要是由蔡英文总统的政治反对者和反蔡的线上活动家主导的。它相对限于台湾的反蔡媒体。鉴于 LSE 和伦敦大学坚定地认为博士学位是合法的—以及其他证据，例如纸本论文的可用性—它不太可能进入任何主流媒体。

可能会有持续的查询来自坚定的反对者，他们可能会发现任何解释都很难接受。我们的建议是我们坚持同意的声明，包括在相关的地方，提供个人查看论文的机会，以及伦敦大学关于证书本身的声明。

Daniel O'Connor
媒体关系主管 | 传播部门
伦敦政经学院
霍顿街，伦敦 WC2A 2AE
电话：+44 （0） 20 7955 7417
电子邮件：oconnord@lse.ac.uk
lse.ac.uk

LSE 在社会科学方面在欧洲排名第一
（QS 世界大学排名 2018）

RE_ [Academic Support Librarians] purchasing a ....

From: Wilson,Clive
To: O'Connor,D
Subject: RE: [Academic Support Librarians] purchasing a copy of Ph. D thesis
Date: 29 July 2019 17:18:28

No problem ☺
thanks

From: O'Connor,D
Sent: 29 July 2019 16:39
To: Wilson,Clive
Subject: RE: [Academic Support Librarians] purchasing a copy of Ph. D thesis

Hi Clive,

Sorry, I didn't respond on this.

Don't reply with the suggested.

I'd say don't bother replying at all.

Danny

From: Wilson,Clive
Sent: 25 July 2019 16:31
To: O'Connor,D <D.O'Connor@lse.ac.uk>
Subject: FW: [Academic Support Librarians] purchasing a copy of Ph. D thesis

Hi Danny

I'll keep my mouth shut in future ...

Trying to think of a way to say we don't have permission to digitise without actually saying we don't have permission ... came up with the following ...

Any better ideas? No particular rush ...
thanks

Clive

[Internal Note] Clive Wilson
Jul 25 2019, 03:09pm via Staff Entry

Dear ▮▮▮▮

I am not entering into an endless backwards and forwards on this. As both LSE and the University of London have confirmed, Dr. Tsai's PhD was correctly awarded.

Although more recent theses are submitted electronically, older theses specifically need the

寄件者：Wilson，Clive
收件者：O"Connor，D
主旨：回复：[学术支援图书馆员] 购买博士论文副本
日期：2019 年 7 月 29 日 17：18：28
没问题，谢谢。

寄件者：O'Connor，D
日期：2019 年 7 月 29 日 16：39
收件者：Wilson，Clive
主旨：回复：[学术支援图书馆员] 购买博士论文副本
嗨，Clive，
抱歉，我之前没有回应这件事。不要按照建议回复。我建议根本不要回复。Danny

寄件者：Wilson，Clive
日期：2019 年 7 月 25 日 16：31
收件者：O'Connor，D D.O'Connor@lse.ac.uk
主旨：转发：[学术支援图书馆员] 购买博士论文副本
嗨，Danny，
我以后会保持沉默……
我在想一种方法，说明我们没有数位化的许可，而实际上我们没有许可……我想到了以下的方式……
有更好的想法吗？不用特别赶……谢谢。
Clive

[内部笔记] Clive Wilson
2019 年 7 月 25 日，下午 03：09，透过员工输入
亲爱的▆▆▆▆，
我不打算进入这个无休止的来回讨论中。正如 LSE 和伦敦大学都已确认的，蔡博士的博士学位是正确授予的。
虽然最近的论文是电子提交的，但较早的论文特别需要

author's permission to be digitised. If Dr Tsai wishes her thesis to be digitised we will happily do so.

[Queue Transfer from Library Enquiries to Academic Support Librarians]

[Status changed to *Pending*]

Jul 25 2019, 01:05pm via Email

Hi Clive,Thanks so much for your response on this matter.
Would you please advise the reason why Mrs.Tsai's thesis is not available from this etheses website?Since your library recently received her personal copy, can we expect her thesis be converted to pdf and open to public for download in the near future?
Thanks,
Jimpo

http://etheses.lse.ac.uk/view/year/1984.html?fbclid=IwAR3HBSoEbY_pawK4ukFzFHYsyJC3fBPk_OD2Tr3EzV97k0a02lfbdgndLP4

Clive Wilson

Jul 24 2019, 05:05pm via System

Hi

yes, the thesis can be viewed. But as I said, you need the author's permission to have it copied.

Clive

Jul 24 2019, 03:04pm via Email

Hi Clive,Thanks for the prompt response to my request.Is this publication open to public at this moment? If yes, can I have someone come to your library to make the copy for me?

Clive Wilson

Jul 24 2019, 02:18pm via System

Dear

even in the US there are plenty of examples of theses where the author has specifically requested that the thesis is neither online nor copied.

Under UK copyright law, the author's permission needs to be given in order to quote or reproduce any part of a thesis. If you have the author's permission you are welcome to arrange to have it copied, however we do not offer a copying service.

作者的许可才能进行数位化。如果蔡博士希望她的论文被数位化，我们将很乐意这么做。

[从图书馆查询转到学术支援图书馆员]

[状态更改为待定]

▮▮▮▮▮

2019 年 7 月 25 日，下午 01：05，透过电子邮件

嗨，Clive，非常感谢您对此事的回应。

可否请您告诉我为什么蔡女士的论文不在这个 etheses 网站上？由于您的图书馆最近收到了她的个人纸本，我们可以期待她的论文在不久的将来被转换为 pdf 并向公众开放下载吗？

谢谢，

Jimpo

http://etheses.lse.ac.uk/view/year/1984.html?fbclid=IwAR3HBSoEbY_pawK4ukFzFHYsyJC3fBPk_OD2Tr3EzV97k0a02lfbdgndLP4

Clive Wilson

2019 年 7 月 24 日，下午 05：05，透过系统

▮▮▮▮▮

是的，可以查看论文。但正如我所说，您需要作者的许可才能复制它。

Clive

▮▮▮▮▮

2019 年 7 月 24 日，下午 03：04，透过电子邮件

嗨，Clive，感谢您对我请求的迅速回应。这份出版物现在对公众开放吗？如果是，我可以请某人来您的图书馆为我复制吗？

Clive Wilson

2019 年 7 月 24 日，下午 02：18，透过系统

亲爱的 ▮▮▮▮▮

即使在美国，也有很多论文的例子，其中作者有特别需求论文不能上线也不能被复制。

根据英国的版权法，需要作者的许可才能引用或重制论文的任何部分。如果您有作者的许可，您可以安排复制，但我们不提供复制服务。

You would also be welcome to visit to view the item.

best wishes

Clive

Clive Wilson
Enquiry Services Manager
LSE Library

Original Question

Jul 24 2019, 12:46pm via Email

purchasing a copy of Ph. D thesis
Dear LSE Library Staff,
I am currently doing some research in the area of unfair trading and found some Ph.D thesis interesting to me.
Based on my experience in U.S.A I believe all theses are public and can be purchased at reasonable cost.
Would you please advise the cost and process of acquiring the copy of the following thesis?

Author: Tsai, Ing-Wen
Title: Unfair trade practices and safeguard actions

Best Regards,

▇▇▇▇▇▇

Questioner Information

Name: ▇▇▇▇▇▇▇▇
Email: ▇▇▇▇▇▇▇▇▇▇▇▇▇

Clive Wilson Enquiry Services LSE Library

This email is sent from LSE Library in relationship to ticket id #2675412.

Read our privacy policy.

您也可以来访以查看该项目。最好的祝愿
Clive
Clive Wilson
查询服务经理
LSE 图书馆

―――――――――――――――――――――

原始问题
2019 年 7 月 24 日，12：16pm，透过电子邮件

购买博士论文副本
亲爱的 LSE 图书馆工作人员，
我目前正在进行有关不公平贸易的研究，并发现一些博士论文对我很有趣。
根据我在美国的经验，我相信所有的论文都是公开的，可以以合理的价格购买。
可否请您告诉我论文副本的价格和获得方法吗？

作者：蔡英文
标题：不公平贸易和防卫机制

最好的祝愿，
███████

提问者资讯
姓名：███████
电子邮件：███████

Clive Wilson 查询服务 LSE 图书馆

这封电子邮件是从 LSE 图书馆发送的，与票据编号 #2675412 有关。
阅读我们的隐私政策。

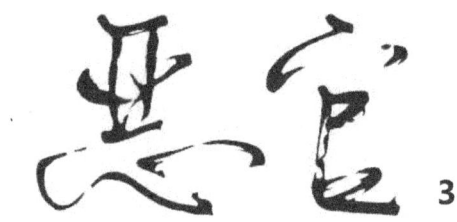

3

LSE 的模糊策略

LSE 的模糊策略

在伦敦，LSE 的几位高层官员"举杯"庆祝。他们成功地将一场可能对学校造成巨大损害的舆论风暴压下来。

但是，这场风暴并没有完全平息。蔡英文的提告消息传来，让他们感到震惊。他们从未想过，这位台湾的领袖会采取如此激烈的行动。在一次内部会议中，一位官员自嘲地说，"我们的证词已经准备好了"。

O'Connor，一位经验丰富的公关专家，建议 Wilson 在回应公众时更模糊其词。他认为，现在是他们必须小心谨慎的时候，因为蔡英文的提告可能会让整个事件再次升级。他们不希望再次成为媒体的焦点。

不久之后，台湾驻英代表处的代表来到 LSE，他们希望确认蔡英文的论文并不是唯一遗失的。这使得 LSE 的高层更加紧张。他们开始担心，如果真的只有蔡英文的论文遗失，那么这将是一个巨大的丑闻。LSE 的高层再次巧妙地用模糊的话术回避了这样的说法。

2019 年 8 月 27 日，林环墙教授发表了 50 页的"蔡英文论文独立调查报告"，直指蔡英文 1984 年并未取得伦敦政经学院的法学博士学位。两天后，贺德芬教授在立法院召开"蔡英文总统博士学位论文说明会"，也提出了相似的结论。

总统府的反应迅速。8 月 29 日，总统府发言人张惇涵召开记者会，宣布对林环墙和贺德芬两位教授提告，认为他们的指控是不实的。

RE_ [Academic Support Librarians] purchasing a ....

From: Cerny,MW
To: O"Connor,D; Wilson,Clive
Subject: RE: [Library Enquiries] PhD thesis search
Date: 09 July 2019 13:33:00

Thanks for keeping me up to date with this. I'm pretty relaxed about this given that there is no question that the thesis existed and was examined. Do people not think that if we were genuinely engaged in a conspiracy we'd have pretty certainly managed to come across a copy that had been misplaced on a shelf in one of the Libraries.

I think that the clarity we are showing in being open about the thesis being lost and the current copy being a recently submitted facsimile replacing the original demonstrates that there is no corruption or cover up.

Once a query becomes a circular correspondence (as one of mine did) I think it's fine to simply ignore after giving the formal response.

Thanks,
Marcus

Marcus Cerny
Deputy Director, PhD Academy
London School of Economics and Political Science
Houghton Street
London WC2A 2AE

Please consider the environment and do not print this email unless absolutely necessary.
Please access the attached hyperlink for an important electronic communications disclaimer:
http://lse.ac.uk/emailDisclaimer

From: O'Connor,D
Sent: 09 July 2019 11:36
To: Wilson,Clive; Cerny,MW
Subject: Re: [Library Enquiries] PhD thesis search

Thanks Clive.

I would be amazed if the Guardian or NYT followed up with a story beyond a short, 'oops, how embarrassing that they lost her PhD'. If our records say she graduated they should take that as confirmation.

(Separately, "panda huggers" !)

Danny

From: Wilson,Clive

寄件者：Cerny，MW　　**收件者**：O"Connor，D； Wilson，Clive
主旨：回复：[图书馆查询] 博士论文搜寻
日期：2019 年 7 月 9 日 13：33：00

感谢您将我与此事保持同步。我对此相当放心，因为毫无疑问论文是存在且已经过审查的。人们难道不认为，如果我们真的参与了某种阴谋，我们肯定能找到一份在图书馆的某个架子上被误放的副本吗？

我认为，我们在公开表示论文遗失，且目前的副本是最近提交的复印本，用以替代原始版本，这样的清晰度表明没有任何腐败或掩盖行为。

一旦查询变成了循环的对话（就像我的其中一封），我认为在提出正式回应后，完全可以选择忽略。

谢谢，
Marcus

Marcus Cerny
博士生学院副主任
伦敦政经学院
霍顿街
伦敦 WC2A 2AE
为了环保，除非绝对必要，否则请不要列印此电邮。请访问附加的超连结，以获取一个重要的电子通讯免责声明：https://lse.ac.uk/emailDisclaimer

---

寄件者：O'Connor，D　**日期**：2019 年 7 月 9 日 11：36
收件者：Wilson，Clive； Cerny，MW
主旨：回复：[图书馆查询] 博士论文搜寻

谢谢你，Clive。

我很惊讶，如果《卫报》或《纽约时报》除了短暂地报导"哎呀，他们竟然遗失了她的博士学位"之外，还有其他跟进的报导。如果我们的记录显示她毕业，他们应该接受这一事实作为确认。

（题外话，"中共的拥戴者"！）

Danny

寄件者：Wilson，Clive

Sent: 09 July 2019 11:28:09
To: Cerny,MW; O'Connor,D
Subject: FW: [Library Enquiries] PhD thesis search

Dear Both

fyi – I'm chasing our making it available right now!!

Clive

From: LSE Library [mailto:Library.enquiries@lse-uk.libanswers.com]
Sent: 09 July 2019 11:23
To: Wilson,Clive
Subject: [Library Enquiries] PhD thesis search

--# Please type your reply above this line, it will be sent as a response to the patron #--
A new reply has been submitted for Ticket #2633151 and is awaiting attention. View this ticket at https://lse-uk.libanswers.com/admin/ticket?qid=2633151.

Hughes,CR
Jul 09 2019, 11:23am via Email
Dear Clive

Thanks so much for this. It is an issue that is being dramatized and distorted for political reasons, so these steps should put the issue to rest.

All the best
Chris

Clive Wilson
Jul 09 2019, 11:21am via System
Dear Both
LSE has made it very clear that the thesis was submitted properly and that the degree could not have been awarded without it. (Some people should just learn how to read.)
I can probably say now that President Tsai has given us two facsimile copies of her thesis which we are trying to rush through to make them available. Due to excessive interest we will not digitise it, though researchers will be very welcome to request it in our Special Collections Reading Room.
best wishes
Clive
Clive Wilson
Enquiry Services Manager
LSE Library

Hughes,CR
Jul 09 2019, 10:07am via Email
Dear ████

日期：2019年7月9日 11：28：09　收件者：Cerny，MW；O'Connor，D
主旨：转发：[图书馆查询]博士论文搜寻

亲爱的二位，

仅供参考—我正在追紧我们现在能够提供的资讯！

Clive

寄件者： LSE 图书馆 [mailto: Library.enquiries@lse-uk.libanswers.com]
日期： 2019年7月9日 11：23
收件者： Wilson，Clive
主旨： [图书馆查询]博士论文搜寻

--# 请在此行上方输入您的回复，它将作为对读者的回应发送 #--

一个新的回复已经提交给票据 #2633151，并等待关注。在 https://lse-uk.libanswers.com/admin/ticket?qid=2633151 查看此票据。

Hughes，CR
2019年7月9日，上午11：23，透过电子邮件

亲爱的 Clive，

非常感谢您。这是一个因政治原因而被戏剧化和扭曲的问题，所以这些步骤应该可以解决这个问题。

祝一切顺利，

Chris

Clive Wilson 2019年7月9日，上午11：21，透过系统

亲爱的二位，

LSE 已经非常清楚地表示，论文是正确提交的，而且如果没有它，学位是不可能被授予的。（有些人应该学会如何阅读）

我现在可以说，蔡总统给了我们两份她论文的复印本，我们正在尝试赶紧使它们可供取得。由于过度的关注，我们不会将其数位化，但研究人员非常欢迎在我们的特藏阅览室借阅。 最好的祝愿，

Clive

Clive Wilson
查询服务经理
LSE 图书馆

Hughes，CR
2019年7月9日，上午10：07，透过电子邮件

亲爱的 ███████

Thanks for cc'ing me into this. It is incredibly frustrating for everybody, esp Pres Tsai. I guess the simple fact is that things do go missing, and given Tsai's high priority, it is certainly possible that someone or some organization with bad intentions has taken the thesis from the library. The fact that the LSE has recorded her as having been awarded the PhD should be enough to close down any allegations that she did not do one. As for quality, the LSE can only stand by the rigour of its examination procedures. Unless Pres Tsai has a copy of the thesis, then I don't see what anyone can do about this now.

Good to hear from you and keep in touch

▮▮▮▮▮▮▮▮▮▮

Jul 08 2019, 10:58pm via Email

Dear Mr. Wilson:

This is ▮▮▮▮▮▮ again. I thought President Tsai's PhD thesis problem had been solved, but it rekindled again, as you may see from the four attached reports and email. It is almost getting out of hand.

The naysayers even use the Guardian report to throw the doubt about the existence and authenticity of Tsai's thesis. See docu #2. I hope this will not happen to Tsai. The best way now seems to me that the LSE finds her thesis committee members to get her thesis and relist/publish it and replace it in the LSE library. (My third book is forthcoming from World Scientific, I even can help her publish it with my commentary).

I think LSE should do something to clarify the thesis ASAP before the Guardian, NYT or Washington Post picks up the news story (it will be a sensational). It seems to me reputation of the LSE is at stake.

▮▮

PS. I am cc to Professor Chris Hughes.
As for #4 about the English writing of Ma (or Tsai), if this is the concern of LSE, I don't think it should be the concern. As Wassily Leontief, a Harvard Professor and a Nobel Prize winner in Economics, once wrote in the introduction of his book, "American Sciences were advanced by broken English."
In fact, everybody knows two birds are plural, you don't need to add s to show it, or worry about the tense or articles. At least 6 billion of people speak Chinese and Japanese without using plural, tense and articles.

Attached Files
- 0Richardson_British_Library_Richardreversal_on_Tsai_Ing-wen's_phantom_thesis_deepens_mystery_of_missing_manuscript.pdf
- 1Richardson_Tsai_Ing-wen's_missing_thesis_was_not_submitted_says_university_library_-_Richardson_Reports.pdf
- 2Richardson_lttr_to.pdf
- 3Richardson_TIW_official_CV_fm_TGov.pdf
- 4Richardson_Tsai_Ing-wen's_missing_doctoral_thesis_follows_Ma_Ying-jeou's_error-filled_thesis.pdf

[Internal Note] Clive Wilson

Jun 20 2019, 12:17pm via System

[Status changed to *Closed*.]

感谢您将我加入寄送副本。这对每个人，尤其是蔡总统，都是极其令人沮丧的。我想，事实很简单，就是事物会遗失，考虑到蔡英文的高度优先级别，很有可能有人或某个组织带着坏意从图书馆拿走了论文。LSE 已经记录她被授予博士学位，这应该足以驳斥她没有完成论文的指控。至于标准，LSE 只能依赖其考试程序的严格性。除非蔡总统有论文的副本，否则我不认为现在有人可以对此做些什么。

很高兴收到您的消息，请保持联系。

▇▇▇▇▇▇▇▇▇▇▇▇▇▇▇▇▇▇▇▇▇▇▇▇▇▇

2019 年 7 月 8 日，晚上 10：58，透过电子邮件

亲爱的 Wilson 先生：

这是再次 ▇▇▇▇▇ 我以为蔡总统的博士论文问题已经解决了，但您可能从附加的四份报告和电子邮件中看到，它再次被重新点燃。这几乎已经失控了。

反对者甚至使用《卫报》的报导来怀疑蔡论文的存在和真实性。参见文件 #2。我希望这不会发生在蔡身上。现在最好的方法似乎是 LSE 找到她的论文委员会成员，取得她的论文，重新列出／发布它，并将其替换到 LSE 图书馆。（我的第三本书即将由 World Scientific 出版，我甚至可以帮助她出版它，并附上我的评论）。

我认为 LSE 应该尽快澄清论文，以免《卫报》、《纽约时报》或《华盛顿邮报》撰写新闻报导（这将是一个轰动的新闻）。我认为 LSE 的声誉岌岌可危。

▇▇▇▇▇

附注：我抄送给 Chris Hughes 教授。

至于关于马（或蔡）的英文写作，如果这是 LSE 的关心，我不认为这应该是关心的事。正如哈佛大学教授、经济学诺贝尔奖得主 Wassily Leontief 在他的书的前言中所写的那样，"美国的科学是由破碎的英语推进的。"

事实上，每个人都知道两只鸟是复数，你不需要加 s 来表示它，或担心时态或冠词。至少有 60 亿的人说中文和日语，而不使用复数、时态和冠词。

附加文件

    0Richardson_British_Library_Richardreversal_on_Tsai_Ing-wen's_phantom_thesis_deepens_mystery_of_missing_manuscript.pdf

    1Richardson_Tsai_Ing-wen's_missing_thesis_was_not_submitted_says_university_library_-_Richardson_Reports.pdf

    2Richardson_lttr_to.pdf

    3Richardson_TIW_official_CV_fm_TGov.pdf

    4Richardson_Tsai_Ing-wen's_missing_doctoral_thesis_follows_Ma_Ying-jeou's_error-filled_thesis.pdf

──────────────────────

[内部注记] Clive Wilson

2019 年 6 月 20 日，下午 12：17，透过系统

[状态更改为已关闭。]

███████████████
Jun 13 2019, 07:17pm via Email
Dear Ms Wilson:

Thank you very much for your confirmation about President Tsai's PhD degree.

Despite a very strong opposition from her own party, Do. Tsai was nominated as the presidential candidate of the Democratic Progressive Party (DPP) yesterday. We hope she will be re-elected as the President of Taiwan for the next four years despite fake news and false news, naysayers spread by the Chinese in and out of Taiwan.

In fact, the situation is much much more complicated than Premier May in England or the current protest in Hong Kong due to the Chinese and panda huggers' interference.

In any case, "missing" means it existed. That also confirm that she had submitted the PhD thesis, and she graduated. One theory here is that the thesis might be stolen by a Chinese to spread rumor that Tsai concocted her degree to question her integrity.

We are very proud of our President, and her achievements. Please continue looking for her Thesis to help her and let us know.

Incidentally, her Thesis topic was innovative and farsighted in 1984, as the topic of "unfair trade practices" is current very hot under Trump administration. The LSE should be proud of having such a student.

Thank you very much.

PS. I am sending cc to ███████████ and ███████████, the current and the former ███████████████████████████

Clive Wilson
Jun 13 2019, 12:23pm via System
Dear ███
in light of recent interest over President Tsai's re-nomination and the possible ambiguity of my previous email, I thought I should add that University of London and LSE records confirm Tsai Ing-wen was correctly awarded a PhD in Law in 1984.
best wishes
Clive

[Internal Note] Clive Wilson
Jun 13 2019, 12:24pm via Staff Entry
[Ownership assigned to Clive Wilson]
[Status changed to *Pending*]

Clive Wilson

2019 年 7 月 13 日，下午 7：17，透过电子邮件
亲爱的 Wilson 女士：
非常感谢您确认蔡英文总统的博士学位。

尽管她自己的党内有非常强烈的反对，蔡博士昨天被提名为民主进步党（DPP）的总统候选人。我们希望她能够在接下来的四年内再次当选台湾总统，尽管有中国在台湾内外散播的假新闻和虚假消息。

实际上，由于中国和"拥抱熊猫派"的干涉，这种情况比英国的梅伊首相或香港的当前抗议活动要复杂得多。

无论如何，"失踪"意味着它曾经存在。这也确认她已经提交了博士论文，并且她已经毕业。这里的一个理论是，论文可能被一名中国人偷走，以传播谣言说蔡英文伪造了她的学位，从而质疑她的诚信。
我们为我们的总统和她的成就感到非常自豪。请继续寻找她的论文以帮助她，并让我们知道。

顺便说一下，她在 1984 年的论文主题是创新和有远见的，因为"不公平的贸易"在川普政府下是当前非常热门的主题。LSE 应该为有这样的学生而感到自豪。
非常感谢您。

Clive Wilson
2019 年 6 月 13 日，下午 12：23，透过系统
亲爱的 ▇▇▇▇▇
鉴于最近对蔡英文总统的重新提名和我之前电子邮件的可能出现含糊之处，我认为我应该补充说，伦敦大学和 LSE 的记录确认蔡英文在 1984 年正确地被授予法学博士学位。
祝好，
Clive

[内部注记] Clive Wilson
2019 年 6 月 12 日，下午 2：24，透过系统入口
[所有权分配给 Clive Wilson]
[状态更改为待定]

Clive Wilson

人类史上最大学位诈骗案　163

Jun 11 2019, 11:56am via System
Dear ███
Unfortunately, LSE Library has never had a copy of this thesis.
All PhDs from that period were awarded under the University of London banner and would have been sent first to Senate House Library. As you can appreciate, over the last few years there has been a lot of interest in Dr Tsai's thesis and we have been in correspondence with the University of London about it and extensive searches made.
Unfortunately Senate House are unable to find their copy.
I am sorry we cannot help further
yours sincerely
Clive
Clive Wilson
Enquiry Services Manager
LSE Library

[Internal Note] Sarah Hayward

Jun 11 2019, 10:35am via System
Hi
Please can you assist with this thesis enquiry?
Please copy us in your reply
Thanks
Sarah
[Status changed to *Pending*.]

Original Question

Jun 11 2019, 06:22am via Email
PhD thesis search
Dear Sir/Madam:
My name is ███████ I beg your pardon to writing to you.

I am looking for the LSE thesis as follows. I could not find any title in the PhD thesis section in your library. There are only three PhD thesis in 1984 but none of them has the following title.

Could you kindly direct me to access the thesis?
The ethos indicate that it is a "restricted access." May I ask why is it restricted?

Your early response will be greatly appreciated.

Title: Unfair trade practices and safeguard actions
Author: **Tsai**, Ing-Wen
Awarding Body: London School of Economics and Political Science (University of London)
Current Institution:
London School of Economics and Political Science (University of London)
Date of Award: 1984
Availability of Full
Text: Full text unavailable from EThOS. Restricted access.

2019 年 6 月 11 日，上午 11：56，透过系统
亲爱的 ████████：
很遗憾，LSE 图书馆从未拥有这份论文的纸本。
那个时期的所有博士学位都是在伦敦大学的名下授予的，并且首先会被送到伦敦大学总图书馆。如您所知，过去几年来，蔡博士的论文引起了很大的关注，我们已经与伦敦大学就此进行了很多通信并进行了广泛的搜索。
很不幸，总图书馆无法找到他们的副本。
很抱歉我们无法提供进一步的帮助。诚挚地，
Clive

Clive Wilson
查询服务经理
LSE 图书馆

[内部注记] Sarah Hayward
2019 年 6 月 11 日，上午 10：55，透过系统 嗨，
您能协助这次的论文查询吗？请在回复中抄送我们。
谢谢，Sarah
[状态更改为待定。]

原始问题
2019 年 6 月 11 日，上午 6：22，透过电子邮件
博士论文搜寻
亲爱的先生 / 女士：
我的名字是 ████████ 我向您道歉写信给您。
我正在寻找以下的 LSE 论文。在您的图书馆的博士论文部分，我找不到任何标题。
1984 年只有三篇博士论文，但没有一篇是以下的标题。
您能指导我如何访问这篇论文吗？
EThOS 指出它是"限制取得"。我可以问问为什么它受到限制吗？您的早日回应将不胜感激。
标题：不公平贸易和防卫机制
作者：蔡英文
授予机构：伦敦政经学院（伦敦大学）
当前机构：伦敦政经学院（伦敦大学）
授予日期：1984 年
全文可用性：
EThOS 无法提供全文。限制取得。

Please contact the current institution's library for further details.

Attached Files
- ▮▮▮▮

Questioner Information
Name: ▮▮▮▮
Email: ▮▮▮▮

This email is sent from LSE Library in relationship to ticket id #2633151.
Read our privacy policy.

请联系当前机构的图书馆以获得更多详细资讯。

附加文件

提问者资讯
姓名：
电子邮件：

此电子邮件是由 LSE 图书馆发送的，与票证编号 #2633151 有关。
阅读我们的隐私政策。

RE_-A-plea-for-LSE-to-elaborate

From: O"Connor,D
To: Wilson,Clive
Subject: RE: A plea for LSE to elaborate
Date: 16 July 2019 11:14:00

Hi Clive,

I think there can be pretty standard reply to this, with some extra information.

Dear █████,

Thank you for your email which has been passed to me.

As has been highlighted in other correspondence, we have checked our records and both the London School of Economics and Political Science and the University of London confirm that Tsai Ing-Wen was correctly awarded a PhD in Law 1984.

President Tsai Ing-wen recently provided the LSE Library with a facsimile copy of the thesis, 'Unfair trade practices and safeguard actions'. This is now available to view in the LSE Library's reading room.

Tsai Ing-wen is the sole author of the thesis listed on the catalogue. The second name --which was of her PhD supervisor - was briefly added to the catalogue in error and has now been removed. We can confirm he was **not** a co-author of the thesis.

Questions regarding a reproduction of the PhD certificate itself should be directed to the University of London.

Kind regards,

From: Directorate
Sent: 16 July 2019 10:53
To: Wilson,Clive <CLIVE.Wilson@lse.ac.uk>
Cc: O'Connor,D <D.O'Connor@lse.ac.uk>
Subject: FW: A plea for LSE to elaborate

Dear Clive,
I think you are the right person to send the below email to. I am copying Danny O'Connor for information.

Best regards,
Kinga

From: ████████████████████████
Sent: 15 July 2019 18:49

寄件者：O'Connor，D
收件者：Wilson，Clive
主旨：回复：LSE 详细说明的请求
日期：2019 年 7 月 16 日 11：14：00

嗨，Clive，
我认为这可以有一个相对标准的回复，并加入一些额外的资讯。
亲爱的 ███████，
感谢您的电子邮件，已转交给我。
如其他通信中所强调的，我们已经检查了我们的记录，伦敦政经学院和伦敦大学都确认蔡英文于 1984 年正确地获得了法学博士学位。

蔡英文总统最近向 LSE 图书馆提供了论文"不公平贸易和防卫机制"的复印本。现在可以在 LSE 图书馆的阅览室查看。

蔡英文是目录上列出的论文的唯一作者。第二个名字—她的博士指导教授的名字 - 因为错误而短暂地被加到目录上，现在已被移除。我们可以确认他不是论文的共同作者。

关于博士学位证书本身的复制问题，应该直接向伦敦大学提出。
诚挚的，

———————————————————

寄件者：Directorate
日期：2019 年 7 月 16 日 10：53
收件者：Wilson，Clive CLIVE.Wilson@lse.ac.uk
副本：O'Connor，D D.O'Connor@lse.ac.uk
主旨：转发：LSE 详细说明的请求

亲爱的 Clive，
我认为你是发送以下电子邮件的正确人选。我抄送 Danny O'Connor 以供参考。

最好的祝福，Kinga

寄件者：███████

To: Directorate <Directorate@lse.ac.uk>
Subject: A plea for LSE to elaborate

Dear Director Minouche:

Facing the gigantic pressure from the Taiwanese electorate, Dr. Tsai Ing-wen at last had to yield and provided as late as this year a copy of her 1984 PhD. thesis to the LSE Library to keep in records. The record of this replacement copy's co-authorship partially explains my earlier questioning of her English writing competence—wasn't high enough to afford a PhD thesis, judged from an English speech transcript she provided to the Center for Strategic and International Studies in 2016.

With the advent of the attached page,

I hereby write to make a plea for LSE to elaborate on the following issues:

1. Is it allowed or not allowed for two LSE PhD students to co-author a PhD thesis?

2. If the answer is negative, then the rest of the questions can be dropped. If, however, the answer is positive, will each of the two students be awarded a doctorate degree?

3. If the answer is negative, then the rest of the questions can be dropped. If, however, the answer is positive, then why wouldn't Mr. Elliott be called Dr. Elliott all his life before he passed away in 2016 while Ms. Tsai has been enjoying the bright tile of doctor?

4. Does the fact that Mr. Elliott was never called Dr. Elliott imply that he was never awarded a PhD? If Mr. Elliott was never awarded a PhD with the co-authored thesis, why was Ms. Tsai and why was her degree claimed to be "awarded correctly"?

5. On July 10 Dr. Tsai showed to the public her replacement degree certificate which carries not only a "different" wording but also "different" signature, while the Head of the Diploma Production Office states that "Replacement certificates…… will of course still be identical to the original document— same wording, same signature." Does the black-and-white discrepancy imply that Dr. Tsai's replacement certificate might be "fake"?

6. Why would a worldwide famous education institute like TSE allow a PhD thesis to be missing for 35 years without requesting the author to re-submit a copy and have to wait for the Taiwanese electorate uproar over the issue to demand an answer?

7. Why would Dr. Shih Fang-long, the Co-director of TSE's Taiwan Research Program, continue to blame the repeated calls for an answer by the Taiwanese electorate, including many highly esteemed professors, and brazenly refused to provide a once-and-for-all answer to the thesis mystery to end everyone's agony? What is to hide?

8. Would TSE look into the wording and signature discrepancies

日期：2019 年 7 月 15 日 18：49
收件者：Directorate Directorate@lse.ac.uk
主旨：LSE 详细说明的请求

亲爱的 Minouche 主任：

面对台湾选民的巨大压力，蔡英文博士最终不得不屈服，并于今年年末前将她 1984 年的纸本博士论文提供给 LSE 图书馆，以作为记录。这份补发纸本的共同作者记录部分解释了我早先对她的英文写作能力的质疑——从她于 2016 年提供给战略与国际研究中心的一篇英文演讲稿来看，她的英文水平不足以完成一篇博士论文。

随着附加页面的出现，我在此写信恳请 LSE 详细说明以下问题：

1. LSE 的两名博士生是否允许共同撰写一篇博士论文？

2. 如果答案是否定的，那么可以忽略其余的问题。然而，如果答案是肯定的，那么这两名学生每人都会被授予博士学位吗？

3. 如果答案是否定的，那么可以忽略其余的问题。然而，如果答案是肯定的，那么为什么 Elliott 先生在他于 2016 年去世之前一直没有被称为 Elliott 博士，而蔡女士一直享有博士的光荣称号？

4. Elliott 先生从未被称为 Elliott 博士的事实是否意味着他从未被授予博士学位？如果 Elliott 先生从未因共同撰写的论文被授予博士学位，为什么蔡女士会被授予，而她的学位被声称是"正确授予"的？

5. 7 月 10 日，蔡博士向公众展示了她的补发学位证书，该证书不仅具有"不同"的措辞，而且还有"不同"的签名，而文凭制作办公室的主管表示："补发证书……当然仍与原始文件相同——相同的措辞，相同的签名。"这种黑白之间的差异是否意味着蔡博士的补发证书可能是"伪造"的？

6. 为什么像 LSE 这样的世界著名教育机构会允许一篇博士论文失踪 35 年，而不要求作者重新提交副本，并且必须等待台湾选民对此问题的强烈反应才要求答案？

7. 为什么 LSE 的台湾研究计划的共同主任施芳珑博士会继续指责台湾选民，包括许多高度受尊敬的教授，对答案的反复要求，并厚颜无耻地拒绝提供一个一劳永逸的答案来结束所有人的痛苦？有什么要隐瞒的？

8. LSE 会不会研究第 5 项问题中描述的措辞和签名的差异，如果公开展示的博士学位证书被证明是"伪造"的，LSE 会怎么做？

described in issue 5 and what would TSE do should the publicly shown PhD certificate prove to be "fake"?

Thank you very much for the patience to read this long email; your answer to any of these eight issues would be highly appreciative to the electorate of the 2020 Taiwanese presidential election. Since Ms. Tsai has been formally nominated a candidate in the election, the Taiwanese electorate's right to know is well justified. Any attempt to lead this issue into a personal privacy should be bluntly rebutted.

Sincerely yours,

非常感谢您耐心阅读这封长邮件；您对这八个问题中的任何一个的答案都将对 2020 年台湾总统选举的选民非常有价值。由于蔡女士已被正式提名为选举的候选人，台湾选民有知的权利是具正当理由的。任何试图将此问题引入个人隐私的尝试都应该被直接驳回。

诚挚的，
███████

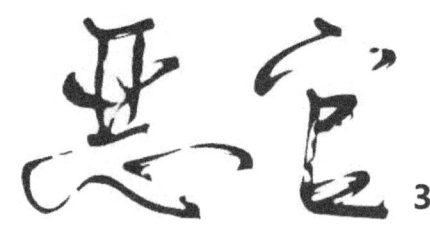

真相的封锁：LSE 内部的真相与策略

真相的封锁：LSE 内部的真相与策略

伦敦政经学院（LSE）一直回避确认蔡英文的证书真实性。总统府的白手套施芳珑特地来到 LSE，要求修改 6 月 24 日的声明。LSE 媒体关系部门负责人 Daniel O'Connor 表示同意，但他对施芳珑的态度感到不满。他觉得施芳珑更新的速度太慢，而且她一再指挥声明的内容。

施芳珑不满意 LSE 的声明中提到蔡英文的论文有双作者，她直接去找 O'Connor，要求他改掉这一点。O'Connor 虽然有些不悦，但他还是答应了。

LSE 内部有一份关于蔡英文的论文、证书和学位的机密通知。O'Connor 在这份通知中修改了一些用字，以规避责任。他还设计了如何更改证书签名的说法，以应对外界的质疑。

2019 年 7 月 10 日，蔡英文访问了台湾的网路媒体 Dcard。她在媒体面前，将其 2015 年补发的 LSE 博士毕业证书以塑胶袋装，晃了 20 秒。

不久之后，台湾教育部的高教司长朱俊彰召开了记者会。他表示，经过台湾驻英代表处的协助，他们确认 LSE 有典藏蔡英文的博士论文。

但在同一天，教育部却将蔡英文在台湾的东吴大学和政治大学的教师聘任及升等资料，以"公文附件"的方式，封锁到 2049 年的 12 月 31 日。

这一系列的事件，让 LSE 和蔡英文的学术真相变得更加模糊。在学术的世界里，真相和谎言交织，政治和学术的界线变得模糊。LSE，这所享有国际声誉的学府，面临的，不仅仅是学术的真伪，还有道德的崩坏。

RE_-A-plea-for-LSE-to-elaborate

From: Wilson, Clive
To: ▇
Subject: RE: further assistance saught for the whereabouts of a dissertation
Date: 12 July 2019 13:25:41

Dear ▇

Ms Orson was using text that I had provided several years ago, and it appears that I had been given incorrect information. It is very unfortunate that Ms Orson's name has been attributed to this text when it was my error. By all means, contact Senate House directly to confirm this.

As to the rest, I'm just a librarian but – as LSE has confirmed the PhD was awarded correctly - I can't see that there are any other questions in your email for LSE to answer.

kind regards

Clive Wilson
Enquiry Services Manager (Academic Services)
London School of Economics   Tel.:   020 7955 7475
10 Portugal Street   Fax.:   020 7955 7454
London WC2A 2HD   Email: Datalibrary@lse.ac.uk
                                        clive.wilson@lse.ac.uk

From: ▇
Sent: 10 July 2019 02:24
To: Wilson, Clive
Cc: Directorate
Subject: further assistance saught for the whereabouts of a dissertation

Dear Manager Wilson:

Thank you very much for the email regarding Dr. Tsai Ing-wen's dissertation. Unfortunately, however, I haven't got the Director's reply as of today, July 9, 2019. Hence my inquiry in the previous email. So, I am particularly appreciative for your email.

寄件者：Wilson，Clive

收件者：▮▮▮▮

主旨：回复：关于一篇论文的位置进一步的协助

日期：2019 年 7 月 12 日 13：25：41

亲爱的 ▮▮▮▮

Orson 女士使用的文本是我几年前提供的，看起来我得到了错误的资讯。很不幸，Orson 女士的名字被归因于这段文字，但这是我的错误。您当然可以直接联系伦敦大学总图书馆以确认此事。

至于其余部分，我只是一名图书馆员，但由于 LSE 已确认博士学位是正确授予的，我看不出您的电子邮件中还有其他问题需要 LSE 回答。

诚挚的问候，

Clive Wilson

查询服务经理（学术服务）

伦敦政经学院

电话：020 7955 7475

地址：10 Portugal Street， 伦敦 WC2A 2HD

电子邮件： Datalibrary@lse.ac.uk， clive.wilson@lse.ac.uk

寄件者：▮▮▮▮

日期：2019 年 7 月 10 日 02：24

收件者：Wilson，Clive

副本：Directorate

主旨：关于一篇论文的位置进一步的协助

亲爱的 Wilson 经理，

非常感谢您关于蔡英文博士的论文的电子邮件。不幸的是，到今天 2019 年 7 月 9 日为止，我还没有收到主任的回复。因此我在之前的电子邮件中提出了我的查询。所以，我特别感谢您的电子邮件。

No one ever doubts that "Tsai Ing-Wen was correctly awarded a PhD." So, this should not be an issue. However, some controversies have been hovering over Taiwan questioning 1). why should her dissertation be "missing" or "unavailable," (attachment 1) for 35 years, as pointed out by Ms. Ruth Orson, an LSE library assistant at the Research Support Services? Wouldn't every PhD holder be proud to show, if not show off, his/her dissertation? If a dissertation author tries best to make the dissertation vanish without a trace, what is there for the author to hide? 2). Why would Dr. Fang-Long Shih, a co-director of Taiwan Research Program, keep trying to translate all questionings regarding this dissertation issue into a political controversy among rivaling candidates in Taiwan's presidential election instead of taking it decently and offering substantial answers since this is really an issue of integrity surrounding a presidential candidate as well as the LSE. Sadly, on June 21, 2019 Dr. Shih again offered the same answer to the same question in the same way as she did four years ago, offering no substantial answers at all except that result

would be made available within 10 days, and yet 18 days have passed and the whereabouts of the dissertation is still a mystery. Why so? I can't help but to start to ponder if she is taking a political side, and 3) why would the only page in the record of the dissertation made known so far show no name of the dissertation's supervisor nor the dissertation's abstract (attachment 2)? How would one blame that there are more and more Taiwanese people of all walks who sense something foul in this dissertation mystery.

Shouldn't LSE, being an outstanding university of the oldest democracy, respect Taiwanese people's rights to know about the whereabouts and the contents of the dissertation, particularly when the author is a presidential candidate? Again, this is more an issue of an individual's academic integrity and the LSE's reputation in the world than a political controversy as Dr. Shih tries to lead it to.

Apart from all arguments from all sides, shouldn't LSE and all parties concerned ask Dr Tsai for another copy to keep as record, at least, since none of these parties can find their copies of the dissertation?

Last but not least, I got confused when I was reading your email since you say "It is clear from Senate House Library records that a copy was received." while Ms. Orson of the LSE library informs her inquirer in the said letter, "Unfortunately Senate House apparently never received a copy…" So, I'd appreciate it if you could kindly further clarify this difference of information.

Thank you so much for your kindness to help look into this issue, the result of which is so important for the Taiwanese people to know before they cast their votes in 2020 to choose their new president. The Taiwanese electorate would really appreciate your understanding and caring for their hunger for the rights to know.

Gratefully,

没有人怀疑"蔡英文正确地获得了博士学位"。所以，这不应该是一个问题。然而，有一些争议在台湾持续存在，问题是：1）为什么她的论文会"失踪"或"无法取得"（附件1）35年，如LSE图书馆助理Ruth Orson所指出的那样？每个博士学位持有者不都会以自己的论文为荣，如果不是炫耀的话？如果论文的作者尽最大努力使论文消失得无影无踪，那么作者隐藏的是什么？2）为什么台湾研究计划的共同主任施芳珑博士会不断试图将关于这篇论文的问题翻译成台湾总统选举中的政治争议，而不是正经地回答，并提供实质性的答案，因为这实际上是围绕着一位总统候选人以及LSE的诚信问题。可悲的是，2019年6月21日，施博士再次以四年前相同的方式回答了同样的问题，除了结果将在10天内公开之外，没有提供任何实质性的答案，但已经过去了18天，论文的下落仍然是一个谜。为什么会这样？我不禁开始思考她是否站在政治的一方，以及3）为什么到目前为止已知的论文记录的唯一页面既没有显示论文指导教授的名字，也没有论文的摘要（附件2）？怎么会有越来越多的台湾人开始觉得这个论文之谜中有些事情不对劲呢？

作为最古老民主国家的优秀大学，LSE不应该尊重台湾人民知道论文的下落和内容的权利吗？尤其是当作者是总统候选人时？再次强调，这更多的是一个个人学术诚信和LSE在世界上的声誉问题，而不是施博士试图将其引导成的政治争议。

撇开所有方面的争论，LSE和所有相关方面不应该至少要求蔡博士提供另一份纸本以作为记录吗？因为这些方面都找不到论文的纸本。

最后，当我阅读您的电子邮件时，我感到困惑，因为您说"从伦敦大学总图书馆的记录中可以清楚地看到已经收到了一份纸本"。而LSE图书馆的Orson女士在上述信中告诉她的询问者，"很不幸，总图书馆显然从未收到纸本……"所以，如果您能够进一步澄清这些资讯的差异，我将不胜感激。

非常感谢您的善意帮助调查这个问题，这个结果对于台湾人民在2020年选择他们的新总统之前知道是如此重要。台湾选民真的很感谢您对他们知情权的渴望的理解和关心。

衷心感谢，█████

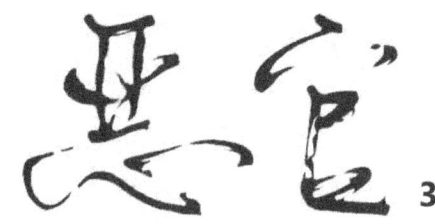

三张证书的谜团：蔡英文学位疑云再起

三张证书的谜团：蔡英文学位疑云再起

施芳珑写了一封信给伦敦大学，要求他们改变学位证书补发的说法，与此同时，总统府的代表也和 LSE 档案管理员 Sue Donnelly 会面，希望能够取得蔡英文的学生纪录。

是一封来自总统府发言人室的信，不仅建议 LSE 加入提告学者的行列，还建议校方依据总统府要求的四点诉求来发出声明。LSE 的高层从未想过，事情会发展到这个地步。台湾教育部的政务次长刘孟奇决定亲自前往 LSE 与伦敦政经学院院长及高层会面。

2019 年 9 月，国立台湾大学前新闻研究所所长彭文正教授连续一星期声援林环墙教授与贺德芬教授两位学者，总统府于中秋节前夕深夜，发表新闻稿追加告诉彭教授。英国牛津大学博士徐永泰，在亲自去看过蔡英文所谓论文后，在《世界日报》发表蔡英文论文观后感上、中、下篇，并提出伦敦政经学院妇女图书馆所展示之黑皮书并非正式论文的观点。徐永泰同时去函 LSE 法律系请求调查蔡英文的博士纪录，LSE 法律系回应"没有保存任何蔡英文博士资料"。

在庞大的舆论压力下，蔡英文终于首度接受媒体访问回应自己的学位疑云，强调"有学位就有论文"。蔡英文以"不会是吧"，否认 LSE 存放的黑皮伪论文严格借阅规定来自作者本人。

与此同时，总统府首度召开论文门记者会，现场以白手套呈现蔡英文一页一页的论文草稿，但内容纸张明显年代不符。同一天民进党籍立委管碧玲首度曝光蔡英文的第三张毕业证书，也就是 2010 年补发的毕业证书。蔡英文出现三张毕业证书，两张补发违反了伦敦大学的补发限一次的规定。

蔡英文南下左营辅选，是最后一次针对论文门事件接受媒体提问。再次强调哪有一页一页，都是一整本一整本的，并表示台湾国家图书馆已经同意收纳并公布论文。2019 年 9 月 27 日，国家图书馆违反学位授予法，收录了蔡英文所谓《不公平贸易和防卫机制》（Unfair Trade Practices and Safeguard Actions）论文到硕博士论文专区。

RE_-A-plea-for-LSE-to-elaborate

From: Begum,SS
To: Cerny,MW
Subject: FW: Ing-wen Tsai"s Ph.D. degree
Date: 24 September 2019 08:51:47
Attachments: DB5445E9994C44FEA0C59E8128FC71D4.png

Hi Marcus

Forwarding this to you for comment.

Thanks

Shuma

From: ▓▓▓▓▓▓▓▓▓▓▓▓▓▓▓▓▓▓▓▓▓▓▓▓▓▓
Sent: 23 September 2019 18:35
To: Begum,SS <S.S.Begum@lse.ac.uk>
Subject: Ing-wen Tsai's Ph.D. degree

Dear Ms Begum,

I am writing to you to check the authenticity of the Ph.D. degree of Ing-wen Tsai who claims she graduated from LSE in 1984. Tsai's integrity is very important to me and many other people. It is why I send you this email.

People find that Tsai's dissertation is not available in the libraries of LSE or any other public place in the world. It is very suspicious.
Could you check the authenticity of Tsai's Ph.D. degree, please? And what has happened to her dissertation if the Ph.D. degree is authentic?

Followed are some details you may need.

寄件者：Begum, SS

收件者：Cerny, MW

主旨：转寄：蔡英文的博士学位

日期：2019年9月24日 08：51：47

附件：DB5445E9994C44FEA0C59E8128FC71D4.png

嗨 Marcus,

我将这封邮件转发给你以便评论。

谢谢

Shuma

寄件：

日期：2019年9月23日 18：35

收件者：Begum, SS S.S.Begum@lse.ac.uk

主旨：蔡英文的博士学位

亲爱的 Begum 女士，

我写这封邮件给您是为了核实蔡英文的博士学位的真实性，她声称她于1984年从 LSE 毕业。蔡的诚信对我和许多其他人来说非常重要，这就是我为什么发送这封邮件给您的原因。

人们发现蔡英文的博士论文在 LSE 的图书馆或世界上的任何其他公共场所都无法找到。这非常可疑。

可否请您核实蔡英文的博士学位的真实性？如果博士学位是真实的，她的博士论文发生了什么事？

下面是您可能需要的一些详细资讯。

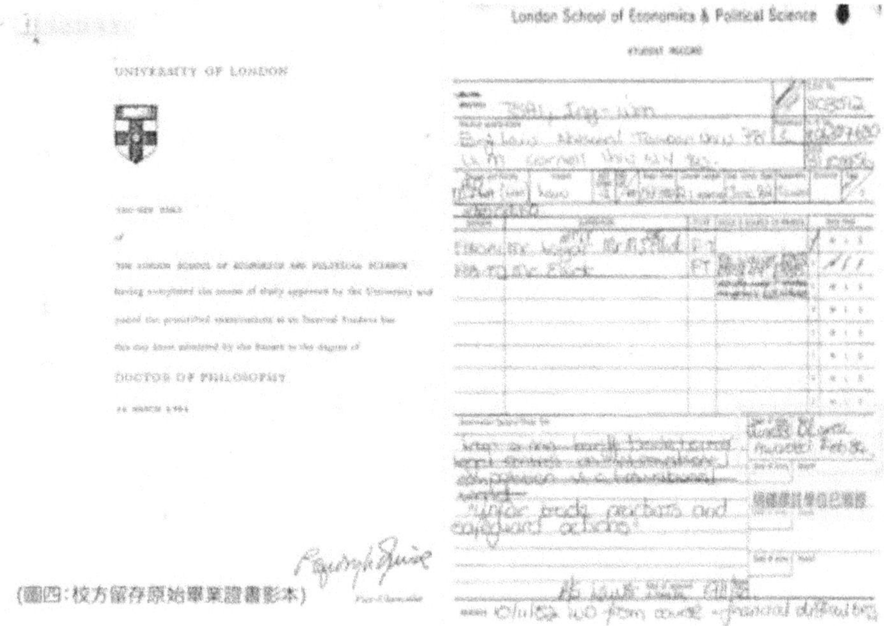

(圖四：校方留存原始畢業證書影本)

Sincerely,

(圖四:校方留存原始畢業證書影本)

诚挚的,

RE_-A-plea-for-LSE-to-elaborate

From: Wilson,Clive
To: Metcalfe,F
Cc: O''Connor,D
Subject: FW: Request for President Tsai''s student record from Presidential office Taiwan
Date: 20 September 2019 11:39:00

Hi Fiona

I'm not sure we would want to do this but this one's also out of my jurisdiction.

Just as far as I can ascertain though: 1 and 2 are definitely correct. 3 and 4 (except for the last point) would come under UoL and not us.

Clive

From: ███████████████
Sent: 18 September 2019 10:37
To: Wilson,Clive
Subject: RE: Request for President Tsai's student record from Presidential office Taiwan

Dear Clive,

As LSE is one of the leading academic institutions in the world, any statement issued by LSE certainly carries weight by itself. We would be truly grateful if you can kindly mention the following points in the statement.

1. University of London and LSE records confirm that Tsai Ing-wen was awarded a PhD in Law in 1984.

2. LSE is in possession of all relevant information pertaining to Dr. Tsai's degree. Dr. Tsai was originally registered as an MPhil student in September 1980. In her second year, upon the recommendation of her supervisor that her work was of doctorate standard, she was retroactively upgraded to PhD status. Dr. Tsai submitted her thesis "Unfair trade practices and safeguard actions", and successfully passed the viva examination in October 1983. She was later awarded a PhD in Law in 1984.

3. This procedure is in line with the School's regulations.

4. A PhD degree is only awarded once a candidate has provided a copy of the successful thesis. While the original copy of Dr. Tsai's thesis cannot currently be located, it is not the only one missing and a hardbound copy of this thesis is currently available at the LSE Library.

As for the channels, is it possible that this statement can be on the LSE website?

Your assistance in clarifying this matter is greatly appreciated.

寄件者：Wilson，Clive

日期：2019 年 9 月 20 日 11：39：00

收件者：Metcalfe，F

副本：O"Connor，D

主旨：转寄：来自台湾总统府的蔡总统学生记录的请求

嗨 Fiona，

我不确定我们是否真的想这么做，但这件事超出了我的职权范围。

但就我所知：1 和 2 确定是正确的。3 和 4（除了最后一点）应该是属于 UoL 的，而不是我们的。Clive

寄件者：█████

日期：2019 年 9 月 18 日 10：37

收件者：Wilson，Clive

主旨：回复：来自台湾总统府的蔡总统学生记录的请求

亲爱的 Clive，

由于 LSE 是世界上领先的学术机构之一，LSE 发出的任何声明都具有一定的分量。如果您能在声明中提及以下几点，我们将非常感激。

1. 伦敦大学和 LSE 的记录确认蔡英文于 1984 年获得法学博士学位。

2. LSE 持有与蔡博士学位相关的所有资讯。蔡博士最初于 1980 年 9 月注册为 MPhil 学生。在她的第二年，根据她的指导教授的建议，认为她的工作达到博士水平，她被追溯升级为博士学位。蔡博士提交了她的论文"不公平的贸易和防卫机制"，并于 1983 年 10 月成功通过口试。她后来于 1984 年被授予法学博士学位。

3. 这个程序符合学校的规定。

4. 只有当候选人提供成功的论文副本时，才会授予博士学位。虽然目前找不到蔡博士论文的原始副本，但这不是唯一一篇失踪的论文，而且这篇论文的精装副本目前在 LSE 图书馆中可用。

至于渠道，这份声明是否可以放在 LSE 的网站上？非常感谢您在此事上的协助。

Sincerely,

From: Wilson,Clive [mailto:CLIVE.Wilson@lse.ac.uk]
Sent: Tuesday, September 17, 2019 11:53 PM
To:
Subject: RE: Request for President Tsai's student record from Presidential office Taiwan

Hi

I'm told that LSE isn't really interested in filing a lawsuit. The Comms team seem to be happy to reissue a statement confirming the correct award of the degree but what channel do you think it should go through?

I still haven't seen (or can't find) an English translation of Lin's report.

best wishes

Clive

From:
Sent: 16 September 2019 13:13
To: Wilson,Clive
Subject: RE: Request for President Tsai's student record from Presidential office Taiwan

Hi Clive,

I extend my cordial thanks for your help these days.

As you might have noticed, the smear campaign regarding President Tsai's PhD degree has not yet over. On the contrary, the situation deteriorates since LSE has also become one of the targets of the campaign. The campaigners are associating the LSE-Gaddafi affair with this case, ridiculously accusing the school of selling a degree to President Tsai.

Some of the accusations can be found in these two pieces:

Tsai Ing-wen's missing thesis was not submitted says university library
https://richardsonreports.wordpress.com/2019/07/04/tsai-ing-wens-missing-thesis-was-not-submitted-says-university-library/

Tsai Ing-wen files lawsuit against two professors in London School of Economics thesis controversy
https://richardsonreports.wordpress.com/2019/09/06/tsai-ing-wen-files-lawsuit-against-two-professors-in-london-school-of-economics-thesis-controversy/

诚挚的，

███████

寄件者：Wilson, Clive [mailto：CLIVE.Wilson@lse.ac.uk]
日期：2019 年 9 月 17 日 11：53 PM
收件者：███████
主旨：回复：来自台湾总统府的蔡总统学生记录的请求

嗨，███，

我被告知 LSE 其实并不真的有兴趣提起诉讼。通讯团队似乎很乐意重新发布一份声明，确认学位的正确授予，但您认为它应该通过哪个渠道？

我仍然没有看到（或找不到）林的报告的英文翻译。最好的祝愿，

Clive

寄件者：███████
日期：2019 年 9 月 16 日 13：13
收件者：Wilson, Clive
主旨：回复：来自台湾总统府的蔡总统学生记录的请求

嗨 Clive，

非常感谢您这些天的帮助。

如您可能已经注意到，关于蔡总统的博士学位的抹黑运动还没有结束。相反，情况恶化了，因为 LSE 也成为了该运动的目标之一。这些运动者将 LSE 格达费事件与此案关联起来，荒谬地指控学校向蔡总统出售学位。

其中一些指控可以在这两篇文章中找到：

蔡英文的失踪论文并未提交，大学图书馆说

https://richardsonreports.wordpress.com/2019/07/04/tsai-ing-wens-missing-thesis-was-not-submitted-says-university-library/

蔡英文在伦敦政经学院论文争议中对两位教授提起诉讼

https://richardsonreports.wordpress.com/2019/09/06/tsai-ing-wen-files-lawsuit-against-two-professors-in-london-school-of-economics-thesis-controversy/

I would like to recommend the LSE consider issuing statements reconfirming that President Tsai had been awarded a PhD, or filing lawsuit against such smear tactics. Please kindly let me know what's your thought on this matter.

Many thanks,

From: Wilson,Clive [mailto:CLIVE.Wilson@lse.ac.uk]
Sent: Wednesday, September 11, 2019 4:41 PM
To:
Subject: RE: Request for President Tsai's student record from Presidential office Taiwan

H

as the copy certificate couldn't be obtained from LSE I do doubt that there will be an 'official record' here, but I have passed it on to colleagues who will know more

Clive

From:
Sent: 11 September 2019 07:57
To: Wilson,Clive
Subject: RE: Request for President Tsai's student record from Presidential office Taiwan

Hi Clive,

Unfortunately, I have not received any response from UoL yet.
Thanks for the information though. I will try to contact .
Further, I would like to confirm if LSE holds official records of President Tsai's applications for a degree certification in August 2010 and in September 2015. If LSE does and is able to provide us with the document, we will very much appreciate that.

Best,

From: Wilson,Clive [mailto:CLIVE.Wilson@lse.ac.uk]
Sent: Tuesday, September 10, 2019 10:46 PM
To:
Subject: RE: Request for President Tsai's student record from Presidential office Taiwan

Hi

我想建议 LSE 考虑发布声明，再次确认蔡总统已获得博士学位，或对这种抹黑策略提起诉讼。请告诉我您对此事的看法。

非常感谢，

━━━━━━━━━━━━━━━━━━━━━━━━━━

寄件者：Wilson, Clive [mailto：CLIVE.Wilson@lse.ac.uk]

日期：2019 年 9 月 11 日 4：41 PM

收件者：

主旨：回复：来自台湾总统府的蔡总统学生记录的请求

嗨

由于从 LSE 无法获得副本证书，我怀疑这里是否会有一个"正式记录"，但我已将其转交给更了解的同事。

Clive

━━━━━━━━━━━━━━━━━━━━━━━━━━

寄件者：

日期：2019 年 9 月 11 日 07：57

收件者：Wilson, Clive

主旨：回复：来自台湾总统府的蔡总统学生记录的请求

嗨 Clive，

很不幸，我还没有收到伦敦大学的回复。

不过，谢谢您的资讯。我会试着联系

此外，我想确认 LSE 是否持有蔡总统在 2010 年 8 月和 2015 年 9 月申请学位认证的正式记录。如果 LSE 有并能够提供我们该文件，我们将非常感激。

最好的祝愿，

━━━━━━━━━━━━━━━━━━━━━━━━━━

寄件者：Wilson, Clive [mailto：CLIVE.Wilson@lse.ac.uk]

日期：2019 年 9 月 10 日 10：46 PM

收件者：

主旨：回复：来自台湾总统府的蔡总统学生记录的请求

嗨，

Have you had a reply yet? The only other person I can think of is ▓▓▓▓▓▓▓▓
▓▓▓▓▓▓▓▓▓▓▓▓▓▓▓▓▓▓▓▓▓▓▓▓▓▓▓▓▓▓▓▓▓▓▓▓ and did most of the
investigation work at their end when President Tsai first stood for office. I don't know if she is still there.

best wishes

Clive

From: ▓▓▓▓▓▓▓▓▓▓▓▓▓▓▓▓▓▓▓▓▓▓
Sent: 06 September 2019 06:32
To: Wilson,Clive
Subject: RE: Request for President Tsai's student record from Presidential office Taiwan

Hi Clive,

Thank you very much for the suggestion. Unfortunately, the contact person at UoL has not replied my email yet.
However, the official records from the school(either LSE or UoL) of President Tsai's applications for a degree certification in August 2010 and in September 2015 are necessary to rebut the accusation, which claims that the certificate we provided was not issued by the school and therefore, was fake.

Do you have suggestion that from which sector I can possibly get this information?

Many thanks,
▓▓

From: Wilson,Clive [mailto:CLIVE.Wilson@lse.ac.uk]
Sent: Tuesday, September 3, 2019 11:06 PM
To: ▓▓▓▓▓▓▓▓▓▓▓▓▓▓▓▓
Subject: RE: Request for President Tsai's student record from Presidential office Taiwan

Hi ▓▓

You might have done this already but it occurs to me that you should also contact the University of London directly. Due to the umbrella nature of the UoL, especially pre 2010, their student record will be different to ours.

best wishes

Clive

From: ▓▓▓▓▓▓▓▓▓▓▓▓▓▓▓▓▓▓▓▓▓▓

您收到回复了吗？我能想到的唯一其他人是 ▓▓▓▓▓ 她在蔡总统首次竞选公职时主要负责调查工作。我不知道她是否还在那里。

最好的祝愿，

Clive

寄件者： ▓▓▓▓▓
日期： 2019年9月6日06：32
收件者： Wilson, Clive
主旨： 回复：来自台湾总统府的蔡总统学生记录的请求

嗨 Clive，

非常感谢您的建议。不幸的是，伦敦大学的联络人还没有回复我的电子邮件。

但是，学校（无论是 LSE 还是伦敦大学）关于蔡总统在 2010 年 8 月和 2015 年 9 月申请学位认证的正式记录对于驳斥指控是必要的，这些指控声称我们提供的证书不是学校发出的，因此是伪造的。

您有建议我可以从哪个部门获得这些资讯吗？

非常感谢，

▓▓▓▓▓

寄件者： Wilson, Clive [mailto：CLIVE.Wilson@lse.ac.uk]
日期： 2019年9月3日11：06 PM
收件者： ▓▓▓▓▓
主旨： 回复：来自台湾总统府的蔡总统学生记录的请求

嗨 ▓▓▓▓▓

您可能已经这么做了，但我想到您应该直接联系伦敦大学。由于伦敦大学的联盟性质，尤其是在 2010 年之前，他们的学生记录将与我们的不同。

最好的祝愿，

Clive

寄件者： ▓▓▓▓▓

Sent: 03 September 2019 06:53
To: Wilson,Clive
Cc: Donnelly,S
Subject: RE: Request for President Tsai's student record from Presidential office Taiwan

Dear Mr. Clive Wilson and Ms. Sue Donnelly,

Attached is the scanned letter signed by President Tsai.

We expect the academic record to contain information such as date of her viva exam, date of notification of the exam results, date of degree awarded, date of her application for a degree certification(If memory serves, it should be in August 2010 and in September 2015).

Please feel free to let me know if there is anything I can help and million thanks for your assistance.

Sincerely,
████

From: Wilson,Clive [mailto:CLIVE.Wilson@lse.ac.uk]
Sent: Monday, September 2, 2019 6:31 PM
To: ████
Cc: Donnelly,S <S.Donnelly@lse.ac.uk>
Subject: RE: Request for President Tsai's student record from Presidential office Taiwan

Dear ████

yes, we heard about the report last week and look forward to seeing an English version.

We can definitely provide a copy of President Tsai's student record but we do need to have a letter actually signed by President Tsai to do this. This can be a scan and it can request that the record is sent to you but as it is her personal data, the letter has to be signed by her.

I have copied this to Ms. Sue Donnelly, the LSE Archivist, so if you can send the scanned letter to both of us we can sort that out for you.

best wishes

Clive

From: ████
Sent: 02 September 2019 11:02
To: Wilson,Clive
Subject: Request for President Tsai's student record from Presidential office Taiwan

日期：2019年9月3日06：53
收件者：Wilson，Clive
副本：Donnelly，S
主旨：回复：来自台湾总统府的蔡总统学生记录的请求

亲爱的 Clive Wilson 先生和 Sue Donnelly 女士，
附件是蔡总统签名的扫描信件。
我们希望学术记录包含如口试日期、考试结果通知日期、学位授予日期、她在2010年8月和2015年9月申请学位认证的日期等资讯。
如果有任何我可以帮助的事情，请随时告诉我，非常感谢您的协助。
诚挚的，
███████

———————————————————————————

寄件者：Wilson，Clive [mailto：CLIVE.Wilson@lse.ac.uk]
日期：2019年9月2日 6：31 PM
收件者：███████
副本：Donnelly，S S.Donnelly@lse.ac.uk
主旨：回复：来自台湾总统府的蔡总统学生记录的请求

亲爱的，███████

是的，我们上周听说了这份报告，并期待看到英文版本。

我们确实可以提供蔡总统的学生记录的副本，但我们确实需要由蔡总统亲自签名的信件才能这么做。这可以是扫描版，并且可以要求将记录发送给您，但由于这是她的个人资料，信件必须由她签名。

我已将此事转发给LSE 的档案管理员Sue Donnelly 女士，所以如果您可以将扫描信件发送给我们两人，我们可以为您解决这个问题。

最好的祝愿，
Clive

———————————————————————————

寄件者：███████
日期：2019年9月2日11：02
收件者：Wilson，Clive
主旨：来自台湾总统府的蔡总统学生记录的请求

Dear Clive,

I trust this e-mail finds you well. It's been a while since our last conversation. Is everything going well with you?

I am writing to again seek your kind assistance with regard to President Tsai's LSE doctoral degree. To rebut the defamatory libel, President Tsai decides to take legal actions against the people behind the malice. For the court proceeding, President Tsai will need her student record, including the beginning and ending dates of study, names of supervisor and viva examiners... etc.

In our email trail, you kindly notified us that LSE has identified related documentation in this regard. I am wondering if it is possible that the above-mentioned information can be retrieved and sent to us? We have applied for the certificate of the degree for her, but more detail would be necessary to clarify the speculation.

There is another thing that I would like you to know. Recently, there is a publication by ▮▮▮▮▮▮▮ titled, "An independent investigation: the authenticity of Tsai, Ing Wen's doctoral degree and thesis." In the report, he states that LSE, as an accomplice, has helped Dr. Tsai to fake her degree. The English version is expected to be released by ▮ this week. You may look into it and decide whether it is necessary for the school to issue a statement against the unreasonable accusation as LSE is one of the leading academic institutions in the world and any statement issued by LSE certainly carries weight by itself.

We appreciate your help on this matter.

Sincerely yours,
▮▮▮▮▮▮
Spokesperson of the President
Office of the President, ROC(Taiwan)

亲爱的 Clive，

希望这封电子邮件能让您感到愉快。自从我们上次交谈以来已经过了一段时间。您一切都好吗？

我写这封信是再次寻求您的帮助，关于蔡总统的 LSE 博士学位。为了驳斥诽谤的谎言，蔡总统决定对背后的恶意行为提起法律诉讼。对于法庭程序，蔡总统将需要她的学生记录，包括学习的开始和结束日期、指导教授和口试考官的名字等。

在我们的电子邮件中，您友善地通知我们 LSE 已经找到了相关的文件。我想知道是否有可能检索上述资讯并发送给我们？我们已经为她申请了学位证书，但更多的细节是必要的，以澄清这种猜测。

还有另一件事我想让您知道。最近，有一份由 ███ 发表的报告，题为《独立调查：蔡英文的博士学位和论文的真实性》。在报告中，他声称 LSE 作为共犯，帮助蔡博士伪造了她的学位。英文版本预计将在本周由 ███ 发布。您可以查看它，并决定学校是否有必要对这种不合理的指控发表声明，因为 LSE 是世界上领先的学术机构之一，LSE 发出的任何声明都具有一定的分量。

我们非常感谢您在此事上的帮助。

诚挚的，
总统发言人
中华民国（台湾）总统府

台北市中正区重庆南路一段 122 号

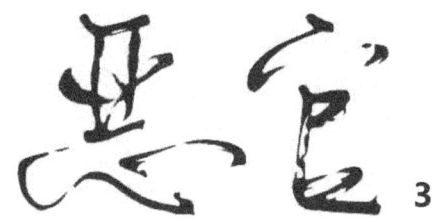

黑皮书的谜团：台湾代表的 LSE 之旅

黑皮书的谜团：台湾代表的 LSE 之旅

2019 年 7 月，整个事件的说法突然发生了变化。所有人都开始说，蔡英文的论文曾经送到伦敦大学总图书馆。

台湾的驻英代表处决定亲自访问 LSE，寻求真相。不久之后，台湾的教育部也派出代表，并在台湾召开了一场记者会，试图澄清整个事件。

但真相似乎越来越远。LSE 内部由蔡英文递交所谓"黑皮书"的论文，被认为是揭示真相的关键，但它似乎被隐藏起来，不让外界看到。

在学术的世界里，真相和谎言、权力和道德、政治和学术，这些界线愈来愈模糊。LSE 咨询服务经理 Clive Wilson、伦敦大学、LSE 和蔡英文，他们都成为了这场风波的主角，而真相，还正在等待被揭露。

FW_ Taiwan Deputy Minister visiting LSE

From: Directorate
To: Ross,LV
Cc: Directorate
Subject: FW: Taiwan Deputy Minister visiting LSE
Date: 18 September 2019 10:17:54

From ▇▇▇▇▇ Ministry of Foreign Affairs – Taiwan. Wanting to speak to Minouche on short notice.

Fri 20 Sept won't work but if Minouche was keen, it looks like Monday 23 Sept might work at 3-5pm?

Best,
Daniel

From: ▇▇▇▇▇
Sent: 18 September 2019 10:13
To: Directorate <Directorate@lse.ac.uk>
Subject: Taiwan Deputy Minister visiting LSE

Dear Dame Minouche,

My office, the Education Division of the Taipei Representative Office in the UK, is the official representation of the Ministry of Education, Taiwan (MoE), and a department of the *de facto* embassy for Taiwan. Our responsibilities include striving to enhance educational relations between the UK and Taiwan, promoting the study of Mandarin at institutions in the UK and facilitating study abroad.

The Deputy Minister for Education in Taiwan, Mr Mon-Chi Lio, will be arriving in London later this week to attend the UK-Taiwan Higher Education Forum. The Forum will be attended by the Presidents of seventeen Taiwanese national universities as well as representatives, including Vice-Chancellors, from around thirty UK universities.

As no representatives from LSE will be joining the Forum, Mr Lio would very much like to pay a courtesy call to your office in order to thank you in person for displaying a copy of President Tsai's thesis in the LSE Library.

Mr Lio has a tight schedule, but could be available on the 20th September from 3:30pm - 6pm or on the 23rd September from 10:30am -12pm / 3pm-5pm.

We appreciate this is very short notice and you must be extremely busy, but would that time potentially be convenient for you for a brief meeting with the Deputy Minister?

I look forward to hearing from you.

Kind regards,

寄件者：Directorate
收件者：Ross,
LV

日期：2019年9月18日 10：17：54
主旨：转寄：台湾次长访问LSE 自（外交部 - 台湾。想在短时间内与Minouche通话。
日期：

9月20日星期五不行，但如果Minouche愿意，9月23日星期一下午3-5点可以吗？

最好的祝福，

Daniel

寄件者

日期：2019年9月18日 10：13
收件者：Directorate Directorate@lse.ac.uk
主旨：台湾次长访问LSE

亲爱的 Dame Minouche，

我的办公室，位于英国的台北代表处教育部门，是台湾教育部的官方代表，并且是台湾事实上的大使馆的一个部门。我们的职责包括努力加强英国和台湾之间的教育关系，促进英国机构的中文学习，并促进海外学习。

台湾教育部次长，刘孟奇先生，将于本周晚些时候抵达伦敦参加英国 - 台湾高等教育论坛。该论坛将由十七所台湾国立大学的校长以及来自大约三十所英国大学的代表（包括副校长）参加。

由于 LSE 没有代表参加论坛，刘先生非常希望能够亲自拜访您的办公室，以亲自感谢您在 LSE 图书馆中展示蔡英文总统的论文。

刘先生的行程很紧，但他在9月20日下午3：30至6：00或9月23日上午10：30至中午12：00/下午3点至5点之间可能有空。

我们知道这是一个非常短的通知，您一定非常忙，但在那个时间您是否可能方便与次长简短地会面？

期待您的回复。

诚挚的问候，

RE_ an odd request for truth

From: O"Connor,D
To: Thomson,MT
Subject: RE: an odd request for truth
Date: 26 September 2019 14:17:35

Thanks Mark.

This is getting quite frustrating.

Danny

From: Thomson,MT
Sent: 26 September 2019 12:23
To: O'Connor,D <D.O'Connor@lse.ac.uk>
Subject: FW: an odd request for truth

Of possible interest.

From: ▓▓▓▓▓▓▓▓▓▓▓▓▓▓▓▓▓▓
Sent: 26 September 2019 12:21
To: Thomson,MT <M.T.Thomson@lse.ac.uk>
Subject: Re: an odd request for truth

Dear Mr. Thomson,

It is truly kind of you to reply this email.

If so, according to Ms. Tsai, LSE did lose her thesis and therefore should take the blame. I just couldn't imagine how this could happen to all three libraries in the University of London, that is, the Senate Library, IALS Library and LSE library. There must be black holes or stargates in those libraries. By the way, in a press conference that was held two days ago, Ms. Tsai admitted that the facsimile copy was merely a manuscript and not a completed thesis.

Thank you so much for your time.

Sincerely yours,
▓▓▓▓▓▓

Thomson,MT <M.T.Thomson@lse.ac.uk> 於 2019年9月26日 週四 上午3:12寫道：

> Dear ▓▓▓▓▓▓,
>
> The London School of Economics and Political Science and the University of London can categorically confirm that Dr Tsai Ing-Wen completed her thesis and was correctly awarded a PhD in Law in 1984.
>
> Dr Tsai Ing-wen recently provided the LSE Library with a facsimile copy of the thesis, 'Unfair trade practices and safeguard actions'. This is available to view in the LSE library reading room upon request.
>
> All best,

寄件者：O"Connor，D　**收件者**：Thomson，MT
主旨：回复：寻求真相的奇怪请求
日期：2019 年 9 月 26 日 14：17：35
感谢 Mark。

这真的让人感到相当沮丧。Danny

寄件者：Thomson，MT
日期：2019 年 9 月 26 日 12：23
收件者：O'Connor，D D.O'Connor@lse.ac.uk
主旨：转寄：寻求真相的奇怪请求
可能对你有兴趣。

寄件者：
日期：2019 年 9 月 26 日 12：21
收件者：Thomson，MT M.T.Thomson@lse.ac.uk
主旨：回复：寻求真相的奇怪请求

亲爱的 Thomson 先生，

您能回复此电邮真是太好了。

如果是这样，根据蔡女士的说法，LSE 确实遗失了她的论文，因此应该承担责任。我无法想象这怎么可能发生在伦敦大学的所有三家图书馆，即总图书馆、IALS 图书馆和 LSE 图书馆。那些图书馆里一定有黑洞或星际之门。顺便说一下，两天前举行的记者会上，蔡女士承认影印本只是手稿，而不是完成的论文。

非常感谢您的时间。

诚挚地，

Thomson，MT M.T.Thomson@lse.ac.uk 2019 年 9 月 26 日 3：12：
亲爱的，

伦敦政经学院和伦敦大学可以明确确认，蔡英文博士于 1984 年完成了她的论文，并正确地获得了法学博士学位。

蔡英文博士最近向 LSE 图书馆提供了论文"不公平贸易和防卫机制"的影印本。此论文可在 LSE 图书馆阅览室应要求查看。

最好的祝福，

Mark Thomson
Academic Registrar

From: ███████████████████████████
Sent: 25 September 2019 03:32
To: Thomson,MT <M.T.Thomson@lse.ac.uk>
Subject: an odd request for truth

Dear Mr. Thomson

This is ████████████████████████████████████
██
██████████ Nonetheless, I do not write this email for my personal matter, but for truth.

Recently, a Taiwanese LSE graduate tried hard to prove that she did get a Ph.D. degree in Law in your school in 1984. And yet, the more evidence she provided, the more curious the truth became. This graduate happens to be the president of Taiwan, Ing-wen Tsai. She provided her LSE student record and notification of examination outcome (please see the attached files), but they just arouse more questions. For example, the notification is lacking a signature of the academic registrar, that is, Mrs. G. F. Roberts, which is very strange. Or, why the registrar crossed out "MPhil" and replace it with "Ph.D." in handwriting without any notes (maybe it was different in 1980). There are still more questions like these.

Many young and high intellectuals in Taiwan like me are playing Sherlock Holmes now -- that is why I send this odd email to you. I don't expect to get all the answers. If you couldn't confirm if those documents came from your office, would you please at least give me a hint about one question -- how would your office put a Taiwanese student's nationality in the student record in the past (1980) and in the present -- Republic of China (ROC) or Taiwan?

Thank you very much for reading this email. Wish you all the best.

P.S.: The first attachment is President Tsai's student record provided by her spokesman, which she said came from LSE. The second attachment is a comparative analysis of the notification of exam outcome by another Holmes on the internet (he found another Ph.D. graduate's letter on the internet) and found many strange things.

Sincerely yours
████

Mark Thomson 学术登记员

寄件者： ▇▇▇▇
日期： 2019 年 9 月 25 日 03：32
收件者： Thomson, MT M.T.Thomson@lse.ac.uk
主旨： 寻求真相的奇怪请求

亲爱的 Thomson 先生，

这是 ▇▇▇▇。尽管如此，我写这封邮件并不是为了我个人的事情，而是为了真理

最近，一位台湾的 LSE 毕业生努力证明她在 1984 年确实在贵校获得了法学博士学位。然而，她提供的证据越多，真相就越令人好奇。这位毕业生恰好是台湾的总统，蔡英文。她提供了她的 LSE 学生记录和考试结果通知（请参阅附件），但这些只引起了更多的问题。例如，通知书缺少学术登记员的签名，即 Mrs. G. F. Roberts，这非常奇怪。或者，为什么登记员会手写删除 "MPhil" 并将其替换为 "Ph.D."，而没有任何注释（也许 1980 年的情况不同）。还有更多这样的问题。

像我这样的许多台湾年轻且高学历的人现在都在扮演福尔摩斯的角色——这就是为什么我给您发这封奇怪的电邮。我不期望得到所有答案。如果您不能确认这些文件是否来自您的办公室，那么您至少可以给我一个提示，关于一个问题——您的办公室在过去（1980 年）和现在如何在学生记录中记录台湾学生的国籍——中华民国（ROC）还是台湾？

非常感谢您阅读这封电邮。祝您一切顺利。

附注：第一个附件是由她的发言人提供的蔡总统的学生记录，她说这是来自 LSE 的。第二个附件是另一位网路上的福尔摩斯对考试结果通知的比较分析（他在网路上找到了另一位博士毕业生的信），并发现了许多奇怪的事情。

诚挚地，
▇▇▇▇

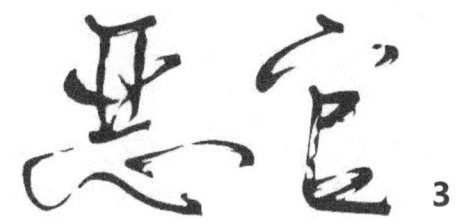

LSE 的策略：罐头答复与形象维护

LSE 的策略：罐头答复与形象维护

在东京大学的法学图书馆，一名东大生在翻阅古老的文献时，意外地发现了一本被称为"红皮书"的文件。这本书的存在，对于 LSE 来说，无疑是一个巨大的惊喜。他们内部的高层人士私下里庆幸，"太好了，如果这本书是真的，那么我们之前的所有疑虑都将烟消云散"。

但这位东大生更进一步表示，他在东大的法学图书馆中，找到了 1985 年的出版品，上头记载着蔡英文的博士论文项目。这似乎证明了蔡英文在 1984 年确实取得了博士学位。但网路节目主持人彭文正教授却质疑，东大生查到的只是书目，有书目不一定有书。他进一步指出，他在英国高等法律研究院的查询系统中查询蔡英文的论文，发现蔡英文的馆藏记录空空如也。

彭文正在其节目《政经关不了》中进一步质疑说，书目跟书不一样，有书不一定就有书目、有书目不一定有书。他认为，蔡英文的论文争议得要走到"正规的大马路"直球对决，就是 36 年从未出现过博士论文，但不是手稿、书或书目。

东大生则反驳说，除非蔡英文真的强大到可以伪造 1985 年的出版品，还记得跨洋连东大的图书馆都要寄藏一本，不然蔡英文有取得博士学位，似乎毫无疑问。

彭文正则再度质疑这份出版品的前言就明确的表示，该书记载的并非真正取得学位的纪录。中国学者李海默也在网路上分析，这份 IALS 索引是变动式的纪录所有法学硕、博士生的法律研究题目，里面也确实有多人之后并未取得博士学位。

但是，这场学术风暴还远远没有结束。LSE 面对外界的质疑，决定采取一种策略：对于那些他们认为不友善的提问，他们会给出一个事先准备好的"罐头答复"。这样的策略，无疑是为了保护学校的形象，但也引起了不少争议。

台湾的官员在总统府的记者会上，面对媒体的质疑，感到压力倍增。他们再度与 LSE 要求见面，希望能够得到更多的资讯。总统府特别要求 LSE 提供 1980

年代的博士生求学流程，希望能够厘清整个事件的真相。

在这场风暴的中心，LSE 媒体关系部门负责人 Daniel O'Connor 是一个关键人物。即使在休假期间，他也会不时地发出群组信，"提醒"大家注意某些事情。

随着教育部政务次长刘孟奇的到来，LSE 开始做好接待的准备。他们知道，这次的会面，将是决定整个事件走向的关键。LSE 内部的情绪也变得复杂。他们面对外界的质疑，决定采取一种策略：对于那些他们认为不友善的提问，他们会给出一个事先准备好的"罐头答复"。这样的策略，无疑是为了保护学校的形象，但也引起了更多争议。

RE_ Evidence of Tsai PhD submission（1）

From: Wilson,Clive
To: O"Connor,D; Phdacademy
Cc: Metcalfe,F; Thomson,MT
Subject: RE: Evidence of Tsai PhD submission
Date: 27 September 2019 13:57:24

I've found our copy of the book the student found and made a quick video (because I am sad!):
https://photos.app.goo.gl/w9GwFXGq2hYn8atFA

This book is in a number of UK libraries and several in Germany, Holland and Spain. It was reviewed in at least two law journals.

And yes, a copy of the thesis with no missing pages would be nice ☺

The National Central Library has now made the digitised version available through https://etds.ncl.edu.tw/cgi-bin/gs32/gsweb.cgi/ccd=9aF5rF/webmge?switchlang=en It is a beautifully clean copy, with none of the scruffy photocopying of our copy ...

And I think they are still hoping LSE will make a repeat statement ... although if they do supply us with an online copy, could we do it then?

thanks

Clive

From: O'Connor,D
Sent: 27 September 2019 10:01
To: Wilson,Clive; Phdacademy
Cc: Metcalfe,F; Thomson,MT
Subject: RE: Evidence of Tsai PhD submission

Thanks Clive.

Probably worth going and taking a photo of the hard copy of the IALS index when you can. This isn't going away!

(I assume you mean to new copy will *include* the missing pages?)

Danny

From: Wilson,Clive
Sent: 27 September 2019 09:54
To: Phdacademy <Phdacademy@lse.ac.uk>; O'Connor,D <D.O'Connor@lse.ac.uk>
Cc: Metcalfe,F <F.Metcalfe@lse.ac.uk>; Thomson,MT <M.T.Thomson@lse.ac.uk>
Subject: RE: Evidence of Tsai PhD submission

Ha, that's fantastic.
I was actually planning a visit to IALS to look at the old printed version of Index to Theses for

寄件者：Wilson，Clive

收件者：O"Connor，D； Phdacademy

副本：Metcalfe，F； Thomson，MT

主旨：回复：蔡英文博士论文提交的证据 日期：2019年9月27日 13：57：24

我发现一位学生找到了我们的书本副本，并快速拍了一段影片（因为我觉得很遗憾！）：https://photos.app.goo.gl/w9GwFXGq2hYn8atFA

这本书在许多英国图书馆以及德国、荷兰和西班牙的几家图书馆都有。至少有两家法律期刊对其进行了评论。

是的，一份没有遗失页面的论文副本会很好。

国家中央图书馆现在已经透过 https://etds.ncl.edu.tw/cgi-bin/gs32/gsweb.cgi/ccd=9aF5rF/webmge?switchlang=en 提供了数位化版本。这是一份非常干净的副本，与我们的副本上的粗糙影印完全不同 …

我认为他们仍然希望 LSE 会再次发表声明 … 不过，如果他们确实给我们提供了一份线上副本，那么我们可以这样做吗？

谢谢，

Clive

寄件者：O'Connor，D 日期：2019年9月27日 10：01

收件者：Wilson，Clive； Phdacademy

副本：Metcalfe，F； Thomson，MT

主旨：回复：蔡英文博士论文提交的证据

谢谢 Clive。

当你可以的时候，可能值得去拍一张 IALS 索引的硬拷贝照片。这件事不会就此结束！

（我猜你的意思是新的副本将包括遗失的页面？）

Danny

寄件者：Wilson，Clive 日期：2019年9月27日 09：54

收件者：Phdacademy Phdacademy@lse.ac.uk； O'Connor，D D.O'Connor@lse.ac.uk

副本：Metcalfe，F F.Metcalfe@lse.ac.uk； Thomson，MT M.T.Thomson@lse.ac.uk

主旨：回复：蔡英文博士论文提交的证据

哈，真的太棒了。

我其实正计划访问 IALS，查看论文索引的旧印刷版本，原因完全相同（一旦它电子化，我们就没有保留它）。目前我都在回击一天一个询问。

exactly the same reason (we didn't keep it once it went electronic).

I'm batting away about one enquiry a day at the moment.

You may also have seen that the President's office announced on Monday that she would put an electronic copy in Taiwan's theses depository. They have also offered us a copy (and a replacement printed copy that doesn't have the missing pages!)

Clive

From: LSE PhD Academy [mailto:phdacademy@lse.ac.uk]
Sent: 27 September 2019 09:44
To: O'Connor,D
Cc: Metcalfe,F; Wilson,Clive; Thomson,MT
Subject: RE: Evidence of Tsai PhD submission

Thanks Danny,

Sporadic queries continue to trickle in as very badly disguised 'official' requests for verification. I'm not sure how authoritative people think a generic yahoo account and a one line signature with a made up job title and organisation looks.

Regards,
Marcus

Marcus Cerny
PhD Academy Deputy Director
The London School of Economics and Political Science
Houghton Street, London WC2A 2AE
t: +44 (0)20 7955 6766
e: m.w.cerny@lse.ac.uk
lse.ac.uk/phdacademy

If you are a current PhD student please remember to send your queries through the PhD Academy Enquiry Form. All other enquirers should contact phdacademy@lse.ac.uk

--------------- Original Message ---------------
From: O'Connor,D [d.o'connor@lse.ac.uk]
Sent: 26/09/2019 16:51
To: clive.wilson@lse.ac.uk; m.t.thomson@lse.ac.uk; phdacademy@lse.ac.uk
Cc: f.metcalfe@lse.ac.uk
Subject: Evidence of Tsai PhD submission

Dear all,

I thought you may be interested to see the recent report in the pro-Tsai Taiwan News.
https://www.taiwannews.com.tw/en/news/3784704

你可能也已经看到,总统办公室在周一宣布,她将在台湾的论文存放处放置一份电子副本。他们还提供给我们一份副本(以及一份没有遗失页面的替换印刷副本!)

Clive

寄件者: LSE PhD Academy [mailto:phdacademy@lse.ac.uk]

日期: 2019年9月27日 09:44

收件者: O'Connor,D

副本: Metcalfe,F; Wilson,Clive; Thomson,MT

主旨: 回复:蔡英文博士论文提交的证据

谢谢 Danny,

零星的查询仍然持续一点一滴的产生,它们都被非常巧妙地伪装成"官方"的验证请求。我不确定人们会相信一个通用的 yahoo 帐户和一行带有虚构职称和组织的签名看起来有多权威。

祝好,Marcus

Marcus Cerny

博士生学院副主任

伦敦政经学院

Houghton Street, London WC2A 2AE

电话:+44 (0) 20 7955 6766

电邮:m.w.cerny@lse.ac.uk

网站:lse.ac.uk/phdacademy

如果您是目前的博士学生,请记得通过 PhD 学院查询表格发送您的查询。所有其他查询者应联系 phdacademy@lse.ac.uk

----------- 原始讯息 -----------

寄件者: O'Connor,D [d.o'connor@lse.ac.uk]

日期: 2019/09/26 16:51

收件者: clive.wilson@lse.ac.uk; m.t.thomson@lse.ac.uk; phdacademy@lse.ac.uk

副本: f.metcalfe@lse.ac.uk

主旨: 蔡英文博士论文提交的证据

各位,

我想您可能会对看到最近在支持蔡英文的《台湾英文新闻》中的报导感兴趣。
https://www.taiwannews.com.tw/en/news/3784704

It seems someone uncovered a IALS listings document which included an entry for her thesis.

Thanks,

Danny

From: Windebank,S
Sent: 26 September 2019 16:38
To: O'Connor,D <D.O'Connor@lse.ac.uk>
Subject: FW: Google Alert - "London School of Economics"

Interesting (it's good news, if true)

From: Google Alerts [mailto:googlealerts-noreply@google.com]
Sent: 26 September 2019 05:57
To: Windebank,S <S.Windebank@lse.ac.uk>
Subject: Google Alert - "London School of Economics"

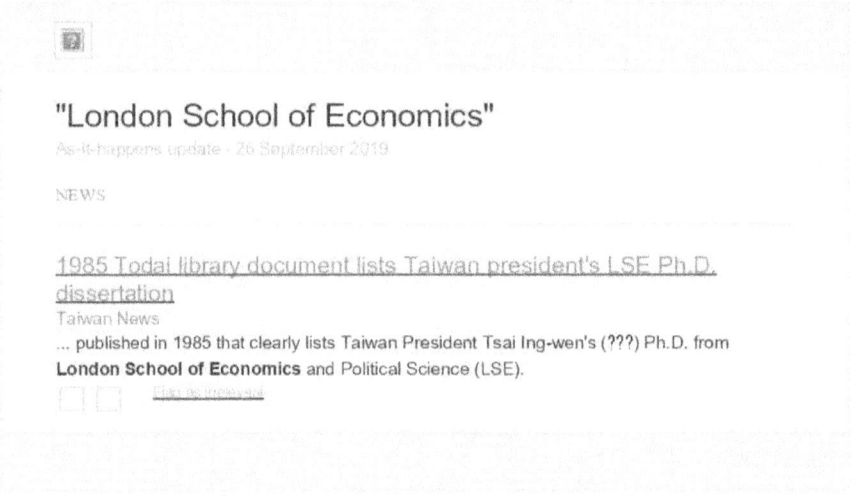

"London School of Economics"
As-it-happens update · 26 September 2019

NEWS

1985 Todai library document lists Taiwan president's LSE Ph.D. dissertation
Taiwan News
... published in 1985 that clearly lists Taiwan President Tsai Ing-wen's (???) Ph.D. from **London School of Economics** and Political Science (LSE).

Flag as irrelevant

You have received this email because you have subscribed to **Google Alerts**.
Unsubscribe

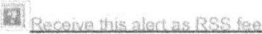
Receive this alert as RSS feed
Send Feedback

ref:_00D58JYzR._5004ItwAJi:ref

似乎有人发现了一份 IALS 的列表文件，其中包括她的论文条目。

谢谢，

Danny

寄件者：Windebank，S
日期：2019 年 9 月 26 日 16：38
收件者：O'Connor，D D.O'Connor@lse.ac.uk
主旨：转发：Google Alert - " 伦敦政经学院 "

有趣（如果是真的话）

寄件者：Google Alerts [mailto：googlealerts-noreply@google.com]
日期：2019 年 9 月 26 日 05：57
收件者：Windebank，S S.Windebank@lse.ac.uk
主旨：Google Alert - "London School of Economics"

" 伦敦政经学院 "

即时更新 · 2019 年 9 月 26 日

新闻

1985 年东大图书馆文件列出台湾总统的 LSE 博士论文

台湾新闻

... 1985 年出版的文件清楚列出台湾总统蔡英文（???）从伦敦政经学院（LSE）获得的博士学位。

标记为不相关

您收到此电邮是因为您已订阅 Google Alerts。

取消订阅

发送反馈 ref:

_00D58JYzR._5004ItwAJi：ref

RE_ Ing Wen Tsai's thesis gate

From: Directorate
To: O'Connor,D
Subject: RE: Ing Wen Tsai's thesis gate
Date: 30 September 2019 17:02:00

Thank you very much for your advice!
Best regards,
Kinga

From: O'Connor,D
Sent: 30 September 2019 17:00
To: Directorate <Directorate@lse.ac.uk>; Wilson,Clive <CLIVE.Wilson@lse.ac.uk>
Subject: RE: Ing Wen Tsai's thesis gate

It may be best if you pass them to Communications so we can reply.

(Though I understand ▬▬▬ has already had a number of replies, so we've exhausted that route).

Kind regards,

Danny

From: Directorate
Sent: 30 September 2019 16:57
To: O'Connor,D <D.O'Connor@lse.ac.uk>; Wilson,Clive <CLIVE.Wilson@lse.ac.uk>
Subject: RE: Ing Wen Tsai's thesis gate

How shall I reply to these in the future? Do you have some kind of a template? Or suggestion on how I should reply?

Best regards,
Kinga

From: O'Connor,D
Sent: 30 September 2019 13:59
To: Directorate <Directorate@lse.ac.uk>; Wilson,Clive <CLIVE.Wilson@lse.ac.uk>
Subject: RE: Ing Wen Tsai's thesis gate

Thanks Kinga.

These individuals are not well-intentioned actors so I think we should still provide only basic information.

Danny

寄件者：Directorate
收件者：O'Connor，D
主旨：回复：蔡英文的论文门事件　**日期**：2019 年 9 月 30 日 17：02：00
非常感谢您的建议！
最佳的问候，
Kinga

寄件者：O'Connor，D
日期：2019 年 9 月 30 日 17：00
收件者：Directorate Directorate@lse.ac.uk；　Wilson，Clive CLIVE.Wilson@lse.ac.uk
主旨：回复：蔡英文的论文门事件

将它们转交给 Communications 部门，以便我们可以回复，可能是最好的方法。
（尽管我理解▇▇▇▇已经收到了多次回复，所以我们已经用尽了那条路。）
亲切的问候，
Danny

寄件者：Directorate
日期：2019 年 9 月 30 日 16：57
收件者：O'Connor，D D.O'Connor@lse.ac.uk；　Wilson，Clive CLIVE.Wilson@lse.ac.uk
主旨：回复：蔡英文的论文门事件

我将来应该如何回复这些？你有没有某种模板？或者有关于我应该如何回复的建议？
最佳的问候，
Kinga

寄件者：O'Connor，D
日期：2019 年 9 月 30 日 13：59
收件者：Directorate Directorate@lse.ac.uk；　Wilson，Clive CLIVE.Wilson@lse.ac.uk
主旨：回复：蔡英文的论文门事件
谢谢你，Kinga。
这些人不是出于善意的行为者，所以我认为我们应该只提供基本的资讯。
Danny

From: Directorate
Sent: 30 September 2019 13:32
To: Wilson,Clive <CLIVE.Wilson@lse.ac.uk>; O'Connor,D <D.O'Connor@lse.ac.uk>
Subject: FW: Ing Wen Tsai's thesis gate

Dear Clive and Daniel,

I keep ignoring this individual as you have mentioned in one of your last emails, but just to let you know he or she is still sending us emails from time to time..

Best regards,
Kinga

Sent: 29 September 2019 13:15
To: Directorate <Directorate@lse.ac.uk>
Subject: Ing Wen Tsai's thesis gate

Dear Director Minouche:

Now that Ing-wen Tsai has publicly denied in a Taipei press conference her knowledge of all the LSE banning restrictions imposed on her Ph.D. thesis, I am eager to know if all the restrictions to the access to her thesis will be lifted immediately. In the public denial, which has been repeatedly played in Taiwan's TV news and comment programs, Tsai clearly stated that she was not aware of any of such banning restrictions. What people can't understand after Tsai's denial is why LSE would state in the first place in the displayed thesis to restrict copying of any part of this thesis". Also, since Tsai's president office has made the thesis available in Taiwan's Central Library, LSE's continuous restrictions on her thesis displayed on campus seems to have become a joke.

Also, I'd appreciate it if you, an honorable and highly respected LSE Director, could lead an investigation to see why Tsai could be awarded a doctorate degree when LSE library, the Senate House Library and the IALSrepeatedly stated that none of them have ever received a copy or unable to find their copy of Tsai's thesis, while Article 58 of the LSERegulations for Research Degrees clearly states that a Ph.D. degree "will not be awarded until the candidate has provided a copy of the successful thesis". Intriguingly, the non-existence of Tsai's thesis remains until Aug 26, 2019, when a photo copy from her personal collection was finally made available by LSE.

As more and more renowned Ph.D. holding scholars getting involved

寄件者：Directorate
日期：2019年9月30日 13：32
收件者：Wilson, Clive CLIVE.Wilson@lse.ac.uk; O'Connor, D D.O'Connor@lse.ac.uk
主旨：转发：蔡英文的论文门事件

亲爱的 Clive 和 Daniel，

我一直在忽略这个人，正如你在上一封邮件中提到的，但只是让你知道他或她仍然不时地给我们发邮件。

最佳的问候，

Kinga

寄件者：█████
日期：2019年9月29日 13：15
收件者：Directorate Directorate@lse.ac.uk
主旨：蔡英文的论文门事件

亲爱的 Minouche 院长：

现在蔡英文在台北的一场记者会上公开否认她知道所有 LSE 对她的博士论文施加的禁止限制，我急于知道是否所有对她论文的查阅限制将立即解除。在公开否认中，这已经在台湾的电视新闻和评论节目中反复播放，蔡清楚地表示她不知道任何这样的禁止限制。人们在蔡的否认之后不能理解的是，为什么 LSE 首先会在展示的论文中声明"限制复制这篇论文的任何部分"。此外，由于蔡的总统办公室已经在台湾的中央图书馆提供了论文，LSE 对校园内展示的她的论文的持续限制似乎已经成为一个笑话。

此外，如果您这位受人尊敬且高度受尊重的 LSE 院长，能够主持一项调查，看看为什么蔡英文可以获得博士学位，当 LSE 图书馆、伦敦大学总图书馆和 IALS 都多次表示他们从未收到或找不到他们的蔡论文副本时，而 LSE 的研究学位规定的第 58 条明确规定，博士学位"不会被授予，直到候选人提供了成功的纸本论文"。有趣的是，蔡的论文的不存在一直持续到 2019 年 8 月 26 日，当她的个人收藏的照片副本终于由 LSE 提供时。

in the proactive investigations of Tsai Ing-wen's "Thesis Gate" and digging out more proof and questioning points, their suspicions over the authenticity of Tsai's thesis has become more and more persuasive and justifiable. An LSE Director over 35 years away, you have everyone's confidence that you are not part of this "potential scandal." As a result, you make an ideal objective third-party to lead an objective investigation into this highly controversial gate. Given the fact that Tsai being one of the three already known candidates in Taiwan's presidential election in January 2020, the importance of this investigation is self-evident. Countless Taiwanese electorates have claimed that a candidate that can't even explained why her thesis should have been missing on records for over 35 years and can't provide a degree certificate carrying a formal embossing LSE seal should be excluded from the candidate list until all the questionable issues have been clarified.

Other questionings raised by American and British Ph.D. holding scholars and the Taiwanese journalists which Tsai Ing-wen has never answered include but are not limited to the followings:

1. why a highly respected university like LSE would accept and display a thesis that has so many defects such as missing 6 pages, carrying so many nonconsecutive pages and most importantly, discussing only the first half of its topic, the unfair trade practices, leaving a total blank on the second part of the thesis, and safeguard actions-not a single sentence/word was contributed to the safeguard actions, let alone a conclusion of the whole thesis.

2. Why would LSE lose Tsai's thesis? Tsai's president office has publicly blamed LSE for losing her thesis and claimed the student who turned in her thesis is not and/or should not be responsible for the loss.

3. In Tsai's publicized thesis, she keeps using the plural first person "we," matching first LSE record of Tsai's thesis showing two author's names. Why would LSE later claim it was a mistake and changed it into a one-authored thesis?

4. Tsai showed on TV programs her self-claimed "original" copy of her Ph.D. degree certificate. Then why would she have to apply twice for replacement copies of her degree copies?

随着越来越多的知名博士学者参与蔡英文的"论文门"事件的积极调查,并挖掘出更多的证据和质疑点,他们对蔡论文的真实性的怀疑变得越来越有说服力和合理性。作为LSE院长,您有每个人的信心,您不是这个"潜在的丑闻"的一部分。因此,您是带领这一高度有争议的门事件的客观调查的理想选择。考虑到蔡英文是2020年1月台湾总统选举中已知的三名候选人之一,这项调查的重要性是不言而喻的。无数的台湾选民声称,一个甚至不能解释为什么她的论文应该在记录上失踪超过35年,且不能提供带有正式LSE印章的学位证书的候选人,应该被排除在候选人名单之外,直到所有有争议的问题都已得到澄清。

美国和英国的博士学者以及台湾记者提出的其他质疑,蔡英文从未回答,包括但不限于以下

1. 为什么像LSE这样受人尊敬的大学会接受和展示一篇有这么多缺陷的论文,例如缺少6页,带有很多不连续的页面,最重要的是,只讨论了其主题的前半部分,即不公平的贸易实践,完全空白在论文的第二部分,以及保护行动 - 没有一个句子/单词被贡献给保护行动,更不用说整篇论文的结论了。

2. 为什么LSE会失去蔡的论文?蔡的总统办公室公开指责LSE失去了她的论文,并声称提交她论文的学生不是和/或不应该对失踪负责。

3. 在蔡的公开论文中,她不断使用复数第一人称"我们",匹配LSE对蔡论文的第一次记录显示两个作者的名字。为什么LSE后来会声称这是一个错误,并将其更改为一篇单一作者的论文?

4. 蔡在电视节目上展示了她自称的"原始"博士学位证书副本。那么她为什么要申请两次替代她的学位副本?

My personal question is as follows: Is this somehow related to a website that sells a Ph.D. thesis under the topic of "Unfair Trade Exercises" for current price of $13.90 a page? Please note that the topic sold carries only "Unfair Trade Practices"—exactly the same wording as the first half of Tsai's thesis topic and doesn't touch the "safe guard" part at all, exactly the same as how Tsai Ing-wen dealt with her thesis.

Thank you very much for your time and patience to read through this message. Your kind investigation into this highly controversial gate would be really appreciated by all Taiwanese electorates.

Sincerely,

███

我的个人问题如下：这是否与一个网站有关，该网站以每份 13.90 美元的当前价格出售一篇以"不公平贸易"为主题的博士论文？请注意，所售主题只带有"不公平贸易"— 与蔡论文主题的前半部分完全相同的措辞，并且根本不涉及"保护"部分，这与蔡英文如何处理她的论文完全相同。

非常感谢您花时间和耐心阅读此消息。您对这一高度有争议的门事件的亲切调查将受到所有台湾选民的真正欣赏。

诚挚地，

RE_ Inquire From Taipei Representative Office

From: Wilson, Clive
To: Cerny, MW
Subject: RE: Inquire From Taipei Representative Office--Education Division
Date: 04 September 2019 10:05:25

Hi Marcus

no problem – I knew the second part was definitely them but thought I'd better start with you 😊

thanks for the confirmation

Clive

From: Cerny, MW
Sent: 04 September 2019 10:04
To: Wilson, Clive
Subject: RE: Inquire From Taipei Representative Office--Education Division

Hi Clive,

I think that is something for the UofL to clarify. My knowledge would go back to the late 1990's and that is not robust.

The physical thesis submission for examination will have been handled by the Research Degrees Office at UofL and the final copy by Senate House Library.

Sorry about this rather unhelpful response. I am confident in my assumption as to what will have been the process even at that time (confirmation that the thesis had been passed by the examiners, hard bound copy to Senate House triggering confirmation of award by RDO and placing in the Library) but this should be clarified by UofL and I would direct President Tsai's office to send queries on this process to them.

Thanks,
Marcus

Marcus Cerny
Deputy Director, PhD Academy
London School of Economics and Political Science
Houghton Street
London WC2A 2AE

Please consider the environment and do not print this email unless absolutely necessary.
Please access the attached hyperlink for an important electronic communications disclaimer: http://lse.ac.uk/emailDisclaimer

From: Wilson, Clive
Sent: 04 September 2019 09:45
To: Cerny, MW
Subject: FW: Inquire From Taipei Representative Office--Education Division

Hi Marcus

Are you able to answer this? Or at least the first part. UoL processes obviously for them to answer.

As a quick update, I don't know if you are aware but a North American-Taiwan professor came in over the summer to look at Ingwen Tsai's thesis. He published a 50 page report (in Chinese) last week, criticising it and alluding to Gaddafi again. President Tsai has decided to take him to court, hence the questions. She has also requested and been sent a copy of her student record.

thanks

Clive

From: ███████
Sent: 04 September 2019 09:39
To: Wilson, Clive
Cc: sztseng
Subject: RE: Inquire From Taipei Representative Office--Education Division

Dear Clive,

寄件者：Wilson Clive

收件者：Cerny MW 日期：2019 年 9 月 4 日 10：06：25

Directorate Directorate@lse.ac.uk

主旨：回复：来自台北代表处教育部门的询问

嗨 Marcus，

没问题 - 我知道第二部分绝对是他们的，但我认为我最好先从你开始。

感谢确认，Clive

寄件者：Cerny，MW

日期：2019 年 9 月 4 日 10：04

收件者：Wilson，Clive 主旨：回复：来自台北代表处教育部门的询问

嗨 Clive，

我认为这是伦敦大学需要澄清的事情。我的知识可以追溯到 1990 年代末，但那不是很确定。

实体论文的提交将由伦敦大学的研究学位办公室处理，最终副本由总图书馆处理。

对于这个不太有帮助的回应，我很抱歉。我对当时的过程充满信心（确认论文已经被口试委员通过，硬皮书到总图书馆触研究学位办公室 RDO 的授予确认与放进图书馆中），但这应该由伦敦大学澄清，我会建议蔡总统的办公室将此过程的查询发送给他们。

谢谢，Marcus

Marcus Cerny

博士生学院副主任

伦敦政经学院

Houghton Street

伦敦 WC2A 2AE

为了环保，除非绝对必要，否则请不要列印此电邮。请访问附加的超连结，以获取一个重要的电子通讯免责声明：https://lse.ac.uk/emailDisclaimer

---

寄件者：█████ 日期：2019 年 9 月 4 日 09：39

收件者：Wilson，Clive

副本：sztseng 主旨：回复：来自台北代表处教育部门的询问

嗨 Marcus，

Thank you so much for your response.

The President's Office has asked me to find out what the procedure was back in the 1980s for PhD students to submit their theses. Do you know what they would be required to do and how the University of London would process and catalogue the theses submitted at that time?

If you are not in a position to answer this question, would you be able to suggest a contact person who might be able to help explain the process?

Kind regards,

███

Taipei Representative Office in the U.K.
Tel: +44+20 7436 5888
-----Original message-----
From: Wilson,Clive<CLIVE.Wilson@lse.ac.uk>
To: ███
Cc: ███,O'Connor,D<D.O'Connor@lse.ac.uk>
Date: Fri, 30 Aug 2019 10:37:12
Subject: RE: Inquire From Taipei Representative Office--Education Division

Hi ███

thanks for the email. All's well here. It had gone quiet briefly and I was made aware that ███ had visited whilst I was on
leave. I did wonder what would happen next.

To answer the questions:

All visitors to LSE must complete the application form at:
https://www.lse.ac.uk/library/using-the-library/secure/join-the-library

and specify which material they wish to view. All applications to view printed theses in our collections will be accepted and an appointment made to view them in our Special Collections Reading Room.

亲爱的 Clive，

非常感谢您的回应。

总统府已要求我查明 1980 年代博士生提交论文的程序是什么。您知道他们需要做什么以及当时伦敦大学如何处理和编目提交的论文吗？

如果您无法回答这个问题，您能否建议一个可能能够帮助解释该过程的联系人？

祝好，

台北驻英代表处
电话：+44+20 7436 5888

------原始讯息------

寄件者： O'Connor，DD.O'Connor@lse.ac.uk
收件者： ▮▮▮▮▮
副本： ▮▮▮▮▮
日期： 2019 年 8 月 30 日 10：37：12
主旨： 回复：来自台北代表处教育部门的询问

嗨，

感谢您的电子邮件。这里一切都好。事情短暂地变得安静，我得知 ▮▮▮ 在我休假时曾来访。我在想接下来会发生什么。

为了回答您的问题：

所有想要参观 LSE 的访客都必须在以下网址完成申请表格：

https://www.lse.ac.uk/library/using-the-library/secure/join-the-library

并指定他们希望查看的材料。我们会接受所有查看我们收藏中的印刷论文的申请，并安排在我们的特藏阅览室查看。

The copy we hold was received on the 10th July 2019.

We do not know if other theses were missing from the transfer list but received over 600 theses that had not originally been presented to LSE at the time of their award.

As we have just seen the news that says President Tsai may take legal action, I am copying my reply to Danny O'Connor our Head of Media
Relations

very best wishes

Clive

Clive Wilson

Enquiry Services Manager (Academic Services)

London School of Economics Tel.: 020 7955 7475

10 Portugal Street Fax.: 020 7955 7454

London WC2A 2HD Email:
Datalibrary@lse.ac.uk

clive.wilson@lse.ac.uk

From:
████████████████████

Sent: 29 August 2019 14:14
To: Wilson,Clive

我们所持有的纸本论文是在 2019 年 7 月 10 日收到的。

我们不知道是否有其他论文从转移清单中遗失，但我们收到了超过 600 篇论文，这些论文在获得学位授予时原本并未呈交给 LSE。

由于我们刚刚看到新闻说蔡英文总统可能会采取法律行动，我将我的回复复制给我们的媒体关系主管 Danny O'Connor。

祝一切顺利，

Clive

Clive Wilson
询问服务经理（学术服务）
伦敦政经学院
电话：020 7955 7475
10 Portugal Street 传真：020 7955 7454
伦敦 WC2A 2HD 电子邮件：Datalibrary@lse.ac.uk
clive.wilson@lse.ac.uk

寄件者： █████
日期： 2019 年 8 月 29 日 14：14
收件者： Wilson，Clive

Cc: ▉▉▉▉▉▉▉▉
Subject: Inquire From Taipei Representative Office--Education Division

Dear Clive,

I hope you have been keeping well and enjoying the hot weather.

It was very kind of you to welcome my colleagues and me to the LSE Library in mid-July and to allow us to view and photograph President Tsai's thesis. You may be aware that another press conference was held in Taiwan today regarding President Tsai's PhD degree. During this press conference, a Professor by the name of ▉▉▉▉▉ ▉▉ concluded that President Tsai's PhD was not valid, raising various questions which we are now obliged to address.

Therefore, could I possibly trouble you to answer the following three questions?

副本: ██████████

主旨：来自台北代表处教育部门的询问

亲爱的 Clive，

希望您近来一切都好，并享受着炎热的天气。

您在七月中旬热情地欢迎我和我的同事来到 LSE 图书馆，并允许我们查看和拍摄蔡英文总统的论文，这真的非常感激。您可能已经知道，今天在台湾又有另一场有关蔡英文总统的博士学位的新闻发布会。在这次的记者会中，一位名为的教授得出结论认为蔡英文总统的博士学位是无效的，他提出了我们现在必须回应的各种问题。

因此，我可以麻烦您回答以下三个问题吗？

1. What is the procedure for a visitor to apply to view President Tsai's thesis in the LSE Library?

2. When did the LSE Library receive the copy of President Tsai's thesis that it currently holds?

3. Was President Tsai's thesis the only one not to be included in the transfer list from the University of London to LSE Library or was this the case with other theses, as well?

If you would prefer to respond to these questions in person, would it be possible for me to arrange another meeting with you at the LSE Library at some point tomorrow (Friday 30th Aug.)? Otherwise, I look forward to receiving your reply by e-mail.

Thank you very much indeed for your continued assistance in this case.

Kind regards,

1. 请问访客申请在 LSE 图书馆查看蔡英文总统论文的程序是什么？

2. LSE 图书馆是何时收到目前所持有的蔡英文总统论文副本的？

3. 蔡英文总统的论文是唯一一篇未被列入从伦敦大学转移到 LSE 图书馆的转移名单中的论文吗？还是其他的论文也有这种情况？

如果您更愿意面对面回答这些问题，我是否可以安排明天（8 月 30 日，星期五）在 LSE 图书馆与您见面？否则，我期待着您透过电子邮件的回复。

非常感谢您在此案件中的持续协助。

诚挚的问候，

3

妇女图书馆的谜团：蔡英文论文的存放之谜

妇女图书馆的谜团：蔡英文论文的存放之谜

彭文正教授发起了对于蔡英文论文不存在的诉求，但 LSE 决定保持沉默，不对外回应。这使得外界对 LSE 的疑虑加深，尤其是关于蔡英文学生纪录的疑点。

LSE 内部的氛围也变得紧张。他们对自己的答复感到有些心虚，尤其是当外界开始追问蔡英文的口试细节时。LSE 一再强调蔡英文已取得学位，但这似乎并未平息外界的质疑。

在这样的背景下，LSE 秘书部门法务团队负责人 Kevin Haynes 成为了焦点。他刚就任时还相当认真，但很快就被卷入这场风波。O'Connor 向他坦承，蔡英文的论文并非最终版本。而 LSE 博士学程校务处副处长 Marcus W Cerny 则提醒他不要多说。Wilson 则表示，蔡英文论文的限制与其他人并无不同。

然而，风波并未就此平息。O'Connor 坚决要求 LSE 不与林环墙教授接触，认为他的行动让学校内部紧张。LSE 内部开始举行会议，讨论如何应对这场危机。

O'Connor 表示，蔡英文的论文不仅存放在妇女图书馆。但 LSE 对于为何蔡英文的论文会放在妇女图书馆给出的解释却相当模糊。O'Connor 因被外界骂为骗子而感到不悦，他认为对学校的质疑都是假新闻政治学，2019 年 10 月，风波达到了高潮。LSE 在官网上发表了一则声明，试图为这场风波划下句点。蔡英文也在脸书上发文，希望大家能够转发，终结这场风波。

但是，风波并未就此平息。立法委员陈学圣在立法院质询时，询问 48 位国立大学校长中，有多少人相信蔡英文的学位是真的。结果只有六位校长举手，这使得风波再次升级。

彭文正教授率团到英国伦敦，进行了第一手的调查。他们与 LSE 的图书馆馆员进行了访谈，并证明学校从未收藏过这本论文。

美国独立记者 Michael Richardson 则透过《自由资讯公开法》，向 LSE 提出公开蔡英文口试委员与口试日期的请求。但 LSE 的回应却引起了更大的争议。

Fwd_ Request for information

From:	Winterstein, J
To:	O"Connor, D
Subject:	Fwd: Request for information
Date:	03 October 2019 08:51:17

Hi Danny

The story that will not die! If you'd like me to get back to him could you send me our latest statement to pass on?

Many thanks
Jess

Begin forwarded message:

From: ████████████████████
Date: 2 October 2019 at 23:56:14 BST
To: j.winterstein@lse.ac.uk
Subject: Request for information

I am working on an article about the controversy surrounding Republic of China in-exile President Tsai Ing-wen's LSE graduate thesis. Ms. Tsai filed her 1984 theis with the LSE Library in 2019 and that has generated much public interest in Taiwan. The name of the thesis is "Unfair Trade Practices and Safeguard Actions."

My questions, for publication, are:

1) What is the name and degree of Tsai Ing-wen's LSE Advisor?
2) What are the names of the thesis Examiners?
3) What is the date of the thesis oral review?
4) What is the date of the Examiner's signatures of approval?

If you are not the correct person to handle this information request please forward to the appropriate individual.

Thank you for your attention to this request.

寄件者：Winterstein，J

收件者：O'Connor，D

日期：2019 年 10 月 3 日 08：51：17

主旨：转寄：资讯请求

嗨 Danny，

这个故事永不消逝！如果你希望我回复他，你能否将我们最新的声明发给我再转发给他？

非常感谢，Jess

开始转寄的讯息：

寄件者：▬▬▬▬

日期：2019 年 10 月 2 日 23：56：14 BST

收件者：j.winterstein@lse.ac.uk

主旨：资讯请求

我正在撰写有关中华民国流亡政府总统蔡英文在 LSE 的研究论文争议的文章。蔡女士在 2019 年将她 1984 年的论文提交给 LSE 图书馆，这在台湾引起了广泛的公众兴趣。论文的名称是"不公平贸易和防卫机制"。

我有一些将用于出版的问题：

1. 蔡英文在 LSE 的指导教授的名字和学位是什么？

2. 口试委员的名字是什么？

3. 论文口试的日期是什么？

4. 审查员批准的签名日期是什么？

如果您不是处理这个资讯请求的正确人士，请将其转发给适当的个人。

感谢您对这个请求的关注。

RE_ for truth and truth only, ligitimately

From: O"Connor,D
To: Haynes,KJ; Cerny,MW
Cc: Metcalfe,F; Thomson,MT
Subject: RE: for truth and truth only, ligitimately
Date: 01 October 2019 16:06:57

On reflection, it seems weird that you've answered one question but ignored all the others.

I've updated a standard reply we've been using below:

Dear xxx

As indicated to a number of enquirers, the London School of Economics and Political Science and the University of London can confirm categorically that Tsai Ing-Wen completed and submitted her thesis and was correctly awarded a PhD in Law in 1984.

[Update] For your information, Dr Tsai Ing-wen recently provided the LSE Library with a facsimile copy of the thesis, *Unfair trade practices and safeguard actions*. I understand a digital copy has also been provided to Taiwan's National Central Library.

https://ndltd.ncl.edu.tw/cgi-bin/gs32/gsweb.cgi?ccd=1wi2HF/webmge?mode=basic

regards,

From: Haynes,KJ
Sent: 01 October 2019 15:58
To: O'Connor,D <D.O'Connor@lse.ac.uk>; Cerny,MW <M.W.Cerny@lse.ac.uk>
Cc: Metcalfe,F <F.Metcalfe@lse.ac.uk>; Thomson,MT <M.T.Thomson@lse.ac.uk>
Subject: RE: for truth and truth only, ligitimately

Thanks, Danny. Are you comfortable with the following response?

Dear ▓▓▓▓▓▓▓▓

Thank you for your email of 1 October 2019.

We can confirm that President Tsai successfully completed a PhD at LSE in 1984. As was normal practice for LSE qualifications in 1984, her academic certificate was issued by the University of London, of which our School has been a member institution since the beginning of the 20th Century.

As do most institutions in the United Kingdom, the University of London has in place a procedure where it is able to re-issue certificates on request. This practice may explain the existence of more recently issued academic certificates to which you refer.

Best wishes, Kevin

LSE Legal Team
Secretary's Division
Room 3.01, 1 Kingsway
London School of Economics and Political Science
Houghton Street
London
WC2A 2AE

020 7955 7823

寄件者：O'Connor，D　**收件者**：Haynes KJ；Cerny，MW

副本：Metcalfe，F；Thomson，MT

主旨：回复：只为真相，合法地

日期：2019 年 10 月 1 日 16：06：57

反思之后，你只回答了一个问题但忽略了所有其他的似乎很奇怪。

我已经更新了我们一直在使用的标准回复，如下所示：

亲爱的 xxx，

正如我们向多位询问者指出的那样，伦敦政治经济学院和伦敦大学可以明确确认蔡英文于 1984 年正确地获得了法学博士学位。

[更新] 供您参考，蔡英文博士最近向 LSE 图书馆提供了论文"不公平贸易和防卫机制"的传真副本。我得知她也提供了一份数位副本在台湾的国家中央图书馆。

此致，

———————————————————

寄件者：Haynes，KJ　**日期**：2019 年 10 月 1 日 15：58

收件者：O'Connor，D；Cerny，MW

副本：Metcalfe，F；Thomson，MT

主旨：回复：只为真相，合法地

谢谢，Danny。你对以下的回复感到满意吗？

亲爱的 ████

感谢您在 2019 年 10 月 1 日的电子邮件。

我们可以确认蔡总统于 1984 年在 LSE 成功完成了博士学位。正如 1984 年 LSE 资格的正常做法一样，她的学位证书是由伦敦大学发出的，我们的学校自 20 世纪初以来一直是该大学的成员机构。

正如英国的大多数机构一样，伦敦大学有一个程序，可以应要求重新发行证书。这种做法可能解释了您提到的更近期发行的学位证书的存在。

最好的祝愿，Kevin

LSE 法律团队

秘书部门

3.01 室，1 Kingsway

伦敦政经学院

霍顿街

伦敦

WC2A 2AE

020 7955 7823

From: O'Connor,D
Sent: 01 October 2019 15:11
To: Haynes,KJ <K.J_Haynes@lse.ac.uk>; Cerny,MW <MW.Cerny@lse.ac.uk>
Cc: Metcalfe,F <F.Metcalfe@lse.ac.uk>; Thomson,MT <M.T.Thomson@lse.ac.uk>
Subject: RE: for truth and truth only, ligitimately

Hi Kevin,

In general we have been giving a two line reply effectively saying, her PhD is legitimate. The main reason for this nonsense is that the UoL/ IALS lost her thesis, probably many years ago.

On the certificates - these were issued by the University of London. Any graduate can ask for certificates to be re-issued if they pay a small fee. I understand from UoL that she did, indeed, ask for two additional copies.

On everything else, I don't have relevant information on signatures and dates, I'm not totally sure it's worth responding to each question as it's just going to invite never-ending questions.

Danny

From: Haynes,KJ
Sent: 01 October 2019 15:05
To: O'Connor,D <D.O'Connor@lse.ac.uk>; Cerny,MW <MWCerny@lse.ac.uk>
Cc: Metcalfe,F <F.Metcalfe@lse.ac.uk>; Thomson,MT <M.T.Thomson@lse.ac.uk>
Subject: FW: for truth and truth only, ligitimately

Hello Danny, Marcus

You'll see below that I've been approached by a me[redacted] staff looking for clarity on President Tsai's qualifications from LSE (or the University of London).

I'm happy to respond, or for anyone else to do so. Could you please confirm the facts (when, where, what) of the situation if you're content for me to respond?

Best wishes, Kevin

LSE Legal Team
Secretary's Division
Room 3.01 1 Kingsway
London School of Economics and Political Science
Houghton Street
London
WC2A2AE

020 7955 7823

Sent: 01 October 2019 02:47
To: Haynes,KJ <KJ Haynes@lse.ac.uk>
Subject: for truth and truth only, ligitimately

寄件者：O'Connor，D　**日期**：2019年10月1日 15：11

收件者：Haynes, KJ；Cerny, MW

副本：Metcalfe, F；Thomson, MT

主旨：回复：只为真相，合法地

嗨 Kevin，

一般来说，我们持续提供两行的回复，实质上说，她的博士学位是合法的。这些胡说八道的主要原因是伦敦大学/IALS 很多年前就丢失了她的论文。

关于证书 - 这些是由伦敦大学发出的。任何毕业生只要支付一小笔费用就可以要求重新发行证书。我从伦敦大学那里了解到，她确实要求了两份额外的纸本论文。

对于其他一切，我没有关于签名和日期的相关资讯，我不完全确定是否值得回答每个问题，因为这只会引来无休止的问题。

Danny

寄件者：Haynes, KJ

日期：2019年10月1日 15：05

收件者：O'Connor, D；Cerny, MW

副本：Metcalfe, F；Thomson, MT

主旨：转发：只为真相，合法地

你好 Danny， Marcus，

你们会看到下面关于一名 ▓▓▓▓ 员工接触我想要寻找蔡总统的LSE（或伦敦大学）资格明确性。

我很乐意回应，或者任何其他人也可以这样做。如果你满意我的回应，可否请你确认情况的事实（何时、何地、什么）？

最好的祝愿，Kevin

LSE 法律团队

秘书部门

3.01 室，1 Kingsway

伦敦政治经济学院

霍顿街伦敦

WC2A 2AE　020 7955 7823

寄件者：▓▓▓▓▓

日期：2019年10月1日 02：47

收件者：Haynes, KJ

主旨：只为真相，合法地

Dear Mr. Haynes,

This is ███ I do not write this email for my personal matter, but for some legal truth. Many young Ph.D.s in Taiwan like me are playing Sherlock Holmes to crack the mystery of President Ing-wen Tsai's LSE Ph.D. degree.

In this email, I attached a few Ms. Tsai's LSE documents (which she said provided by LSE). However, these documents did not solve people's doubts about her LSE certificate but aroused even more suspicion.

First of all, Ms. Tsai had three Ph.D. certificates that she obtained from 1984, 2010 and 2015 -- How come LSE issued her so many certificates at different times? Are they all legitimate? My second question is, some important documents are lacking signatures of the persons in charge -- Are these documents coming from LSE? Without signatures, are they legitimate? (Attached documents are published by the President's spokesman on his FB and in a press conference.)

I am very sorry if this email is bothering you or LSE, but this matter has caused much disturbance in Taiwan's society in the past few months. Families and friends fought with each other or broke off relations because of this. It has become it is either LSE's fault (missing Ms. Tsai's thesis in three libraries, issuing documents without signatures, missing details between 1983-84 in the student record) or it is Ms. Tsai's fault (if she did not follow the right procedure to get her Ph.D. degree). How could she graduate without a principle supervisor after 1982 as shown in the student record? (It is said that her supervisor Mr. Michael Elliot left LSE in 1982.)

I am not in nature a political person. It is the first time that I care about a political issue so much because it is related to academic dignity and truth. I realize it is not an easy matter. All I can do is just writing this email.

Sincerely yours,

████

亲爱的 Haynes 先生，

这里是 ███。我写这封电子邮件并非为了我的私人事务，而是为了寻求某些法律上的真相。像我这样的许多台湾年轻博士都在扮演福尔摩斯，试图解开蔡英文总统在 LSE 的博士学位之谜。

在这封邮件中，我附上了几份蔡女士的 LSE 文件（她说是由 LSE 提供的）。然而，这些文件并没有解决人们对她的 LSE 证书的疑虑，反而引起了更多的怀疑。

首先，蔡女士从 1984 年、2010 年和 2015 年获得了三张博士学位证书——LSE 怎么会在不同的时间给她发放这么多的证书呢？它们都是合法的吗？我的第二个问题是，一些重要的文件缺少负责人的签名——这些文件是来自 LSE 的吗？没有签名的文件是合法的吗？（附件中的文件是由总统的发言人在他的 FB 和记者会上公开的。）

如果这封邮件打扰了您或 LSE，我深感抱歉，但这件事在过去的几个月中已经在台湾社会引起了很大的骚动。因为这件事，家人和朋友之间发生了争执，甚至断绝了关系。这已经成为是 LSE 的错（在三家图书馆都找不到蔡女士的论文、发放没有签名的文件、在学生记录中的 1983-84 年间缺少细节）还是蔡女士的错（如果她没有按照正确的程序获得她的博士学位）。她在学生记录中显示，1982 年后没有主要的指导教授，她是如何毕业的？（据说她的指导教授 Michael Elliot 在 1982 年离开了 LSE。）

我本质上不是一个政治人物。这是我第一次如此关心一个政治问题，因为它与学术尊严和真相有关。我意识到这不是一件简单的事情。我能做的只是写这封电子邮件。

诚挚的，

███

Re_ Ing-Wen Tsai's PhD of 1984

From: Withers,IF
To: Phdacademy
Cc: Haynes,KJ; Metcalfe,F; Wilson,Clive; Thomson,MT
Subject: Re: Ing-Wen Tsai"s PhD of 1984
Date: 03 October 2019 22:32:08

Hi Marcus

It seems appropriate to give some background and guidance to colleagues if we think more staff are being contacted, although do we have an idea of academic faculty likely to have been approached?

Happy to speak tomorrow to discuss and to also get Danny's expertise to make sure we are aligned with external comms.

Best wishes
Imogen

Sent from my IPhone

On 3 Oct 2019, at 21:55, LSE PhD Academy <phdacademy@lse.ac.uk> wrote:

> The one Kevin has attached has been sent to several people including the Simon Hix, Rita Astuti and Max Shulze. I have advised Rita to ignore but should we do some internal comms to academics likely to receive such queries?
>
> Thanks,
>
> Marcus
>
> **Marcus Cerny**
> **PhD Academy Deputy Director**
> The London School of Economics and Political Science
> Houghton Street, London WC2A 2AE
> t: +44 (0)20 7955 6766
> e: m.w.cerny@lse.ac.uk
> lse.ac.uk/phdacademy
>
> If you are a current PhD student please remember to send your queries through the PhD Academy Enquiry Form. All other enquirers should contact phdacademy@lse.ac.uk
>
> --------------- Original Message ---------------
> **From:** Haynes,KJ [k.j.haynes@lse.ac.uk]
> **Sent:** 03/10/2019 16:24
> **To:** phdacademy@lse.ac.uk; m.t.thomson@lse.ac.uk; i.f.withers@lse.ac.uk
> **Cc:** clive.wilson@lse.ac.uk; f.metcalfe@lse.ac.uk; k.j.haynes@lse.ac.uk
> **Subject:** FW: Ing-Wen Tsai's PhD of 1984
>
> Hi Danny

寄件者：Withers，IF　**收件者**：Phdacademy

副本：Haynes，KJ； Metcalfe，F； Wilson，Clive； Thomson，MT

主旨：回复：蔡英文1984年的博士学位

日期：2019年10月3日22：32：08

Marcus，

如果我们觉得有许多同事一直被联系，提供一些背景和指导似乎是适当的，尽管我们是否有学院教职员工可能已被接触的想法

明天我很乐意谈谈，也获得Danny的专业知识，以确保我们与外部沟通保持一致。

最好的祝愿，

Imogen

从我的iPhone发送

2019年10月3日，晚上21：55，伦敦政治经济学院博士学院发送的电子邮件：

Kevin附上的那份文件已经发送给包括Simon Hix、Rita Astuti和Max Shulze在内的几位人士。我已建议Rita不予理会，但我们是否应该对可能收到此类查询的学者进行一些内部沟通？

谢谢，Marcus

Marcus Cerny

伦敦政经学院博士生学院副院长

Houghton街，伦敦WC2A 2AE

电话：+44（0）20 7955 6766

电子邮件：m.w.cerny@lse.ac.uk

网址：lse.ac.uk/phdacademy

如果您是目前的博士生，请记得通过博士学院询问表格发送您的查询。其他查询者应联系 phdacademy@lse.ac.uk

----------- 原始讯息-----------

寄件者：Haynes，KJ [k.j.haynes@lse.ac.uk]

日期：2019年10月3日16：24

收件者：phdacademy@lse.ac.uk； m.t.thomson@lse.ac.uk； i.f.withers@lse.ac.uk

副本：clive.wilson@lse.ac.uk； f.metcalfe@lse.ac.uk； k.j.haynes@lse.ac.uk

主旨：转发：蔡英文1984年的博士学位

嗨，Danny

I've attached another that you may already have seen. I think our party line more or less answers why we wouldn't be embarking on an investigation.

Best wishes, Kevin

LSE Legal Team

Secretary's Division

Room 3.01, 1 Kingsway

London School of Economics and Political Science

Houghton Street

London

WC2A 2AE

020 7955 7823

From: O'Connor,D
Sent: 03 October 2019 16:13
To: Phdacademy <Phdacademy@lse.ac.uk>; Thomson,MT <M.T.Thomson@lse.ac.uk>; Withers,IF <I.F.Withers@lse.ac.uk>
Cc: Wilson,Clive <CLIVE.Wilson@lse.ac.uk>; Metcalfe,F <F.Metcalfe@lse.ac.uk>; Haynes,KJ <K.J.Haynes@lse.ac.uk>
Subject: FW: Ing-Wen Tsai's PhD of 1984

Colleagues,

To note, the Director's office continue to receive emails from Hwan Lin.

I have advised against engaging with him at all. He has received a response from LSE on numerous occasions, and his subsequent allegations are weak and far-fetched.

我附上了另一份你可能已经看过的文件。我认为我们的官方立场或多或少已经回答了为什么我们不会开始进行调查的原因。

祝好，Kevin

伦敦政经学院法律团队

秘书处 3.01 室，1 Kingsway

Houghton 街，伦敦 WC2A 2AE

020 7955 7823

寄件者：O'Connor，D

日期：2019 年 10 月 3 日 16：13

收件者：Phdacademy Phdacademy@lse.ac.uk； Thomson，MT M.T.Thomson@lse.ac.uk；Withers，IF I.F.Withers@lse.ac.uk

副本：Wilson，Clive CLIVE.Wilson@lse.ac.uk； Metcalfe，F F.Metcalfe@lse.ac.uk；Haynes，KJ K.J.Haynes@lse.ac.uk

主旨：转发：蔡英文 1984 年的博士学位

同事们，

请注意，校长办公室继续收到来自 Hwan Lin 的电子邮件。

我建议完全不要与他接触。他已经多次收到伦敦政治经济学院的回应，他随后的指控是薄弱且牵强的。

Kind regards,

Danny

From: ▓▓▓▓▓▓▓▓▓▓▓▓▓▓▓▓▓▓▓▓▓
Sent: 09 September 2019 03:29
To: Gajewska,M <M.Gajewska@lse.ac.uk>
Subject: Ing-Wen Tsai's PhD of 1984

Dear LSE Director Shafik:

I hope this email finds you well. I am writing to make inquiries about the authenticity of Ms. Tsai's LSE PhD in law, which, she claimed, was awarded in 1984. I am an academic economist in the US and I made my inquiries for the sake of academic honesty and integrity. As you may have noticed, Ms. Ing-Wen Tsai is President of Republic of China (Taiwan).

For your information, some new startling evidence just came up recently. On September 6, 2019, Ms. Ing-Wen Tsai's spokesperson displayed three documents in public in order to prove the authenticity of her so-called PhD in law. These documents are attached in this email for your review. To me, these documents instead prove that she was actually not awarded a PhD in 1984. My explanations of each document are in order:

#1. The first document is Ing-Wen Tsai's Student Records while she was a graduate student at LSE. This document clearly says that she was on a M. Phil. program between October, 1980 and November 10, 1982. In the entire course of study, she had two supervisors (Mr. Lazar and Mr. Elliott) for the academic year of 1980-81 and only one supervisor (Mr. Elliott) for the next academic year of 1981-82. The duration of the course of study was 21 months, much less than the duration of 3 - 4 years for a typical PhD program. The M. Phil program was clearly a master's program. Note that she withdrew from the course of study on November 10, 1982 for the sake of financial difficulties. All these are specified on the Student Records.

It is evident that she did not have any course of study at LSE starting from the day of November 10, 1982. But how could it be possible that the M. Phil program was later changed to a PhD program on the Student Records? And when was this change being made? For these questions, the Student Records

此致，

Danny

寄件者：▉▉▉▉
日期：2019 年 9 月 9 日 03：29
收件者：Gajewska, M M.Gajewska@lse.ac.uk
主旨：蔡英文 1984 年的博士学位

亲爱的伦敦政经学院校长 Shafik：

希望这封邮件能让您感到安好。我写这封邮件是为了询问蔡英文女士所声称在 1984 年获得的伦敦政经学院法学博士学位的真实性。我是美国的一名经济学者，我提出这些问题是出于对学术诚信的关心。您可能已经注意到，蔡英文女士是中华民国（台湾）的总统。

供您参考，最近有一些令人震惊的新证据浮现。2019 年 9 月 6 日，蔡英文女士的发言人在公开场合展示了三份文件，以证明她所谓的法学博士学位的真实性。这些文件附在此电子邮件中供您审查。对我来说，这些文件反而证明她在 1984 年实际上并未获得博士学位。我对每份文件的解释如下：

#1. 第一份文件是蔡英文在伦敦政经学院攻读研究生时的学生记录。这份文件清楚地说明她在 1980 年 10 月至 1982 年 11 月 10 日之间参加了 M. Phil. 课程。在整个学习过程中，她在 1980-81 学年有两位指导教授（Lazar 先生和 Elliott 先生），在 1981-82 学年只有一位指导教授（Elliott 先生）。学习期间为 21 个月，远少于典型博士课程的 3-4 年。M. Phil 课程显然是硕士课程。请注意，她在 1982 年 11 月 10 日因财务困难而退出了学习。所有这些都在学生记录上有所说明。

很明显，她从 1982 年 11 月 10 日起在伦敦政经学院就没有任何学习课程了。但 M. Phil 课程后来如何在学生记录上被更改为博士课程呢？这一变更是何时进行的？对于这些问题，学生记录

provide no information at all. More absurd is that an undisclosed degree was awarded to her in February, 1984, which occurred about 16 months after she withdrew from the course of study. Moreover, the date of recording the degree-awarding event was about one year earlier than the occurrence of this event itself. How could one predict and record a far-away future event on Student Records?

Another serious problem is that the Student Records indicate nobody supervising Ing-Wen Tsai's doctoral study after she withdrew from the course of study on November 10, 1982. Even if we assume that Mr. Elliott continued to serve as Supervisor, it is still unbelievable that LSE could permit a bachelor-degree supervisor to direct a doctoral study. Note that Mr. Elliott graduated from Oxford University with a bachelor's degree and he was very young in the early 1980s. He left LSE in 1982 and joined the Central Policy Review Staff (CPRS) in 1983, which was the cabinet office's Think-Tank.

All these weird problems revealed that Ms. Tsai's Student Records are problematic and can never be a proof that she was awarded a PhD in 1984, given that she had not been an LSE student since November 10, 1982.

#2. The second document is a letter dated February 8, 1984 that Mrs. G. F. Roberts mailed to Ms. Ing-Wen Tsai's home address in Taipei, Taiwan. According to this letter, Mrs. G. F. Roberts was Academic Registrar from the University's Senate House. Ms. Tsai claimed that this letter was a proof that she passed her viva exam for a PhD. However, the letter did not mention the examination as a viva exam, and the two viva examiners were never mentioned at all in the letter and elsewhere, either. More seriously, Mrs. G. F. Roberts did not sign on the letter. Thus, how could such an unsigned letter be a formal proof of passing a viva exam for her PhD.

#3. The third document is a carbon copy of Ms. Tsai's so-called PhD diploma. According to Ms. Tsai, such a carbon copy was kept in the University of London and she got a copy of it from the University. Note that in the year of 2015, Ms. Tsai said that she applied for a replacement diploma from the University. She then displayed this replacement diploma in public on July 10, 2019. A month ago, an image file of this replacement was sent to you, as attached. According to the University's Head of Diploma Production Office, any replacement must be identical to the original diploma. However, the replacement that Ms. Tsai obtained in 2015 is totally different from the carbon copy of the so-called original diploma she obtained from the University. In other words, it is highly possible that the replacement is fake and came illegally from some unknown sources.

完全没有提供任何资讯。更荒谬的是，她在退出学习约 16 个月后于 1984 年 2 月被授予了一个未公开的学位。而且，记录学位授予事件的日期比这一事件本身的发生日期早了大约一年。如何能在学生记录上预测和记录一个遥远的未来事件呢？

另一个严重的问题是，学生记录表明，在 1982 年 11 月 10 日退出学习课程后，没有人指导蔡英文的博士研究。即使我们假设 Elliott 先生继续担任指导教授，伦敦政经学院也不可能允许一位只有学士学位的指导教授指导博士研究。请注意，Elliott 先生毕业于牛津大学，拥有学士学位，并且在 1980 年代初非常年轻。他于 1982 年离开伦敦政治经济学院，于 1983 年加入了内阁办公室的智囊团 Central Policy Review Staff（CPRS）。

所有这些奇怪的问题都揭示了蔡英文的学生记录存在问题，并且绝对不能证明她在 1984 年获得了博士学位，因为她自 1982 年 11 月 10 日起就不再是伦敦政治经济学院的学生。

#2. 第二份文件是 1984 年 2 月 8 日由 G. F. Roberts 女士寄往台北，台湾的蔡英文家庭地址的一封信。根据这封信，G. F. Roberts 女士是大学行政办公室的教务长。蔡英文声称这封信证明她通过了博士口试。然而，这封信并未提及考试为口试，而且两位口试考官在信中和其他地方都从未被提及。更严重的是，G. F. Roberts 女士并未在信上签名。那么，这样一封未签名的信如何能成为通过博士口试的正式证明呢？

#3. 第三份文件是蔡英文所谓的博士学位证书的副本。根据蔡英文的说法，这份副本是由伦敦大学保存的，她从大学那里获得了它的副本。请注意，2015 年，蔡英文说她向大学申请了补发学位证书。然后，她于 2019 年 7 月 10 日在公开场合展示了这份补发学位证书。一个月前，这个补发的图像文件被发送给您，如附件所示。根据大学的学位产制办公室主任的说法，任何补发都必须与原始学位证书完全相同。然而，蔡英文在 2015 年获得的替代与她从大学获得的所谓原始学位证书的纸本完全不同。换句话说，这个补发很可能是假的，并且是从一些未知的来源非法获得的。

I was pulled into the investigation of Ms. Tsai's PhD diploma about three months ago when I tried to check out her thesis titled "Unfair Trade Practices and Safeguard Actions" from LSE Library. The librarian told me that the University's Senate House Library had never received a copy of the thesis over the past 35 years, neither had the University's Institute of Advanced Legal Studies. This was a shock to me and then the investigation has since then continued.

On June 28, 2019, Ms. Tsai sent a facsimile copy of a so-called thesis to LSE Library for the first time in 35 years. It was bound into a hard-cover book and cataloged in the Library. This thesis then become searchable, starting from July 13, on the Library's online search system. On August 6 - 8, 2019, I visited LSE Library and reviewed this thesis. What shocked me was that I was not allowed to copy any part of the thesis's contents. You can see such illegal restrictions indicated on a white-colored paper band on the thesis, as attached. I found that the thesis has six missing pages in Chapter One (pages 5, 6, 7, 8, 9, 10 are missing) and its editorial checks and corrections were quite sloppy. It does not look like a PhD-level thesis.

After a three-month investigation, I have documented a 47-page report in Chinese, which is downloadable at my Facebook Page hwanclin. And an English-version of this report will be available soon. The report concludes that Ms. Ing-Wen Tsai was not awarded an LSE PhD in law in 1984.

I admire the global reputation of LSE. I sincerely hope that we all can work together to uphold the noble values of academic honesty and integrity. I believe that LSE would never compromise these values simply because Ms. Ing-Wen Tsai is President of Republic of China (Taiwan).

I hereby make a Freedom-of-Information-Act request that LSE should verify formally whether Ms. Ing-Wen Tsai was correctly awarded an LSE PhD in law in 1984.

Yours faithfully,

ref:_00D58JYzR._5004Itx0ND:ref

当我三个月前尝试从伦敦政经学院图书馆查阅她的论文《不公平贸易和防卫机制》时，我被吸引进入对蔡英文的博士学位证书的调查中。图书馆员告诉我，大学的总图书馆在过去的 35 年里从未收到过这篇论文的副本，大学的高等法律研究所也没有。这对我来说是一个震惊，从那时起，调查就一直在继续。

2019 年 6 月 28 日，蔡英文首次在 35 年内将一份所谓的论文传真副本发送到伦敦政经学院图书馆。它被装订成硬皮书并在图书馆中编目。从 7 月 13 日开始，这篇论文在图书馆的在线搜索系统上成为可搜索的。2019 年 8 月 6 日至 8 日，我访问了伦敦政治经济学院图书馆并审阅了这篇论文。令我震惊的是，我不被允许复制论文的任何部分内容。您可以看到这种非法限制在论文上的白色纸带上有所表示，如附件所示。我发现论文的第一章有六页消失（第 5、6、7、8、9、10 页丢失），而且其编辑检查和修正相当马虎。它看起来不像一篇博士水平的论文。

经过三个月的调查，我已经记录了一份 47 页的中文报告，可以在我的 Facebook 页面 hwanclin 上下载。这份报告的英文版本将很快提供。报告得出的结论是，蔡英文在 1984 年并未获得伦敦政治经济学院的法学博士学位。

我很欣赏伦敦政治经济学院的全球声誉。我真诚地希望我们都能共同努力，维护学术诚信和正直的崇高价值。我相信，仅仅因为蔡英文是中华民国（台湾）的总统，伦敦政治经济学院绝不会妥协这些价值。

我在此根据《资讯自由法》提出请求，希望伦敦政治经济学院正式验证蔡英文是否在 1984 年正确地获得了伦敦政治经济学院的法学博士学位。

顺颂时祺

ref:_00D58JYzR._5004Itx0ND:ref

RE_-Is-it-possible_-To-award-a-Ph.d.-degree-in-.1

From:	O'Connor,D
To:	Metcalfe,F
Subject:	RE: Is it possible? To award a Ph.d. degree in Law without submission of the thesis?
Date:	07 October 2019 13:49:00
Attachments:	image002.png
	image003.png
	image005.png

Seems fine, though they can't find a digital copy either!

Added a little more to the end.

From: Metcalfe,F
Sent: 07 October 2019 13:47
To: O'Connor,D <D.O'Connor@lse.ac.uk>
Subject: RE: Is it possible? To award a Ph.d. degree in Law without submission of the thesis?

Fair enough

What about

LSE statement on PhD of Tsai Ing-wen

LSE has received a number of queries regarding the academic status of our alumna, Dr Tsai Ing-Wen, President of Taiwan.

We can be clear that the records of LSE and of the University of London - the degree awarding body at the time - confirm that Dr Ing-Wen was correctly awarded a PhD in Law in 1984.

All degrees from that period were awarded via the University of London and the thesis would have been sent first to their Senate House Library. However, it has recently been discovered that the University of London Senate House Library are unable to find the hard copy of the thesis.

The Senate House Library records confirm that a copy was received and sent by them to the Institute for Advanced Legal Studies (IALS) and there is a listing of Dr Ing-Wen's thesis 'Unfair trade practices and safeguard actions' In the IALS index document "Legal Research in the United Kingdown 1905-1984", which was published in 1985.

Dr Ing-wen recently provided the LSE Library with a facsimile of a personal copy of the thesis, *Unfair trade practices and safeguard actions* which is available to view in the Library Reading Room. We understand Dr Tsai has also provided a digital version of her personal copy to the National Central Library of Taiwan.

/END

Fiona Metcalfe
X2892

寄件者：O"Connor.D
收件者：Metcalfe E
主旨：这有可能吗？关于不提交论文是否可能授予法学博士学位？
日期：2019 年 10 月 7 日 13：49：00
附件：imaaeoo2.png、image003.png、imaaeoos.png

看起来没问题，尽管他们也找不到数位副本！我在结尾加了一点内容。

寄件者：Metcalfe，F
日期：2019 年 10 月 7 日 13：47
收件者：O'Connor, D D.O'Connor@lse.ac.uk
主旨：回复：这有可能吗？关于不提交论文是否可能授予法学博士学位？那么这样呢？

LSE 关于蔡英文博士学位的声明

LSE 收到了许多关于我们的校友，台湾总统蔡英文博士的学术地位的查询。

我们可以明确地说，LSE 和当时的学位授予机构－伦敦大学的记录都证实，蔡英文博士在 1984 年正确地获得了法学博士学位。

那段时期的所有学位都是通过伦敦大学授予的，论文首先会被送到他们的总图书馆。但是，最近发现伦敦大学总图书馆找不到论文的纸本副本。

总图书馆的记录证实，他们收到了一份副本并将其发送给高等法律研究所（IALS），并且在 IALS 的索引文件 "Legal Research in the United Kingdown 1905-1984" 中，有蔡英文博士的论文 'Unfair trade practices and safeguard actions' 的列表，该文件于 1985 年出版。

蔡英文博士最近向 LSE 图书馆提供了论文《不公平贸易和防卫机制》的传真副本，该副本可以在图书馆阅览室查看。我们了解蔡博士还向台湾国家中央图书馆提供了她个人副本的数位版本。

/ 结束

Fiona Metcalfe

X2892

From: O'Connor,D
Sent: 07 October 2019 13:39
To: Metcalfe,F
Subject: RE: Is it possible? To award a Ph.d. degree in Law without submission of the thesis?

I think that's fine.

I don't know if we need to acknowledge that UoL did lose her original thesis.

From: Metcalfe,F
Sent: 07 October 2019 13:31
To: O'Connor,D <D.O'Connor@lse.ac.uk>
Subject: RE: Is it possible? To award a Ph.d. degree in Law without submission of the thesis?

What about this:

Fiona Metcalfe
X2892

From: O'Connor,D
Sent: 07 October 2019 12:58
To: Metcalfe,F
Subject: RE: Is it possible? To award a Ph.d. degree in Law without submission of the thesis?

Hey,

Have put together this for a web statement, I suspect it's too discursive but prefer to start long and then edit down.

D

LSE statement on PhD of Tsai Ing-wen

LSE has received a number of queries regarding the academic status of our alumna, Dr Tsai Ing-Wen, President of Taiwan.

We can be clear that the records of LSE and of the University of London - the degree awarding body at the time - confirm that Dr Ing-Wen was correctly awarded a PhD in Law in 1984.

All degrees from that period were awarded via the University of London and the thesis would have been sent first to their Senate House Library.

The Senate House Library records confirm that a copy was received and sent by them to the Institute for Advanced Legal Studies (IALS) and there is a listing of Dr Ing-Wen's thesis 'Unfair trade practices and safeguard actions' In the IALS index document "Legal Research in the United Kingdown 1905-1984", which was published in 1985.

寄件者：O'Connor，D
日期：2019年10月7日13：39　收件者：Metcalfe，F
主旨：回复：这有可能吗？关于不提交论文是否可能授予法学博士学位？

我认为这样很好。

我不知道我们是否需要承认UoL确实丢失了她的原始论文。

寄件者：Metcalfe，F
日期：2019年10月7日13：31
收件者：O'Connor，D D.O'Connor@lse.ac.uk
主旨：回复：这有可能吗？关于不提交论文是否可能授予法学博士学位？

那又怎样呢：

Fiona Metcalfe

X2892

寄件者：O'Connor，D
日期：2019年10月7日12：58
收件者：Metcalfe，F
主旨：回复：这有可能吗？关于不提交论文是否可能授予法学博士学位？

嗨，

我已经为网站声明写了这篇文章，我怀疑它太冗长了，但我更喜欢从长篇开始，然后再编辑。

D

LSE关于蔡英文博士学位的声明

LSE收到了许多关于我们的校友，台湾总统蔡英文博士的学术地位的查询。

我们可以明确地说，LSE和当时的学位授予机构－伦敦大学的记录都证实，蔡英文博士在1984年正确地获得了法学博士学位。

那段时期的所有学位都是通过伦敦大学授予的，论文首先会被送到他们的总图书馆。

总图书馆的记录证实，他们收到了一份纸本论文并将其发送给高等法律研究所（IALS)，并且在IALS的索引文件 "Legal Research in the United Kingdown 1905-1984" 中，有蔡英文博士的论文《不公平贸易和防卫机制》的列表，该文件于1985年出版。

Dr Ing-wen recently provided the LSE Library with a facsimile of a personal copy of the thesis, *Unfair trade practices and safeguard actions* and has provided a digital copy to the National Central Library of Taiwan.

/END

From: Metcalfe,F
Sent: 07 October 2019 12:11
To: O'Connor,D <D.O'Connor@lse.ac.uk>
Subject: RE: Is it possible? To award a Ph.d. degree in Law without submission of the thesis?

I think we need to stop engaging

Can you put statement on website and only signpost
?

Fiona Metcalfe
X2892

From: O'Connor,D
Sent: 07 October 2019 11:38
To: Metcalfe,F
Subject: RE: Is it possible? To award a Ph.d. degree in Law without submission of the thesis?

Hi,

Does this seem ok to you? I realise I shouldn't be replying to all this stuff but it's sending me a bit insane.

Danny

Dear ▓▓▓▓▓▓,

I refer you back to our statement that the London School of Economics and Political Science and the University of London can confirm that Tsai Ing-Wen was correctly awarded a PhD in Law in 1984. The records of both institutions have been checked and both confirm this was correct.

With regards to your other questions: the School has received a number of emails from members of the public with false allegations about this issue. To avoid duplicate responses, the media relations office has been asked to collate and reply to many of these messages.

Thank you for the Wikipedia link but I am aware of the position of the Women's Library at LSE. You are, however, incorrect in your assertions. The dissertation is housed in LSE's central library catalogue. The Women's Library Reading Room (which is part of LSE) was used for those wishing to read it. [check with Clive]

蔡英文博士最近向 LSE 图书馆提供了论文《不公平贸易和防卫机制》的传真副本，并向台湾国家中央图书馆提供了数位副本。

/ 结束

寄件者：Metcalfe，F
日期：2019 年 10 月 7 日 12：11
收件者：O'Connor，D D.O'Connor@lse.ac.uk
主旨：回复：这有可能吗？关于不提交论文是否可能授予法学博士学位？

我认为我们需要停止接触

你能在网站上发表声明并只指示吗？

Fiona Metcalfe

X2892

寄件者：O'Connor，D
日期：2019 年 10 月 7 日 11：38
收件者：Metcalfe，F
主旨：回复：这有可能吗？关于不提交论文是否可能授予法学博士学位？

嗨，

这对你来说看起来还好吗？我意识到我不应该回复所有这些东西，但它让我有点疯狂。

Danny

亲爱的

我转交给你我们的声明，是伦敦政治经济学院和伦敦大学确认蔡英文在 1984 年正确地获得了法学博士学位。两所机构的记录都已经检查，并且都确认这是正确的。

关于您的其他问题：学校收到了来自公众的许多电子邮件，其中包含关于此问题的虚假指控。为了避免重复的回应，已要求媒体关系办公室汇整并回复这些消息。

谢谢您提供的维基百科连结，但我知道 LSE 妇女图书馆的位置。但是，您的断言是不正确的。论文存放在 LSE 的中央图书馆目录中。妇女图书馆阅览室（是 LSE 的一部分）用于那些希望阅读它的人。[与 Clive 确认]

As indicated in previous correspondence, this is a facsimile of the personal copy of Dr Tsai's thesis for those interested. The copy submitted for examination in 1980s could not be located by the University of London's Senate House.

We consider this matter closed.

Regards,

Daniel O'Connor

From: █████████████████████████
Sent: 07 October 2019 09:11
To: O'Connor,D <D.O'Connor@lse.ac.uk>
Cc: Media.Relations <Media.Relations@lse.ac.uk>; Carter,HC <H.C.Carter@lse.ac.uk>
Subject: Re: Is it possible? To award a Ph.d. degree in Law without submission of the thesis?

Dear Mr. O'Connor,

I am writing in relation to the following statement of your response dated 16th of September:

... For your information, Dr Tsai Ing-wen recently provided the LSE Library with a facsimile copy of the thesis, *Unfair trade practices and safeguard actions*. This is available to view in the LSE library reading room upon request.

Since it is not clear which LSE library you referred to that housed Ms. Tsai's thesis copy., I did some research and found it is housed at the LSE Women's Library.

I also found that Women's Library has been in the custody of the LSE, it is in fact not a formal LSE library that will house theses of LSE graduates.

For your information, below is a brief background information on the LSE Women's Library which was downloaded from Wikipedia:

" The **Women's Library @ LSE** is England's main library and museum resource on women and the women's movement, concentrating on Britain in the 19th and 20th centuries. It has an institutional history as a coherent collection dating back to the mid-1920s, although its "core" collection dates from a library established by Ruth Cavendish Bentinck in 1909. Since 2013, the library has been in the custody of the London School of Economics and Political Science (LSE), which manages the collection as part of the British Library of Political and Economic Science in a dedicated area known as the Women's Library @ LSE."

In view of the nature of the collections the Women's Library under the custody of LSE, the copy on Tsai's thesis displayed in LSE Women's Library is unlikely the one submitted to the

如之前的通信所示，这是蔡博士的论文的传真副本，供有兴趣的人查看。在 1980 年代提交的副本无法被伦敦大学的总图书馆找到。

我们认为此事已经结束。问候，
Daniel O'Connor

_____

寄件者： ▓▓▓▓▓▓
日期： 2019 年 10 月 7 日 09：11
收件者： O'Connor, D D.O'Connor@lse.ac.uk
副本： Media.Relations Media.Relations@lse.ac.uk； Carter, HC H.C.Carter@lse.ac.uk
主旨： 回复：这有可能吗？关于不提交论文是否可能授予法学博士学位？

亲爱的 O'Connor 先生，

我写信是关于您在 9 月 16 日的回应中的以下声明：

... 供您参考，蔡英文博士最近向 LSE 图书馆提供了论文《不公平贸易和防卫机制》的传真副本。这可以在 LSE 图书馆阅览室根据要求查看。

由于您提到的 LSE 图书馆中存放蔡女士的论文副本不清楚，我做了一些研究，发现它存放在 LSE 妇女图书馆。

我还发现，尽管妇女图书馆已经在 LSE 的保管下，但它实际上不是一个正式的 LSE 图书馆，将存放 LSE 毕业生的论文。

供您参考，以下是从维基百科下载的 LSE 妇女图书馆的简短背景资讯：

"妇女图书馆 @ LSE 是英国关于妇女和妇女运动的主要图书馆和博物馆资源，专注于 19 和 20 世纪的英国。它有一个从 20 世纪中期开始的机构历史，尽管其'核心'收藏始于 Ruth Cavendish Bentinck 于 1909 年建立的图书馆。自 2013 年以来，该图书馆一直在伦敦政治经济学院的保管下，该学院将该收藏品管理为政治和经济科学的大英图书馆的一部分，称为妇女图书馆 @ LSE"。

Law Department for the doctoral degree. The copy looks more like a personal collection. In addition, there were no signatures of the internal and external examiners.

Thank you for your attention.

Sincerely,

▓▓▓▓▓

From: ▓▓▓▓▓
Sent: Saturday, September 28, 2019 19:35
To: O'Connor,D <D.O'Connor@lse.ac.uk>
Cc: Media.Relations <Media.Relations@lse.ac.uk>; h.c.carter@lse.ac.uk <h.c.carter@lse.ac.uk>
Subject: Re: Is it possible? To award a Ph.d. degree in Law without submission of the thesis?

Dear Mr. O'Connor,

Thank you for your reply dated 16/09 my captioned query.

Having read your response, I have further questions which I will list below:

1. Why is it that Mrs. Carter from the Law Department cannot respond to me directly since it is obviously her job to know about Tsai's thesis in the Law Department.

2. Why should you in the Media/Communication Division respond to inquiries about LES's theses when it should be the responsibility of the relevant department such as the Law Department to do so where the theses are handled?

3. When was the copy of Tsai's thesis submitted? If it were in 1984, why there was no record of such; if it were in 2019, why?

4. Did LES award Tsai's degree based on the thesis in LES's Wemen's Library? If that is the case, then a whole series of questions raised by both Professor Lin of North Carolina and Dr. Xu, a ph.d. from Oxford U., can be asked as to why can LES accept a thesis like this-- sloppy format including different layout of the lines, corrections by hand, missing pages, no signatures of the advisers, etc.?

5. How can a thesis be without a conclusion at the end while in each chapter there is? Was this the common practice among the LES thesis awardees back in 1984?

Thank you.

Sincerely,

▓▓▓▓▓

From: O'Connor,D <D.O'Connor@lse.ac.uk>
Sent: Monday, September 16, 2019 16:59
To: ▓▓▓▓▓
Cc: Media.Relations <Media.Relations@lse.ac.uk>

考虑到 LSE 保管下的妇女图书馆的收藏性质，LSE 妇女图书馆中展示的蔡的论文副本不太可能是提交给法律系以获得博士学位的那一份。这份副本看起来更像是个人收藏。此外，没有内部和外部审查人的签名。

谢谢您的关注。

诚挚地，

___

寄件者：

日期：2019 年 9 月 28 日 19：35

收件者：O'Connor，D D.O'Connor@lse.ac.uk

副本：Media.Relations Media.Relations@lse.ac.uk； h.c.carter@lse.ac.uk b.c.carter@lse.ac.uk

主旨：回复：这有可能吗？关于不提交论文是否可能授予法学博士学位？

亲爱的 O'Connor 先生，

感谢您在 16/09 回复我的查询。

阅读了您的回应后，我有以下几个进一步的问题：

为什么法律系的 Carter 女士不能直接回复我，因为她显然应该知道法律系蔡的论文。

为什么您在媒体／通讯部门应该回应有关 LES 论文的查询，而不是由相关部门如法律系这样做，因为论文是由他们处理的？

蔡的论文是何时提交的？如果是在 1984 年，为什么没有这样的记录；如果是在 2019 年，为什么？

LES 是否基于 LES 的妇女图书馆中的论文授予了蔡的学位？如果是这样，那么北卡罗来纳州的林教授和牛津大学的徐博士都可以问为什么 LES 可以接受这样的论文 - 格式混乱，包括行的不同排列，手工修正，缺少页面，没有教授的签名等？

一篇论文在每章都有结论，但最后却没有结论，这是 1984 年 LES 论文把关者的常见做法吗？

谢谢。诚挚地，

___

寄件者：O'Connor，D D.O'Connor@lse.ac.uk

日期：2019 年 9 月 16 日 16：59

收件者：

副本：Media.Relations Media.Relations@lse.ac.uk

Subject: RE: Is it possible? To award a Ph.d. degree in Law without submission of the thesis?

Dear ▓▓▓▓▓,

Thank you for your email to Ms Carter, I have been asked to respond.

As indicated to a number of enquirers, the London School of Economics and Political Science and the University of London can confirm categorically that Tsai Ing-Wen completed and submitted her thesis and was correctly awarded a PhD in Law in 1984.

For your information, Dr Tsai Ing-wen recently provided the LSE Library with a facsimile copy of the thesis, *Unfair trade practices and safeguard actions*. This is available to view in the LSE library reading room upon request.

Kind regards,

Daniel O'Connor

Daniel O'Connor
Head of Media Relations | Communications Division
The London School of Economics and Political Science
Houghton Street, London WC2A 2AE
t: +44 (0)20 7955 7417
e: oconnord@lse.ac.uk
lse.ac.uk

LSE is ranked #1 in Europe for social sciences
(QS World University Ranking 2019)

From: ▓▓▓▓▓
Sent: 14 September 2019 08:41
To: Carter, HC
Subject: Fwd: Is it possible? To award a Ph.d. degree in Law without submission of the thesis?

Dear Madam,

Following my previous email message to you (attached below), I also enclose my university email address for your reference.

▓▓▓▓▓▓▓▓▓▓▓▓▓

Thank you.

主旨： 回复：这有可能吗？关于不提交论文是否可能授予法学博士学位？
亲爱的 ▓▓▓▓▓▓▓▓▓▓

感谢您发给 Carter 女士的电子邮件，我被要求回应。

如之前对多位查询者所指出的，伦敦政治经济学院和伦敦大学可以明确地确认蔡英文完成并提交了她的论文，并在 1984 年正确地获得了法学博士学位。

供您参考，蔡英文博士最近向 LSE 图书馆提供了论文《不公平贸易和防卫机制》的传真副本。这可以在 LSE 图书馆阅览室根据要求查看。

诚挚的问候，
Daniel O'Connor

Daniel O'Connor
媒体关系主管 | 传播部门
伦敦政经学院
霍顿街，伦敦 WC2A 2AE
电话：+44（0）20 7955 7417
电子邮件：oconnord@lse.ac.uk
lse.ac.uk

LSE 在社会科学方面在欧洲排名第一
(QS 世界大学排名 2018)

寄件者： ▓▓▓▓▓▓▓▓▓▓
日期： 2019 年 9 月 14 日 08：41
收件者： Carter，HC
主旨： 回复：这有可能吗？关于不提交论文是否可能授予法学博士学位？

亲爱的女士，
根据我之前发给您的电子邮件消息，我也附上了我的大学电子邮件地址供您参考。

▓▓▓▓▓▓▓▓▓▓

谢谢。

Sincerely,

---------- Forwarded message ---------
寄件者:
Date: 2019年9月14日 週六 下午3:33
Subject: Is it possible? To award a Ph.d. degree in Law without submission of the thesis?
To: <h.c.carter@lse.ac.uk>

Dear Mrs. Carter,

Sorry to bother you about the captioned issue on the possibility of LSE Law Department awarding a ph.d. in law without submission of a ph.d. thesis.

My name is ▇▇▇▇▇▇▇▇▇▇▇▇▇▇▇▇▇▇▇▇▇▇▇▇▇ I am currently visiting my hometown in Taipei. As there will be a presidential election held in January 2020, potential voters are careful in examining the candidates. The issue on incumbent president Tsai Ing-wen who is seeking for a 2nd term in the coming election, is whether or not LSE law department awarded her a ph.d. degree in 1984, as she spent less than two years (1982-83) with LSE law department, and her ph.d. thesis was missing from the U of London library.

As this issue is in relation to a candidate's integrity, many of us, as valid voters, would like to seek clarification from your department on this issue.

The article attached below entitled "Tsai Ing-wen's missing thesis was not submitted says university library" raised questions on why the Law Department awarded Tsai a ph.d. degree in law without receiving her ph.d. thesis?

https://richardsonreports.wordpress.com/2019/07/04/tsai-ing-wens-missing-thesis-was-not-submitted-says-university-library/

As this issue has also become a most talk-about issues on local TV programs here in Taiwan.

Would be grateful if you could help resolve this puzzle.
Any exceptional case could happen?

Thank you very much for your time.

Sincerely yours,

诚挚地，

---------- 转发讯息----------
寄件者：
日期：2019年9月14日 周六 下午 3：33
主旨：回复：这有可能吗？关于不提交论文是否可能授予法学博士学位？
收件者： h.c.carter@lse.ac.uk

Cruier 女士，

很抱歉打扰您，关于 LSE 法律系是否可能在不提交博士论文的情况下授予法学博士学位的问题。

我是 ▮▮▮▮ 我最近正在故乡—台北探亲。由于 2020 年 1 月将举行总统选举，潜在的选民在审查候选人时都很小心。现任总统蔡英文在即将举行的选举中寻求第二个任期的问题是，LSE 法律系是否在 1984 年授予她博士学位，因为她在 LSE 法律系只待了不到两年（1982-83），而她的博士论文从伦敦大学图书馆中失踪了。

由于这个问题与候选人的诚信有关，我们许多合法的选民都希望从您的部门那里对此问题进行澄清。

以下附上的文章题为 "Tsai Ing-wen's missing thesis was not submitted says university library"，该文章质疑为什么法律系在没有收到蔡的博士论文的情况下授予她博士学位？

由于这个问题在台湾的当地电视节目中也成为了热门话题。

如果您能帮助解决这个谜题，我们将不胜感激。有没有可能发生任何特殊情况？

非常感谢您的时间。

诚挚地，

人类史上最大学位诈骗案 267

RE_-Is-it-possible_-To-award-a-Ph.d.-degree-in-1-1

From: Wilson,Clive
To: O'Connor,D
Subject: RE: Is it possible? To award a Ph.d. degree in Law without submission of the thesis?
Date: 07 October 2019 14:50:45
Attachments: image002.png
image003.png
image005.png

Hi Danny

All of our theses, together with all unique or rare items, are housed within our Archives and Special Collections and can only be viewed in the Women's Library Reading Room. We are very proud to have named the reading room for the amazing collections that form the Women's Library but many other collections are also only viewable in that reading room: pamphlets, archived newspapers, papers and letters from many politicians, academics and organisations, maps, our extensive microfilm and fiche collections, to name but a few.

Feel free to rewrite that as you think appropriate !

Clive

From: O'Connor,D
Sent: 07 October 2019 09:37
To: Wilson,Clive
Subject: FW: Is it possible? To award a Ph.d. degree in Law without submission of the thesis?

Hi Clive,

New conspiracy angle that it's housed in the Women's Library –.

I'm not sure if it's worth a response but do let me know if there is any particular angle you'd want to highlight.

Danny

From: ███████████████████████████████
Sent: 07 October 2019 09:11
To: O'Connor,D <D.O'Connor@lse.ac.uk>
Cc: Media.Relations <Media.Relations@lse.ac.uk>; Carter,HC <H.C.Carter@lse.ac.uk>
Subject: Re: Is it possible? To award a Ph.d. degree in Law without submission of the thesis?

Dear Mr. O'Connor,

I am writing in relation to the following statement of your response dated 16th of September:

... For your information, Dr Tsai Ing-wen recently provided the LSE Library with a facsimile copy

寄件者：Wilson，Clive
收件者：O"Connor，D
主旨：回复：是否可能在不提交论文的情况下授予法学博士学位？
日期：2019 年 10 月 7 日 14：50：45
附件：image002.png、image003.png、image005.png

嗨 Danny，

我们所有的论文，以及所有独特或稀有的物件，都存放在我们的档案和特藏中，只能在妇女图书馆阅览室中查看。我们非常自豪地为阅览室命名，这个由许多令人惊艳收藏品所组成的妇女图书馆，但还有许多其他的收藏也只能在该阅览室中查看：小册子、存档的报纸、许多政治家、学者和组织的文件和信件、地图、我们广泛的微缩影片和胶片收藏，仅列举几例。

请随意按照您认为合适的方式重写！

Clive

寄件者：O'Connor，D
日期：2019 年 10 月 7 日 09：37
收件者：Wilson，Clive
主旨：转发：是否可能在不提交论文的情况下授予法学博士学位？

嗨 Clive，

新的阴谋角度是它被存放在女性图书馆。

我不确定是否值得回应，但如果有任何特定的角度您想要强调，请告诉我。

Danny

寄件者：████████
日期：2019 年 10 月 7 日 09：11
收件者：O'Connor，D D.O'Connor@lse.ac.uk
副本：Media.Relations Media.Relations@lse.ac.uk； Carter，HC H.C.Carter@lse.ac.uk
主旨：回复：是否可能在不提交论文的情况下授予法学博士学位？

尊敬的 O'Connor 先生，

我写这封信是关于您在 9 月 16 日的回应中的以下声明：

... 供您参考，蔡英文博士最近向 LSE 图书馆提供论文《不公平贸易和防卫机制》的传真副本。这可以在 LSE 图书馆阅览室根据要求查看。

of the thesis, *Unfair trade practices and safeguard actions*. This is available to view in the LSE library reading room upon request.

Since it is not clear which LSE library you referred to that housed Ms. Tsai's thesis copy., I did some research and found it is housed at the LSE Women's Library.

I also found that Women's Library has been in the custody of the LSE, it is in fact not a formal LSE library that will house theses of LSE graduates.

For your information, below is a brief background information on the LSE Women's Library which was downloaded from Wikipedia:

" The **Women's Library @ LSE** is England's main library and museum resource on women and the women's movement, concentrating on Britain in the 19th and 20th centuries. It has an institutional history as a coherent collection dating back to the mid-1920s, although its "core" collection dates from a library established by Ruth Cavendish Bentinck in 1909. Since 2013, the library has been in the custody of the London School of Economics and Political Science (LSE), which manages the collection as part of the British Library of Political and Economic Science in a dedicated area known as the Women's Library @ LSE."

In view of the nature of the collections the Women's Library under the custody of LSE, the copy on Tsai's thesis displayed in LSE Women's Library is unlikely the one submitted to the Law Department for the doctoral degree. The copy looks more like a personal collection. In addition, there were no signatures of the internal and external examiners.

Thank you for your attention.

Sincerely,

████████

From: ████████
Sent: Saturday, September 28, 2019 19:35
To: O'Connor,D <D.O'Connor@lse.ac.uk>
Cc: Media.Relations <Media.Relations@lse.ac.uk>; h.c.carter@lse.ac.uk <h.c.carter@lse.ac.uk>
Subject: Re: Is it possible? To award a Ph.d. degree in Law without submission of the thesis?

Dear Mr. O'Connor,

Thank you for your reply dated 16/09 my captioned query.

Having read your response, I have further questions which I will list below:

1. Why is it that Mrs. Carter from the Law Department cannot respond to me directly since it is obviously her job to know about Tsai's thesis in the Law Department.

由于您提到的 LSE 图书馆中存放蔡女士的论文副本的具体位置不清楚，我进行了一些研究，发现它被存放在 LSE 女性图书馆。

我还发现，尽管女性图书馆一直在 LSE 的监管下，但它实际上不是一个正式的 LSE 图书馆，会存放 LSE 毕业生的论文。

供您参考，以下是从 Wikipedia 下载的有关 LSE 女性图书馆的简短背景资讯：

"妇女图书馆 @LSE 是英格兰主要的关于女性和女性运动的图书馆和博物馆资源，主要集中在 19 和 20 世纪的英国。它从 20 世纪中期开始就有一个作为一个连贯收藏的机构历史，尽管它的 " 核心 " 收藏来自 Ruth Cavendish Bentinck 于 1909 年建立的图书馆。自 2013 年以来，该图书馆一直在伦敦政经学院的监管下，该学院将该收藏作为政治和经济科学的英国图书馆的一部分，在一个称为女性图书馆 @LSE 的专用区域中管理"。

考虑到 LSE 监管下的女性图书馆的收藏性质，展示在 LSE 女性图书馆中的蔡的论文副本不太可能是提交给法律系用于博士学位的。该副本更像是个人收藏。此外，内部和外部审查人的签名都没有。

感谢您的关注。

诚挚地，

_____

寄件者：

日期：2019 年 9 月 28 日 19：35

收件者：O'Connor, D D.O'Connor@lse.ac.uk

副本：Media.Relations Media.Relations@lse.ac.uk； h.c.carter@lse.ac.uk h.c.carter@lse.ac.uk

主旨：回复：是否可能在不提交论文的情况下授予法学博士学位？

尊敬的 O'Connor 先生，

感谢您在 9 月 16 日对我的查询的回复。

阅读了您的回应后，我有以下几个进一步的问题：

1. 为什么 Carter 女士从法律系不能直接回复我，因为她显然应该知道蔡英文在法律系的论文。

2. Why should you in the Media/Communication Division respond to inquiries about LES's theses when it should be the responsibility of the relevant department such as the Law Department to do so where the theses are handled?

3. When was the copy of Tsai's thesis submitted? If it were in 1984, why there was no record of such; if it were in 2019, why?

4. Did LES award Tsai's degree based on the thesis in LES's Wemen's Library? If that is the case, then a whole series of questions raised by both Professor Lin of North Carolina and Dr. Xu, a ph.d. from Oxford U., can be asked as to why can LES accept a thesis like this-- sloppy format including different layout of the lines, corrections by hand, missing pages, no signatures of the advisers, etc.?

5. How can a thesis be without a conclusion at the end while in each chapter there is? Was this the common practice among the LES thesis awardees back in 1984?

Thank you.

Sincerely,

████████

From: O'Connor,D <D.O'Connor@lse.ac.uk>
Sent: Monday, September 16, 2019 16:59
To: ████████████████████████
Cc: Media.Relations <Media.Relations@lse.ac.uk>
Subject: RE: Is it possible? To award a Ph.d. degree in Law without submission of the thesis?

Dear ████████,

Thank you for your email to Ms Carter, I have been asked to respond.

As indicated to a number of enquirers, the London School of Economics and Political Science and the University of London can confirm categorically that Tsai Ing-Wen completed and submitted her thesis and was correctly awarded a PhD in Law in 1984.

For your information, Dr Tsai Ing-wen recently provided the LSE Library with a facsimile copy of the thesis, *Unfair trade practices and safeguard actions*. This is available to view in the LSE library reading room upon request.

Kind regards,

Daniel O'Connor

Daniel O'Connor
Head of Media Relations | Communications Division
The London School of Economics and Political Science
Houghton Street, London WC2A 2AE
t: +44 (0)20 7955 7417
e: oconnord@lse.ac.uk
lse.ac.uk

1. 为什么您在媒体／通讯部门应该回应有关 LES 论文的查询，而这应该是相关部门如法律系的责任，因为论文是在那里处理的？

2. 蔡的论文副本是何时提交的？如果是在 1984 年，为什么没有这样的记录；如果是在 2019 年，为什么？

3. LES 是否基于 LES 妇女图书馆中的论文授予蔡的学位？如果是这样，那么北卡罗来纳州的林教授和牛津大学的徐博士都可以提出一系列问题，为什么 LES 可以接受这样的论文——格式混乱，包括行的不同布局、手工修正、缺少页面、没有顾问的签名等？

4. 一篇论文在每一章都有结论，但最后却没有结论，这是 1984 年 LES 论文获得者的常见做法吗？

谢谢。

诚挚地，

███

寄件者： O'Connor，D D.O'Connor@lse.ac.uk
日期： 2019 年 9 月 16 日 16：59
收件人：
副本： Media.Relations Media.Relations@lse.ac.uk
主旨： 回复：是否可能在不提交论文的情况下授予法学博士学位？

亲爱的，

感谢您发给 Carter 女士的电子邮件，我已被要求回复。

如之前对多位查询者所指出的，伦敦政治经济学院和伦敦大学可以明确地确认蔡英文完成并提交了她的论文，并在 1984 年正确地获得了法学博士学位。

供您参考，蔡英文博士最近向 LSE 图书馆提供了论文《不公平贸易和防卫机制》的传真副本。这可以在 LSE 图书馆阅览室根据要求查看。

诚挚的问候，

Daniel O'Connor

Daniel O'Connor

媒体关系部主管 | 通讯部门

伦敦政经学院 Houghton Street，London WC2A 2AE

电话：+44（0）20 7955 7417

电子邮件：oconnord@lse.ac.uk

网站：lse.ac.uk

LSE is ranked #1 in Europe for social sciences (QS World University Ranking 2019)

From: ▬
Sent: 14 September 2019 08:41
To: Carter,HC
Subject: Fwd: Is it possible? To award a Ph.d. degree in Law without submission of the thesis?

Dear Madam,

Following my previous email message to you (attached below), I also enclose my university email address for your reference.

▬

Thank you.

Sincerely,

▬

---------- Forwarded message ----------
寄件者: ▬
Date: 2019年9月14日 週六 下午3:33
Subject: Is it possible? To award a Ph.d. degree in Law without submission of the thesis?
To: <h.c.carter@lse.ac.uk>

Dear Mrs. Carter,

Sorry to bother you about the captioned issue on the possibility of LSE Law Department awarding a ph.d. in law without submission of a ph.d. thesis.

My name is ▬ ▬. I am currently visiting my hometown in Taipei. As there will be a presidential election held in January 2020, potential voters are careful in examining the candidates. The issue on incumbent president Tsai Ing-wen who is seeking for a 2nd term in the coming election, is whether or not LSE law department awarded her a ph.d. degree in 1984, as she spent less than two years (1982-83) with LSE law department, and her ph.d. thesis was missing from the U of London library.

As this issue is in relation to a candidate's integrity, many of us, as valid voters, would like

LSE 在社会科学领域中被评为欧洲第一

（QS 世界大学排名 2019）

寄件者：

日期：

收件者： Carter，HC

主旨： 转发：是否可能在不提交论文的情况下授予法学博士学位？

女士，

根据我之前发给您的电子邮件消息，我也附上了我的大学电子邮件地址供您参考。

谢谢。

诚挚地，

---------- 转发讯息 ----------

寄件者：

日期： 2019 年 9 月 14 日 周六 下午 3：33

主旨： 回复：这有可能吗？关于不提交论文是否可能授予法学博士学位？

收件者： h.c.carter@lse.ac.uk

Cruier 女士，

很抱歉打扰您，关于 LSE 法律系是否可能在不提交博士论文的情况下授予法学博士学位的问题。

我是　　　　　我最近正在故乡—台北探亲。由于 2020 年 1 月将举行总统选举，潜在的选民在审查候选人时都很小心。现任总统蔡英文在即将举行的选举中寻求第二个任期的问题是，LSE 法律系是否在 1984 年授予她博士学位，因为她在 LSE 法律系只待了不到两年（1982-83），而她的博士论文从伦敦大学图书馆中失踪了。

to seek clarification from your department on this issue.

The article attached below entitled "Tsai Ing-wen's missing thesis was not submitted says university library" raised questions on why the Law Department awarded Tsai a ph.d. degree in law without receiving her ph.d. thesis?

https://richardsonreports.wordpress.com/2019/07/04/tsai-ing-wens-missing-thesis-was-not-submitted-says-university-library/

As this issue has also become a most talk-about issues on local TV programs here in Taiwan.

Would be grateful if you could help resolve this puzzle.
Any exceptional case could happen?

Thank you very much for your time.

Sincerely yours,

由于这个问题与候选人的诚信有关，我们许多合法的选民都希望从您的部门那里对此问题进行澄清。

以下附上的文章题为 "Tsai Ing-wen's missing thesis was not submitted says university library"，该文章质疑为什么法律系在没有收到蔡的博士论文的情况下授予她博士学位？

https://richardsonreports.wordpress.com/2019/07/04/tsai-ing-wens-missing-thesis-was-not-submitted-says-university-library/

由于这个问题在台湾的当地电视节目中也成为了热门话题。

如果您能帮助解决这个谜题，我们将不胜感激。有没有可能发生任何特殊情况？

非常感谢您的时间。

诚挚地，

…

RE_ Report on President Tsai degree

From: Haynes,KJ
To: Thomson,MT
Subject: RE: Report on President Tsai degree
Date: 01 October 2019 14:55:10

From: Thomson,MT
Sent: 01 October 2019 14:53
To: Haynes,KJ <K.J.Haynes@lse.ac.uk>
Subject: RE: Report on President Tsai degree

From: Haynes,KJ
Sent: 01 October 2019 14:52
To: O'Connor,D <D.O'Connor@lse.ac.uk>; Phdacademy <Phdacademy@lse.ac.uk>; Wilson,Clive <CLIVE.Wilson@lse.ac.uk>
Cc: Metcalfe,F <F.Metcalfe@lse.ac.uk>; Thomson,MT <M.T.Thomson@lse.ac.uk>; Withers,IF <I.F.Withers@lse.ac.uk>
Subject: RE: Report on President Tsai degree

HI

Sorry, this has been a spectator sport for me. I'd also let nature run its course if the thesis is now available online.

Best wishes, Kevin

LSE Legal Team
Secretary's Division
Room 3.01, 1 Kingsway
London School of Economics and Political Science
Houghton Street
London
WC2A 2AE

020 7955 7823

From: O'Connor,D
Sent: 01 October 2019 14:06
To: Phdacademy <Phdacademy@lse.ac.uk>; Wilson,Clive <CLIVE.Wilson@lse.ac.uk>
Cc: Metcalfe,F <F.Metcalfe@lse.ac.uk>; Haynes,KJ <K.J.Haynes@lse.ac.uk>; Thomson,MT <M.T.Thomson@lse.ac.uk>; Withers,IF <I.F.Withers@lse.ac.uk>
Subject: RE: Report on President Tsai degree

Thanks Marcus.

I realise the thesis is now available to view online via Taiwan's National Central Library, so hopefully this will reduce some of the nonsense.

Danny

寄件者： Haynes, KJ

收件者： Thomson, MT

主旨： 回复：关于蔡英文总统的学位报告　**日期：** 2019 年 10 月 1 日 14：55：10

寄件者： Thomson, MT　**日期：** 2019 年 10 月 1 日 14：53

收件者： Haynes, KJ K.J.Haynes@lse.ac.uk

主旨： 回复：关于蔡英文总统的学位报告

寄件者： Haynes, KJ　**日期：** 2019 年 10 月 1 日 14：52

收件者： O'Connor, D D.O'Connor@lse.ac.uk； Phdacademy Phdacademy@lse.ac.uk； Wilson, Clive CLIVE.Wilson@lse.ac.uk

副本： Metcalfe, F F.Metcalfe@lse.ac.uk； Thomson, MT M.T.Thomson@lse.ac.uk； Withers, IF I.F.Withers@lse.ac.uk

主旨： 回复：关于蔡英文总统的学位报告

嗨，

很抱歉，这对我来说只是一场旁观的运动。如果论文现在可以在线上查看，我也会让事情自然发展。

祝好，Kevin

LSE 法律团队

秘书部门

Room 3.01， 1 Kingsway

伦敦政经学院

Houghton Street

London WC2A 2AE

020 7955 7823

寄件者： O'Connor, D　**日期：** 2019 年 10 月 1 日 14：06

收件者： Phdacademy Phdacademy@lse.ac.uk； Wilson, Clive CLIVE.Wilson@lse.ac.uk

副本： Metcalfe, F F.Metcalfe@lse.ac.uk； Haynes, KJ K.J.Haynes@lse.ac.uk； Thomson, MT M.T.Thomson@lse.ac.uk； Withers, IF I.F.Withers@lse.ac.uk

主旨： 回复：关于蔡英文总统的学位报告

感谢 Marcus。

我意识到论文现在可以通过台湾的国家中央图书馆在线上查看，所以希望这将减少一些胡闹的事情。 Danny

From: LSE PhD Academy [mailto:phdacademy@lse.ac.uk]
Sent: 01 October 2019 13:43
To: Wilson,Clive <CLIVE.Wilson@lse.ac.uk>
Cc: Metcalfe,F <F.Metcalfe@lse.ac.uk>; O'Connor,D <D.O'Connor@lse.ac.uk>; Haynes,KJ <K.J.Haynes@lse.ac.uk>; Thomson,MT <M.T.Thomson@lse.ac.uk>; Withers,IF <I.F.Withers@lse.ac.uk>
Subject: RE: Report on President Tsai degree

Thanks Danny,

I have read it and it doesn't raise anything new in terms of issues relating to the School, University, IALTS etc. to which we have already responded. However, the addition of personal accusations of lying against identified individuals is something we haven't responded to and we should keep an eye on this to make sure that these are addressed if necessary.

Marcus

Marcus Cerny
PhD Academy Deputy Director
The London School of Economics and Political Science
Houghton Street, London WC2A 2AE
t: +44 (0)20 7955 6766
e: m.w.cerny@lse.ac.uk
lse.ac.uk/phdacademy

If you are a current PhD student please remember to send your queries through the PhD Academy Enquiry Form. All other enquirers should contact phdacademy@lse.ac.uk

--------------- Original Message ---------------
From: Wilson,Clive [clive.wilson@lse.ac.uk]
Sent: 01/10/2019 12:26
To: m.t.thomson@lse.ac.uk; phdacademy@lse.ac.uk; d.o'connor@lse.ac.uk; k.j.haynes@lse.ac.uk
Cc: f.metcalfe@lse.ac.uk; i.f.withers@lse.ac.uk
Subject: RE: Report on President Tsai degree

One hopes his own doctoral research was of a higher standard than this report ...
Clive

From: O'Connor,D
Sent: 01 October 2019 12:24
To: Phdacademy; Thomson,MT; Haynes,KJ
Cc: Metcalfe,F; Wilson,Clive; Withers,IF
Subject: RE: Report on President Tsai degree

Just to add, this was shared by a contact in the Taiwanese Govt who has been in touch with Clive.

Regards,

寄件者：LSE PhD Academy [mailto：phdacademy@lse.ac.uk]

日期：2019 年 10 月 1 日 13：43　收件者：Wilson，Clive CLIVE.Wilson@lse.ac.uk

副本：Metcalfe，F F.Metcalfe@lse.ac.uk；O'Connor，D D.O'Connor@lse.ac.uk；Haynes，KJ K.J.Haynes@lse.ac.uk；Thomson，MT M.T.Thomson@lse.ac.uk；Withers，IF I.F.Withers@lse.ac.uk

主旨：回复：关于蔡英文总统的学位报告

感谢 Danny，

我已经阅读了它，并且它没有提出任何新的问题，这些问题与学校、大学、IALS 等有关，我们已经回应了。但是，增加对可识别的个人进行撒谎的指控是我们尚未回应的，我们应该密切关注这一点，以确保必要时解决这些问题。

Marcus

Marcus Cerny

博士生学院副主任

伦敦政经学院

Houghton Street，London WC2A 2AE

电话：+44（0）20 7955 6766

电子邮件：m.w.cerny@lse.ac.uk

网站：lse.ac.uk/phdacademy

如果您是现任博士生，请记住通过 PhD 学院查询表格发送您的查询。所有其他查询者应联系 phdacademy@lse.ac.uk。

------------- 原始消息 -------------

寄件者：Wilson，Clive [clive.wilson@lse.ac.uk]　日期：2019 年 10 月 1 日 12：26

收件者：m.t.thomson@lse.ac.uk；phdacademy@lse.ac.uk；d.o'connor@lse.ac.uk；k.j.haynes@lse.ac.uk

副本：f.metcalfe@lse.ac.uk；i.f.withers@lse.ac.uk

主旨：回复：关于蔡英文总统的学位报告

希望他自己的博士研究比这份报告的水平更高 …

Clive

寄件者：O'Connor，D　日期：2019 年 10 月 1 日 12：24

收件者：Phdacademy；Thomson，MT；Haynes，KJ

副本：Metcalfe，F；Wilson，Clive；Withers，IF

主旨：关于蔡英文总统的学位报告

只是补充一下，这是由一位与 Clive 有联系的台湾政府的联络人分享的。

问候，

Danny

From: O'Connor,D
Sent: 01 October 2019 12:23
To: Phdacademy <Phdacademy@lse.ac.uk>; Thomson,MT <M.T.Thomson@lse.ac.uk>; Haynes,KJ <K.J.Haynes@lse.ac.uk>
Cc: Metcalfe,F <F.Metcalfe@lse.ac.uk>; Wilson,Clive <CLIVE.Wilson@lse.ac.uk>; Withers,IF <I.F.Withers@lse.ac.uk> <I.F.Withers@lse.ac.uk>
Subject: Report on President Tsai degree

Dear colleagues,

For information, please see attached an English translation of the report by ▓▓▓▓▓ against Tsai and LSE, claiming LSE is illegally covering up for President Tsai regarding the PhD matter

I haven't read it fully - It is long, rambling, incoherent and moves from Gaddafi to accusations against Fang-long and to repeated accusations that I am "lying", among other things.

(Page 40) "This public relations head Mr. D.O. stated: the 'records' of both the LSE and the University of London confirm that Tsai Ing-Wen received a Ph.D. in Law in 1984, and the student record shows Tsai had submitted the dissertation. Obviously this public relations head is lying!"

(p 42) "This investigation's search results proves that the LSE Research Support Services' library assistant Ms. R.O. was correct, and that LSE public relations head Mr. D.O. was clearly attempting to lie and cover up for Tsai Ing-Wen."

Plus (p43, p 44)

As frustrating as this is, I am not sure it'll do much good to start issuing detailed denials, or to engage with ▓▓▓▓. He seemed to be a somewhat vindictive individual throughout the process.

(Kevin FYI - you probably haven't seen much of this but there is a conspiracy theory going round parts of Taiwan that the President never got her PhD from LSE).

Kind regards,

Danny

From: Wilson,Clive
Sent: 01 October 2019 09:44
To: O'Connor,D <D.O'Connor@lse.ac.uk>
Subject: FW: English version of Lin's report

Hi Danny

FYI. I haven't read it yet, won't have time until later, but if you think anyone else needs to see it please do pass it on.

I'm sure it will just make me cross!!

Clive

Danny

寄件者：O'Connor, D
日期：2019 年 10 月 1 日 12：23
收件者：Phdacademy Phdacademy@lse.ac.uk; Thomson, MT M.T.Thomson@lse.ac.uk; Haynes, KJ K.J.Haynes@lse.ac.uk
副本：Metcalfe, F F.Metcalfe@lse.ac.uk; Wilson, Clive CLIVE.Wilson@lse.ac.uk; Withers, IF I.F.Withers@lse.ac.uk
主旨：关于蔡英文总统的学位报告

亲爱的同事，

供您参考，请参见附件中的报告的英文翻译，该报告由 ▇▇▇ 针对蔡英文和 LSE 提出，声称 LSE 非法为蔡英文博士事宜掩盖。

我还没有完全阅读它 - 它很长，杂乱，不连贯，从格达费到对施芳珑的指控，再到反复指控我"撒谎"等等。

（第 40 页）"这位公关主管 D.O. 先生表示：LSE 和伦敦大学的'记录'确认蔡英文于 1984 年获得法学博士学位，学生记录显示蔡已提交论文。很明显，这位公关主管在撒谎！"

（第 42 页）"这次调查的搜索结果证明，LSE 研究支持服务的图书馆助理 R.O. 女士是正确的，LSE 公关主管 D.O. 先生明显试图为蔡英文撒谎和掩盖。"

加上（第 43 页，第 44 页）

尽管这很令人沮丧，但我不确定开始发布详细的否认或与 ▇▇▇ 互动会有多大好处。在整个过程中，他似乎是一个有些报复性的人。

（Kevin FYI - 你可能还没有看到这个，但台湾的某些部分有一个阴谋论，认为总统从未从 LSE 获得博士学位）。

祝好，
Danny

寄件者：Wilson, Clive
日期：2019 年 10 月 1 日 09：44
收件者：O'Connor, D D.O'Connor@lse.ac.uk
主旨：转发：林的报告的英文版本

嗨，Danny

供您参考。我还没有阅读它，直到晚些时候我都没有时间，但如果你认为其他人需要看到它，请转发给他们。

我确信这只会让我生气！

Clive

From: █████████
Sent: 01 October 2019 09:24
To: Wilson,Clive
Subject: English version of Lin's report

Hi Clive,

I would like to share the English version of ███ report with you. ███ accusation of LSE begins from page 26, which I believe is quite ridiculous.
Please let me know what you have in mind about this.

Many thanks,
███

ref:_00D58JYzR._5004Itwd3V:ref

寄件者： ▇▇▇▇▇

日期： 2019 年 10 月 1 日 09：24

收件者： Wilson，Clive

主旨： 林的报告的英文版本

嗨，Clive，

我想与您分享 ▇▇▇▇ 报告的英文版本。从第 26 页开始是对 LSE 的 ▇▇▇▇ 指控，我相信这是相当荒谬的。

请告诉我您对此有什么看法。

非常感谢，

▇▇▇▇▇

---

ref：_00D58JYzR._5004Itwd3V：ref

RE_ Report on President Tsai degree（2）

To: Phdacademy; Thomson,MT; Haynes,KJ
Cc: Metcalfe,F; Wilson,Clive; Withers,IF
Subject: RE: Report on President Tsai degree
Date: 01 October 2019 13:41:46

Hi all,

Further to this, a few more relevant points.

Tsai Ing-wen's thesis is now available to download from the Taiwanese National Central library.

████████ report is from the end of August…so has moved on somewhat now.

This makes me think any

From: O'Connor,D
Sent: 01 October 2019 12:24
To: Phdacademy <Phdacademy@lse.ac.uk>; Thomson,MT <M.T.Thomson@lse.ac.uk>; Haynes,KJ <K.J.Haynes@lse.ac.uk>
Cc: Metcalfe,F <F.Metcalfe@lse.ac.uk>; Wilson,Clive <CLIVE.Wilson@lse.ac.uk>; Withers,IF (I.F.Withers@lse.ac.uk) <I.F.Withers@lse.ac.uk>
Subject: RE: Report on President Tsai degree

Just to add, this was shared by a contact in the Taiwanese Govt who has been in touch with Clive.

Regards,
Danny

From: O'Connor,D
Sent: 01 October 2019 12:23
To: Phdacademy <Phdacademy@lse.ac.uk>; Thomson,MT <M.T.Thomson@lse.ac.uk>; Haynes,KJ <K.J.Haynes@lse.ac.uk>
Cc: Metcalfe,F <F.Metcalfe@lse.ac.uk>; Wilson,Clive <CLIVE.Wilson@lse.ac.uk>; Withers,IF (I.F.Withers@lse.ac.uk) <I.F.Withers@lse.ac.uk>
Subject: Report on President Tsai degree

Dear colleagues,

For information, please see attached an English translation of the report by ████████ against Tsai and LSE, claiming LSE is illegally covering up for President Tsai regarding the PhD matter

I haven't read it fully - it is long, rambling, incoherent and moves from Gaddafi to accusations against Fang-long and to repeated accusations that I am "lying", among other things.

(Page 40) "This public relations head Mr. D.O. stated: the 'records' of both the LSE and the University of London confirm that Tsai Ing-Wen received a Ph.D. in Law in 1984, and the student

收件者：Phdacademy； Thomson，MT； Haynes，KJ
副本：Metcalfe，F； Wilson，Clive； Withers，IF
主旨：回复：关于蔡英文总统的学位报告
日期：2019 年 10 月 1 日 13：41：46

大家好，

关于这点，还有一些更相关的要点。

蔡英文的论文现在可以从台湾国家中央图书馆下载 ▇▇▇ 报告是从八月底的...所以现在有些进展。

这让我想到任何 ...

寄件者：O'Connor，D
日期：2019 年 10 月 1 日 12：24
收件者：Phdacademy； Thomson，MT； Haynes，KJ
副本：Metcalfe，F； Wilson，Clive； Withers，IF
主旨：回复：关于蔡英文总统的学位报告

只是补充一下，这是由一位与 Clive 有联系的台湾政府的联络人分享的。

问候，

Danny

寄件者：O'Connor， D
日期：2019 年 10 月 1 日 12：23
收件者：Phdacademy Phdacademy@lse.ac.uk； Thomson， MT M.T.Thomson@lse.ac.uk； Haynes， KJ K.J.Haynes@lse.ac.uk
副本：Metcalfe， F F.Metcalfe@lse.ac.uk； Wilson， Clive CLIVE.Wilson@lse.ac.uk； Withers， IF I.F.Withers@lse.ac.uk
主旨：关于蔡英文总统的学位报告

亲爱的同事，

供您参考，请参见附件中的报告的英文翻译，该报告由 ▇▇▇ 针对蔡英文和 LSE 提出，声称 LSE 非法为蔡英文博士事宜掩盖。

我还没有完全阅读它 - 它很长，杂乱，不连贯，从格达费到对施芳珑的指控，再到反复指控我"撒谎"等等。

（第 40 页）"这位公关主管 D.O. 先生表示：LSE 和伦敦大学的'记录'确认蔡英文于 1984 年获得法学博士学位，学生记录显示蔡已提交论文。很明显，这位公关主管在撒谎！"

record shows Tsai had submitted the dissertation. Obviously this public relations head is lying!"

(p 42) "This investigation's search results proves that the LSE Research Support Services' library assistant Ms. R.O. was correct, and that LSE public relations head Mr. D.O. was clearly attempting to lie and cover up for Tsai Ing-Wen."

Plus (p43, p 44)

As frustrating as this is, I am not sure it'll do much good to start issuing detailed denials, or to engage with ▓▓▓. He seemed to be a somewhat vindictive individual throughout the process.

(Kevin FYI - you probably haven't seen much of this but there is a conspiracy theory going round parts of Taiwan that the President never got her PhD from LSE).

Kind regards,

Danny

From: Wilson,Clive
Sent: 01 October 2019 09:44
To: O'Connor,D <D.O'Connor@lse.ac.uk>
Subject: FW: English version of Lin's report

Hi Danny

FYI. I haven't read it yet, won't have time until later, but if you think anyone else needs to see it please do pass it on.

I'm sure it will just make me cross!!

Clive

From: ▓▓▓
Sent: 01 October 2019 09:24
To: Wilson,Clive
Subject: English version of Lin's report

Hi Clive,

I would like to share the English version of ▓▓▓ report with you. ▓▓▓ accusation of LSE begins from page 26, which I believe is quite ridiculous.
Please let me know what you have in mind about this.

Many thanks,

▓▓▓

（第42页）"这次调查的搜索结果证明，LSE研究支持服务的图书馆助理R.O.女士是正确的，LSE公关主管D.O.先生明显试图为蔡英文撒谎和掩盖。"

加上（第43页，第44页）

尽管这很令人沮丧，但我不确定开始发布详细的否认或与 ▇▇▇▇ 互动会有多大好处。在整个过程中，他似乎是一个有些报复性的人。

（Kevin FYI - 你可能还没有看到这个，但台湾的某些部分有一个阴谋论，认为总统从未从LSE获得博士学位）。

祝好，
Danny

寄件者：Wilson, Clive
日期：2019年10月1日 09：44
收件者：O'Connor, D D.O'Connor@lse.ac.uk
主旨：转发：林的报告的英文版本

嗨，Danny

供您参考。我还没有阅读它，直到晚些时候我都没有时间，但如果你认为其他人需要看到它，请转发给他们。

我确信这只会让我生气！
Clive

寄件▇▇▇▇
日期：2019年10月1日 09：24
收件者：Wilson, Clive
主旨：林的报告的英文版本

嗨，Clive，

我想与您分享 ▇▇▇▇ 报告的英文版本。从第26页开始是对LSE的 ▇▇▇▇ 指控，我相信这是相当荒谬的。

请告诉我您对此有什么看法。

非常感谢，
▇▇▇▇

LSE面对质疑的策略：都是假帐号攻击！

LSE 面对质疑的策略：都是假帐号攻击！

LSE 媒体关系部门负责人 Daniel O'Connor 面对外界有关口试的询问信，他决定将这封信转交给 FOIA 与 LSE 资讯暨纪录经理 Rachael Maguire，希望能够拒绝回答。

就在此时，另一封信进入了他的电子邮箱。这是一封来自某人的信，希望 LSE 的声明也能透过伦敦大学的高等研究学院（School of Advanced Study）的网站发送。O'Connor 认为这是一个很好的机会，可以让 LSE 的立场得到更多的支持。

但是，事情并没有那么简单。O'Connor 在与一位神秘人物会面后，决定对声明进行修改。他担心声明太过"流传"，可能会引起更大的争议。于是，他决定与 Wilson 合作，帮助总统府偷渡论文。

但是，谎言总是需要更多的谎言来圆。当声明提到伦敦大学有收录蔡英文的论文时，外界开始质疑其当时收录的编号。总统府的代表施芳珑更是毫不客气的希望 LSE 能够协助"新增"编号，以平息外界的质疑。

LSE 的法律部门则提出希望声明能提供更多的连结，让 LSE 的态度更加坚定。但 O'Connor 坚决反对。他认为，这只会让事情变得更加复杂。

此时，台湾的律师童文熏加入指控蔡英文的论文自我抄袭 1983 年的中文期刊，并表示她的纽约律师资格已被停权。LSE 的高层对此笑称，申诉者只是故意留下激怒他人言论的人。

面对外界的一再质疑，LSE 决定用一份声明来应对。他们的口气相当冷硬，甚至开始指控外界使用假帐号来攻击他们。他们决定使用《资讯自由法》来处理这些问题。

在发布声明之前，LSE 决定先告知施芳珑。他们希望能够得到她的支持。

而对于彭文正教授誓言提告的反应，LSE 则选择保持沉默。他们知道，这场学术风暴还远远没有结束。

RE_ Request for information (4)

From: Donnelly,S
To: O"Connor,D; Maguire,RE
Subject: RE: Request for Information
Date: 03 October 2019 10:25:46
Attachments: image002.png
image003.png
image005.png
image006.png

I'll check the file later today and see what information we actually have – as this is a University of London degree.

Sue

Sue Donnelly
LSE Archivist | Secretary's Division
The London School of Economics and Political Science
Houghton Street, London WC2A 2AE
t: +44 (0)20 3486 2840
e: s.donnelly@lse.ac.uk
lse.ac.uk

LSE is ranked #1 in Europe for social sciences
(QS World University Ranking 2018)

From: O'Connor,D
Sent: 03 October 2019 10:14
To: Maguire,RE <R.E.Maguire@lse.ac.uk>; Donnelly,S <S.Donnelly@lse.ac.uk>
Subject: RE: Request for information

Thanks Rachael.

I am minded to say that a lot of this information is restricted under Data protection...but – as you suggest - it may be that Tsai herself wants the information to come out.

Danny

From: Maguire,RE
Sent: 03 October 2019 10:05
To: Donnelly,S <S.Donnelly@lse.ac.uk>
Cc: O'Connor,D <D.O'Connor@lse.ac.uk>
Subject: RE: Request for information

Hello Sue,

My comments are below.

寄件者：O"Connor，D； Maguire，RE
主旨：回复：资讯请求
日期：2019 年 10 月 3 日 10：25：46

我稍后会检查档案，看看我们实际上有什么资讯 - 因为这是伦敦大学的学位。

Sue

Sue Donnelly

LSE 档案管理员 | 秘书部门

伦敦政经学院

Houghton 街， 伦敦 WC2A 2AE

电话： +44（0）20 3486 2840

电邮： s.donnelly@lse.ac.uk

网站： lse.ac.uk

LSE 在社会科学方面在欧洲排名第一
（QS 世界大学排名 2018）

寄件者：O'Connor，D
日期：2019 年 10 月 3 日 10：14
收件者：Maguire，RE； Donnelly，S
主旨：回复：资讯请求

感谢 Rachael。

我倾向于说，许多这些资讯受到资料保护的限制 ... 但是 - 正如你所建议的 - 蔡英文本人可能希望这些资讯被公开。

Danny

寄件者：Maguire，RE
日期：2019 年 10 月 3 日 10：05
收件者：Donnelly，S
副本：O'Connor，D
主旨：回复：资讯请求

你好 Sue，

我的评论如下。

Rachael

From: Donnelly,S
Sent: 03 October 2019 09:55
To: Maguire,RE <R.E.Maguire@lse.ac.uk>
Subject: FW: Request for information

From: O'Connor,D
Sent: 03 October 2019 09:49
To: Cerny,MW <M.W.Cerny@lse.ac.uk>; Donnelly,S <S.Donnelly@lse.ac.uk>; Thomson,MT <M.T.Thomson@lse.ac.uk>
Cc: Wilson,Clive <CLIVE.Wilson@lse.ac.uk>
Subject: FW: Request for information

Dear all,

(See below) This individual is one of the main characters stirring up this story.

His blog is effectively the main English-language outlet for the conspiracy theory.

While I don't want to keep doing a back-and-forth can we answer these questions in a dry factual way (if data protection etc allows).

(We may be able to put this to our FoI team as well go be clear on the 20 day response time).

Danny

Begin forwarded message:

From: ██████████████████████████
Date: 2 October 2019 at 23:56:14 BST
To: j.winterstein@lse.ac.uk
Subject: Request for information

I am working on an article about the controversy surrounding Republic of China in-exile President Tsai Ing-wen's LSE graduate thesis. Ms. Tsai filed her 1984 theis with the LSE Library in 2019 and that has generated much public interest in Taiwan. The name of the thesis is "Unfair Trade Practices and Safeguard Actions."

My questions, for publication, are:

Rachael

_____

寄件者：Donnelly，S
日期：2019 年 10 月 3 日 09：55
收件者：Maguire，RE
主旨：转发：资讯请求

_____

寄件者：O'Connor，D
日期：2019 年 10 月 3 日 09：49
收件者：Cerny，MW； Donnelly，S； Thomson，MT
副本：Wilson，Clive
主旨：转发：资讯请求

各位，

（见下文） 这个人是激起这个故事的主要角色之一。他的部落格实际上是这个阴谋论的主要英语媒体。

虽然我不想一直反驳，但我们可以用冷静的事实方式回答这些问题吗（如果资料保护等允许的话）。

（我们也可能可以将这个问题提交给我们的资讯自由小组，以确定 20 天的回应时间）。Danny

开始转发的讯息：

寄件者：▮▮▮▮▮▮▮▮▮▮
日期：2019 年 10 月 2 日 23：56：14 BST
收件者：j.winterstein@lse.ac.uk
主旨：资讯请求

我正在撰写一篇关于中华民国流亡总统蔡英文在 LSE 的研究生论文的争议的文章。蔡女士在 2019 年将她 1984 年的论文提交给 LSE 图书馆，这在台湾引起了很大的公众兴趣。论文的名称是"不公平贸易和防卫机制"。

我的问题，供出版使用，是：

1) What is the name and degree of Tsai Ing-wen's LSE Advisor? – As he is deceased, this is no longer covered by data protection, so can be released.

2) What are the names of the thesis Examiners? - We normally do not release examiner names under any circumstances. However, considering the situation, it's whether there would be any harm to the examiners from releasing this information. If they are deceased, it's the same situation as for the supervisor. If they are retired, there is unlikely to be any harm to their careers, but intense media interest could come their way. If they are still working, there could be potential harm to their careers due to intense media interest. To summarise, assuming we hold this info and not UoL, if the examiners are dead – release the names. If they are not – don't release the names as this could bring them under media interest that would be out of all proportion to the role they played. This would fit under the Section 40(2) exemption.

3) What is the date of the thesis oral review? – Could be released, it's personal data but it is in Ms Tsai's interests that we confirm the review.

4) What is the date of the Examiner's signatures of approval? - Could be released, it's personal data but it is in Ms Tsai's interests that we confirm the approval.

If you are not the correct person to handle this information request please forward to the appropriate individual.

Thank you for your attention to this request.

1. 蔡英文的 LSE 指导教授的名字和学位是什么？- 由于他已经去世，这不再受到资料保护的限制，所以可以被公开。

2. 口试委员的名字是什么？- 我们通常在任何情况下都不公开审查员的名字。但是，考虑到情况，这是从释放这些资讯中可能对审查员造成的任何伤害。如果他们已经去世，这与指导教授的情况相同。如果他们已经退休，他们的职业生涯不太可能受到任何伤害，但可能会受到激烈的媒体关注。如果他们仍然在工作，由于激烈的媒体关注，他们的职业生涯可能会受到潜在的伤害。总之，假设我们持有这些资讯而不是伦敦大学，如果审查员已经去世 - 公开名字。如果他们没有 - 不要公开名字，因为这可能会使他们受到与他们所扮演的角色完全不成比例的媒体关注。这将适用于第 40（2）豁免条款。

3. 论文口头审查的日期是什么？- 可以被公开，这是个人资料，但我们确认审查是符合蔡女士的利益的。

4. 审查员的批准签名的日期是什么？- 可以被公开，这是个人资料，但我们确认批准是符合蔡女士的利益的。

如果您不是处理这个资讯请求的正确人员，请转发给适当的个人。

感谢您对这次请求的关注。

RE_ Statement on LSE website

From: O'Connor, D
To: ▮
Cc: ▮
Subject: RE: Statement on LSE website
Date: 10 October 2019 09:45:00

Dear colleagues,

This has now been posted: http://www.lse.ac.uk/News/Latest-news-from-LSE/2019/j-October-2019/LSE-statement-on-PhD-of-Dr-Tsai-Ing-wen

Best wishes,
Danny

From: ▮
Sent: 10 October 2019 09:31
To: O'Connor,D <D.O'Connor@lse.ac.uk>; ▮
Subject: RE: Statement on LSE website

Dear All,

Just to let you know that the LSE are proposing to post the statement below on their website, if it hasn't already been posted. Danny from the LSE press office, and I have been through the pros and cons on this. I recognise the need for the LSE to do this and I am happy with this as the final version.

I have copied Danny into this email to confirm whether or not it has been posted and perhaps we could have a link to it?

▮ in SAS is off, not sure who else to send it to in SAS – ▮ can you help with this please?

In the meantime, any enquiries on this matter at our end, please continue to refer them to me.
I am on leave today and tomorrow. If anything urgent comes up please feel free to call or email me.

Many thanks

寄件者：O'Connor，D
收件者：█████████
副本：█████████
主旨：关于 LSE 网站上的声明
日期：2019 年 10 月 10 日 09：45：00

各位同仁，

这已经被发布了：http://www.lse.ac.uk/News/Latest-news-from-LSE/2019/j-October-2019/LSE-statement-on-PhD-of-Dr-Tsai-Ing-wen

祝好，

Danny

寄件者：█████████

日期：2019 年 10 月 10 日 09：31

收件者：O'Connor，D

主旨：回复：关于 LSE 网站上的声明

各位，

只是让大家知道，LSE 打算在他们的网站上发布以下的声明，如果还没有被发布的话。我和 LSE 的新闻办公室的 Danny 已经讨论了这件事的利与弊。我认识到 LSE 需要这么做，并且我对这作为最终版本感到满意。

我已经把 Danny 加入到这封邮件中，以确认是否已经发布，也许我们可以有一个连结到它？

在 SAS 中的█████是关闭的，不确定还要发送给 SAS 中的谁 - █████你能帮忙吗？

与此同时，关于我们这边的这个问题的任何查询，请继续将它们转介给我。

我今天和明天都在休假。如果有任何紧急事情，请随时打电话或给我发邮件。

非常感谢

LSE statement on PhD of Dr Tsai Ing-wen

LSE has received a number of queries regarding the academic status of our alumna, Dr Tsai Ing-wen, President of Taiwan.

We can be clear the records of LSE and of the University of London - the degree awarding body at the time - confirm that Dr Tsai was correctly awarded a PhD in Law in 1984.

All degrees from that period were awarded via the University of London and the thesis would have been sent first to their Senate House Library.

The Senate House Library records confirm that a copy was received and sent by them to the Institute for Advanced Legal Studies (IALS). There is a listing of Dr Tsai's thesis 'Unfair trade practices and safeguard actions' in the IALS index document "Legal Research in the United Kingdom 1905-1984", which was published in 1985.

Dr Tsai recently provided the LSE Library with a facsimile of a personal copy of the thesis, Unfair trade practices and safeguard actions which is available to view in the Library Reading Room. We understand Dr Tsai has also provided a digital version of her personal copy to the National Central Library of Taiwan.

LSE 关于蔡英文博士的博士学位的声明

LSE 收到了许多关于我们的校友，台湾总统蔡英文的学术地位的查询。

我们可以清楚地说，LSE 和当时的学位授予机构 - 伦敦大学的记录确认蔡博士在 1984 年正确地获得了法学博士学位。

那段时期的所有学位都是通过伦敦大学授予的，论文首先会被发送到他们的总图书馆。

总图书馆的记录确认他们收到了一份副本，并将其发送到高等法律研究所（IALS）。蔡博士的论文"不公平贸易和防卫机制"在 IALS 的索引文件"1905-1984 年英国的法律研究"中有列出，该文件于 1985 年出版。

蔡博士最近向 LSE 图书馆提供了论文"不公平贸易和防卫机制"的个人纸本的复制品，该复制品可以在图书馆阅览室查看。我们了解蔡博士还向台湾的国家中央图书馆提供了她个人副本的数位版本。

Re_ Statement for the LSE website（1）

From:	Donnelly,S
To:	Phdacademy; Wilson,Clive
Cc:	Metcalfe,F; Media.Relations; O'Connor,D; Thomson,MT; Comms.Socialmedia
Subject:	Re: Statement for the LSE website
Date:	08 October 2019 17:10:28
Attachments:	image002.png
	image003.png
	image005.png

That's fine with me

Sue

Sent from my Samsung Galaxy smartphone. Kk

-------- Original message --------
From: LSE PhD Academy <phdacademy@lse.ac.uk>
Date: 08/10/2019 16:34 (GMT+00:00)
To: "Wilson,Clive" <CLIVE.Wilson@lse.ac.uk>
Cc: "Metcalfe,F" <F.Metcalfe@lse.ac.uk>, "Media.Relations" <Media.Relations@lse.ac.uk>, "O'Connor,D" <D.O'Connor@lse.ac.uk>, "Thomson,MT" <M.T.Thomson@lse.ac.uk>, "Donnelly,S" <S.Donnelly@lse.ac.uk>, "Comms.Socialmedia" <Comms.Socialmedia@lse.ac.uk>
Subject: RE: Statement for the LSE website

Happy for that to be deleted.

Thanks,

Marcus

Marcus Cerny
PhD Academy Deputy Director
The London School of Economics and Political Science
Houghton Street, London WC2A 2AE
t: +44 (0)20 7955 6766
e: m.w.cerny@lse.ac.uk
lse.ac.uk/phdacademy

If you are a current PhD student please remember to send your queries through the PhD Academy Enquiry Form. All other enquirers should contact phdacademy@lse.ac.uk

--------------- Original Message ---------------
From: Wilson,Clive [clive.wilson@lse.ac.uk]
Sent: 08/10/2019 16:10
To: phdacademy@lse.ac.uk; d.o'connor@lse.ac.uk
Cc: f.metcalfe@lse.ac.uk; m.t.thomson@lse.ac.uk; s.donnelly@lse.ac.uk; media.relations@lse.ac.uk; comms.socialmedia@lse.ac.uk

寄件者：Donnelly，S

收件者：Phdacademy； Wilson，Clive

副本：Metcalfe，F； Media.Relations； O"Connor，D； Thomson，MT； Comms.Socialmedia

主旨：回复：LSE 网站的声明

日期：2019 年 10 月 8 日 17：10：28

附件：image002.png image003.png image005.png

我觉得没问题。 Sue

从我的 Samsung Galaxy 智慧型手机发送。Kk

---------- 原始讯息 ----------

寄件者：LSE PhD Academy phdacademy@lse.ac.uk

日期：2019 年 10 月 8 日 16：34 （GMT+00：00）

收件者："Wilson，Clive" CLIVE.Wilson@lse.ac.uk

副本："Metcalfe，F" F.Metcalfe@lse.ac.uk， "Media.Relations" Media.Relations@lse.ac.uk， "O'Connor，D" D.O'Connor@lse.ac.uk， "Thomson，MT" M.T.Thomson@lse.ac.uk， "Donnelly，S" S.Donnelly@lse.ac.uk， "Comms.Socialmedia" Comms.Socialmedia@lse.ac.uk

主旨：回复：LSE 网站的声明

我觉得可以删除那句。谢谢，

Marcus

Marcus Cerny

博士生学院副主任

伦敦政经学院 Houghton Street， London WC2A 2AE

电话：+44 （0） 20 7955 6766

电邮：m.w.cerny@lse.ac.uk

网站：lse.ac.uk/phdacademy

如果您是目前的博士学生，请记得透过博士生学院查询表格发送您的查询。其他查询者请联系 phdacademy@lse.ac.uk。

---------- 原始讯息 ----------

寄件者：Wilson，Clive [clive.wilson@lse.ac.uk]

日期：2019 年 10 月 8 日 16：10

收件者：phdacademy@lse.ac.uk； d.o'connor@lse.ac.uk

副本：f.metcalfe@lse.ac.uk； m.t.thomson@lse.ac.uk； s.donnelly@lse.ac.uk； media.relations@lse.ac.uk； comms.socialmedia@lse.ac.uk

Subject: RE: Statement for the LSE website

☺ no worries

From: O'Connor,D
Sent: 08 October 2019 16:10
To: Wilson,Clive; Phdacademy
Cc: Metcalfe,F; Thomson,MT; Donnelly,S; Media.Relations; Comms.Socialmedia
Subject: RE: Statement for the LSE website

Thanks Clive.

I understand the reasoning but I think that might just add to the confusion.

From: Wilson,Clive
Sent: 08 October 2019 16:03
To: O'Connor,D <D.O'Connor@lse.ac.uk>; Phdacademy <Phdacademy@lse.ac.uk>
Cc: Metcalfe,F <F.Metcalfe@lse.ac.uk>; Thomson,MT <M.T.Thomson@lse.ac.uk>; Donnelly,S <S.Donnelly@lse.ac.uk>; Media.Relations <Media.Relations@lse.ac.uk>; Comms.Socialmedia <Comms.Socialmedia@lse.ac.uk>
Subject: RE: Statement for the LSE website

Hi Danny

that sounds fine to me.   But just thinking aloud - if that sentence comes out, do we want to add 'Although many students did, there was no requirement to submit a second copy to LSE Library'

Clive

From: O'Connor,D
Sent: 08 October 2019 15:19
To: Phdacademy
Cc: Metcalfe,F; Wilson,Clive; Thomson,MT; Donnelly,S; Media.Relations; Comms.Socialmedia

主旨：回复：LSE 网站的声明

没问题。

寄件者：O'Connor，D
日期：2019 年 10 月 8 日 16：10
收件者：Wilson，Clive； Phdacademy
副本：Metcalfe，F； Thomson，MT； Donnelly，S； Media.Relations； Comms.Socialmedia
主旨：回复：LSE 网站的声明

谢谢你，Clive。

我理解这个原因，但我认为这可能只会增加混淆。

寄件者：Wilson，Clive
日期：2019 年 10 月 8 日 16：03
收件者：O'Connor，D D.O'Connor@lse.ac.uk； Phdacademy Phdacademy@lse.ac.uk
副本：Metcalfe，F F.Metcalfe@lse.ac.uk； Thomson，MT M.T.Thomson@lse.ac.uk； Donnelly，S S.Donnelly@lse.ac.uk； Media.Relations Media.Relations@lse.ac.uk； Comms.Socialmedia Comms.Socialmedia@lse.ac.uk
主旨：回复：LSE 网站的声明

嗨，Danny

我觉得这样很好。但是，只是大声思考 - 如果那句话被删除，我们是否想要加入"尽管许多学生确实这么做了，但当时没有要求提交第二份副本给 LSE 图书馆"？

Clive

寄件者：O'Connor，D
日期：2019 年 10 月 8 日 15：19
收件者：Phdacademy
副本：Metcalfe，F； Wilson，Clive； Thomson，MT； Donnelly，S； Media.Relations； Comms.Socialmedia

Subject: RE: Statement for the LSE website

Dear all,

▓▓▓▓▓▓▓▓▓▓▓▓▓▓▓ The University of London is quite concerned by the statement, specifically this part

"However, it has recently been discovered that the University of London Senate House Library are unable to find the hard copy of the thesis."

Would colleagues object if this sentence was just deleted? On reflection, it doesn't seem to impact the overall message.

Best wishes,

Danny

From: O'Connor,D
Sent: 08 October 2019 13:39
To: LSE PhD Academy <phdacademy@lse.ac.uk>
Cc: Metcalfe,F <F.Metcalfe@lse.ac.uk>; Wilson,Clive <CLIVE.Wilson@lse.ac.uk>; Thomson,MT <M.T.Thomson@lse.ac.uk>; Donnelly,S <S.Donnelly@lse.ac.uk>; Media.Relations <Media.Relations@lse.ac.uk>; Comms.Socialmedia <Comms.Socialmedia@lse.ac.uk>
Subject: RE: Statement for the LSE website

Dear all,

The statement is live here: http://www.lse.ac.uk/News/Latest-news-from-LSE/2019/j-October-2019/LSE-statement-on-PhD-of-Dr-Tsai-Ing-wen

Media/ social media colleagues – this is a statement on President Tsai's PhD on our website.

主旨：回复：LSE 网站的声明

各位，

████ 伦敦大学对这个声明感到非常担忧，特别是这部分：

"然而，最近发现伦敦大学总图书馆无法找到论文的纸本副本。"

如果这句话只是被删除，同事们会反对吗？经过反思，似乎不会影响整体的讯息。

祝好，

Danny

寄件者：O'Connor, D
日期：2019 年 10 月 8 日 13：39
收件者：LSE PhD Academy phdacademy@lse.ac.uk
副本：Metcalfe, F F.Metcalfe@lse.ac.uk； Wilson, Clive CLIVE.Wilson@lse.ac.uk； Thomson, MT M.T.Thomson@lse.ac.uk； Donnelly, S S.Donnelly@lse.ac.uk； Media.Relations Media.Relations@lse.ac.uk； Comms.Socialmedia Comms.Socialmedia@lse.ac.uk
主旨：回复：LSE 网站的声明

各位，

这个声明已经在这里发布：https://www.lse.ac.uk/News/Latest-news-from-LSE/2019/j-October-2019/LSE-statement-on-PhD-of-Dr-Tsai-Ing-wen

媒体 / 社交媒体的同事 - 这是我们网站上关于蔡总统的博士学位的声明。

Best wishes,

Danny

From: LSE PhD Academy [mailto:phdacademy@lse.ac.uk]
Sent: 08 October 2019 10:26
To: O'Connor,D <D.O'Connor@lse.ac.uk>
Cc: Metcalfe,F <F.Metcalfe@lse.ac.uk>; Wilson,Clive <CLIVE.Wilson@lse.ac.uk>; Thomson,MT <M.T.Thomson@lse.ac.uk>; Donnelly,S <S.Donnell@lse.ac.uk>
Subject: RE: Statement for the LSE website

That looks good to me. If everybody else agrees let me know when and where it is up and I'll respond to queries directing to this.

I will also contact the Law Dept and those that have sent on queries to me to let them know. Do we need to do anything else via internal comms so that people are aware? It is hard to guess who exactly might receive a random query.

Thanks,
Marcus

Marcus Cerny
PhD Academy Deputy Director
The London School of Economics and Political Science
Houghton Street, London WC2A 2AE
t: +44 (0)20 7955 6766
e: m.w.cerny@lse.ac.uk
lse.ac.uk/phdacademy

If you are a current PhD student please remember to send your queries through the PhD Academy Enquiry Form. All other enquirers should contact phdacademy@lse.ac.uk

--------------- Original Message ---------------
From: O'Connor,D [d.o'connor@lse.ac.uk]
Sent: 08/10/2019 09:35
To: phdacademy@lse.ac.uk; m.t.thomson@lse.ac.uk
Cc: clive.wilson@lse.ac.uk; f.metcalfe@lse.ac.uk; s.donnelly@lse.ac.uk
Subject: Statement for the LSE website

Dear colleagues,

祝好，

Danny

寄件者：LSE PhD Academy [mailto：phdacademy@lse.ac.uk]

日期：2019年10月8日 10：26

收件者：O'Connor，D D.O'Connor@lse.ac.uk

副本：Metcalfe，F F.Metcalfe@lse.ac.uk； Wilson，Clive CLIVE.Wilson@lse.ac.uk； Thomson，MT M.T.Thomson@lse.ac.uk； Donnelly，S S.Donnelly@lse.ac.uk

主旨：回复：LSE网站的声明

我觉得这样很好。如果其他人都同意，请告诉我何时和在哪里发布，我将回应查询并指向这个声明。

我还将联系法律系和那些已经转发查询给我的人，让他们知道。我们是否需要通过内部通讯做其他事情，以便人们知道？很难猜测谁可能会收到随机查询。

谢谢，

Marcus

---------- 原始讯息 ----------

寄件者：O'Connor，D [d.o'connor@lse.ac.uk]

日期：2019年10月8日 09：35

收件者：phdacademy@lse.ac.uk； m.t.thomson@lse.ac.uk

副本：clive.wilson@lse.ac.uk； f.metcalfe@lse.ac.uk； s.donnelly@lse.ac.uk

主旨：LSE网站的声明

各位同事，

Further to the correspondence yesterday, Fiona and I have put together a draft statement (below) which can go on the LSE website. It is based on previously agreed statements and deliberately does not go into the range of claims and counter-claims being circulated

Please let me know if there is anything of concern or anything you believe needs to be added/ deleted.

Ideally we would like to get this uploaded later today.

Best wishes,

Danny

LSE statement on PhD of Tsai Ing-wen

LSE has received a number of queries regarding the academic status of our alumna, Dr Tsai Ing-Wen, President of Taiwan.

We can be clear that the records of LSE and of the University of London - the degree awarding body at the time - confirm that Dr Ing-Wen was correctly awarded a PhD in Law in 1984.

All degrees from that period were awarded via the University of London and the thesis would have been sent first to their Senate House Library.

The Senate House Library records confirm that a copy was received and sent by them to the Institute for Advanced Legal Studies (IALS) and there is a listing of Dr Ing-Wen's thesis 'Unfair trade practices and safeguard actions' In the IALS index document "Legal Research in the United Kingdown 1905-1984", which was published in 1985.

Dr Ing-wen recently provided the LSE Library with a facsimile of a personal copy of the thesis, *Unfair trade practices and safeguard actions* which is available to view in the Library Reading Room. We understand Dr Tsai has also provided a digital version of her personal copy to the National Central Library of Taiwan.

/END

Daniel O'Connor

根据昨天的通信，Fiona 和我已经整理了一份草稿声明（如下），可以放在 LSE 网站上。它基于先前同意的声明，并且特意不涉及正在发布的一系列声明和反驳。

请告诉我是否有什么令人担忧的事情，或者您认为需要添加 / 删除的东西。

理想情况下，我们希望今天晚些时候上传这个。

祝好，

Danny

LSE 关于蔡英文博士的博士学位的声明

LSE 收到了许多关于我们的校友，台湾总统蔡英文的学术地位的查询。

我们可以清楚地说，LSE 和当时的学位授予机构 - 伦敦大学的记录确认蔡博士在 1984 年正确地获得了法学博士学位。

那段时期的所有学位都是通过伦敦大学授予的，论文首先会被发送到他们的总图书馆。

总图书馆的记录确认他们收到了一份副本，并将其发送到高等法律研究所（IALS）。蔡博士的论文"不公平贸易和防卫机制"在 IALS 的索引文件 "1905-1984 年英国的法律研究"中有列出，该文件于 1985 年出版。

蔡博士最近向 LSE 图书馆提供了论文"不公平贸易和防卫机制"的个人纸本的复制品，该复制品可以在图书馆阅览室查看。我们了解蔡博士还向台湾的国家中央图书馆提供了她个人纸本的数位版本。

/ 结束

Daniel O'Connor

Head of Media Relations | Communications Division

The London School of Economics and Political Science

Houghton Street, London WC2A 2AE

t: +44 (0)20 7955 7417

e: oconnord@lse.ac.uk

lse.ac.uk

LSE is ranked #1 in Europe for social sciences

(QS World University Ranking 2019)

ref:_00D58JYzR._5004ItxPeD:ref

媒体关系主管 | 传播部门

伦敦政经学院

霍顿街，伦敦 WC2A 2AE

电话：+44（0）20 7955 7417

电邮：oconnord@lse.ac.uk

网站：lse.ac.uk

LSE 在社会科学领域中在欧洲排名第一
（QS 世界大学排名 2018）

ref：_00D58JYzR._5004ItxPeD：ref

RE_ Statement for the LSE website（8）

From: O"Connor,D
To: Wilson,Clive; Phdacademy; Thomson,MT
Cc: Donnelly,S; Metcalfe,F
Subject: RE: Statement for the LSE website
Date: 08 October 2019 10:16:54
Attachments: image002.png
image003.png
image005.png

Good spot Clive.

I think it's ok to make available as electronic copy though inevitably we'll be asked a flurry of questions about the process behind this.

Danny

From: Wilson,Clive
Sent: 08 October 2019 10:04
To: O'Connor,D <D.O'Connor@lse.ac.uk>; Phdacademy <Phdacademy@lse.ac.uk>; Thomson,MT <M.T.Thomson@lse.ac.uk>
Cc: Donnelly,S <S.Donnelly@lse.ac.uk>; Metcalfe,F <F.Metcalfe@lse.ac.uk>
Subject: RE: Statement for the LSE website

HI Danny (and everyone)

I still get confused as to the correct way to address people and whether it should be Tsai Ing-Wen or Ing-Wen Tsai, but Tsai is the family name so it should be Dr Tsai in the 2nd line.

I was given permission from her office yesterday to upload the electronic copy. If we host it on LSE theses online, it also means we can revert to the 'normal' copyright statement on the print copy. Uploading copy from it will still be illegal, but if it's online anyway that is less of an issue. It might mitigate some of the 'unreasonable restrictions' emails.

We will still describe it as a copy ...

thanks

Clive

From: O'Connor,D
Sent: 08 October 2019 09:36
To: Phdacademy; Thomson,MT
Cc: Wilson,Clive; Donnelly,S; Metcalfe,F
Subject: Statement for the LSE website

寄件者：O"Connor，D

收件者：Wilson，Clive； Phdacademy； Thomson，MT

副本：Donnelly，S； Metcalfe，F

主旨：回复：LSE 网站的声明

日期：2019 年 10 月 8 日 10：16：54

附件：image002.png image003.png image005.png

好眼力，Clive。

我认为提供电子副本是可以的，虽然我们不可避免地会被问到关于这背后的流程的一系列问题。

Danny

寄件者：Wilson，Clive

日期：2019 年 10 月 8 日 10：04

收件者：O'Connor，D D.O'Connor@lse.ac.uk； Phdacademy Phdacademy@lse.ac.uk； Thomson，MT M.T.Thomson@lse.ac.uk

副本：Donnelly，S S.Donnelly@lse.ac.uk； Metcalfe，F F.Metcalfe@lse.ac.uk

主旨：回复：LSE 网站的声明

嗨，Danny（和大家），

我仍然对如何正确称呼人感到困惑，不确定应该是 Tsai Ing-Wen 还是 Ing-Wen Tsai，但 Tsai 是姓氏，所以第二行应该是 Dr Tsai。

昨天她的办公室允许我上传电子副本。如果我们将其放在 LSE 线上论文，这也意味着我们可以恢复打印副本上的"正常"版权声明。从中上传副本仍然是非法的，但如果它已经在线上，那就不太是问题了。

这可能会减少一些"不合理的限制"的电子邮件。

我们仍然会描述它是一份副本 ... 谢谢，

Clive

寄件者：O'Connor，D

日期：2019 年 10 月 8 日 09：36

收件者：Phdacademy； Thomson，MT

副本：Wilson，Clive； Donnelly，S； Metcalfe，F

主旨：LSE 网站的声明

Dear colleagues,

Further to the correspondence yesterday, Fiona and I have put together a draft statement (below) which can go on the LSE website. It is based on previously agreed statements and deliberately does not go into the range of claims and counter-claims being circulated

Please let me know if there is anything of concern or anything you believe needs to be added/ deleted.

Ideally we would like to get this uploaded later today.

Best wishes,

Danny

LSE statement on PhD of Tsai Ing-wen

LSE has received a number of queries regarding the academic status of our alumna, Dr Tsai Ing-Wen, President of Taiwan.

We can be clear that the records of LSE and of the University of London - the degree awarding body at the time - confirm that Dr Ing-Wen was correctly awarded a PhD in Law in 1984.

All degrees from that period were awarded via the University of London and the thesis would have been sent first to their Senate House Library. However, it has recently been discovered that the University of London Senate House Library are unable to find the hard copy of the thesis.

The Senate House Library records confirm that a copy was received and sent by them to the Institute for Advanced Legal Studies (IALS) and there is a listing of Dr Ing-Wen's thesis 'Unfair trade practices and safeguard actions' In the IALS index document "Legal Research in the United Kingdown 1905-1984", which was published in 1985.

Dr Ing-wen recently provided the LSE Library with a facsimile of a personal copy of the thesis, *Unfair trade practices and safeguard actions* which is available to view in the Library Reading Room. We understand Dr Tsai has also provided a digital version of her personal copy to the National Central Library of Taiwan.

/END

Daniel O'Connor
Head of Media Relations | Communications Division
The London School of Economics and Political Science
Houghton Street, London WC2A 2AE
t: +44 (0)20 7955 7417
e: oconnord@lse.ac.uk
lse.ac.uk

各位同事，

根据昨天的通信，Fiona 和我已经整理了一份草稿声明（如下），可以放在 LSE 网站上。它基于先前商定的声明，并且特意不涉及正在发布的一系列声明和反驳。

请告诉我是否有什么令人担忧的事情，或者您认为需要添加/删除的东西。

理想情况下，我们希望今天晚些时候上传这个。
祝好，
Danny

LSE 关于蔡英文博士的博士学位的声明

LSE 收到了许多关于我们的校友，台湾总统蔡英文的学术地位的查询。

我们可以清楚地说，LSE 和当时的学位授予机构 - 伦敦大学的记录确认蔡博士在 1984 年正确地获得了法学博士学位。

那段时期的所有学位都是通过伦敦大学授予的，论文首先会被发送到他们的总图书馆。

总图书馆的记录确认他们收到了一份副本，并将其发送到高等法律研究所（IALS）。蔡博士的论文"不公平贸易和防卫机制"在 IALS 的索引文件"1905-1984 年英国的法律研究"中有列出，该文件于 1985 年出版。

蔡博士最近向 LSE 图书馆提供了论文"不公平贸易和防卫机制"的个人纸本的复制品，该复制品可以在图书馆阅览室查看。我们了解蔡博士还向台湾的国家中央图书馆提供了她个人纸本的数位版本。

/ 结束

Daniel O'Connor
媒体关系主管 | 传播部门
伦敦政经学院
霍顿街，伦敦 WC2A 2AE
电话：+44 （0) 20 7955 7417　　　　LSE 在社会科学领域中在欧洲排名第一
电邮：oconnord@lse.ac.uk　　　　　　（QS 世界大学排名 2019）
网站：lse.ac.uk

Re_-Statement-on-the-LSE-website1

From:	O'Connor,D
To:	Fang-Long Shih
Subject:	Re: Statement on the LSE website
Date:	09 October 2019 10:43:14

Hi Fang-long,

Thanks for your email, though I haven't got a new job!

I'll ask library colleagues about the catelogue number.

Best wishes,
Danny

From: Fang-Long Shih <fgshih@gmail.com>
Sent: 09 October 2019 05:12
To: O'Connor,D <D.O'Connor@lse.ac.uk>
Subject: Statement on the LSE website

Dear Danny,
Congratulations to your new position as Head of Media Relations and Communications Division!
It is a good idea to put a statement on the LSE website. Thank you for drafting this statement which looks good.
However, if U of London's Senate House Library still keeps its original paper version of the "book-search index cards" before the library collections became digitized? If so, whether there was a catalogue number assigned to the original thesis copy by the Senate House Library when the thesis was submitted?
It is believed if one can locate the catalogue number assigned to the original thesis, it's the exact proof that President Tsai completed the process. One can no longer cast any further doubt. As to what happened to the submitted copy (even missing), it's another story.

Do you think if you could assist to find and add this catalogue number? Many thanks!
I am currently in Seattle and will fly to Taiwan in 4 hours for an intensive international course until 17 Oct, and then will teach in Masaryk University in Czech and be back in London on 28 October. If I could help do anything while I am here, please don't hesitate to let me know.
All the very best,
Fang-long

寄件者：O"Connor，D
收件者：Fang-Long Shih
主旨：回复：LSE 网站上的声明
日期：2019 年 10 月 9 日 10：43：14

嗨施芳珑，

感谢您的电子邮件，不过我没有换新工作！我会询问图书馆的同事关于目录编号的事情。

祝好，Danny

_____

寄件者：Fang-Long Shih fgshih@gmail.com
日期：2019 年 10 月 9 日 05：12
收件者：O'Connor，D D.O'Connor@lse.ac.uk
主旨：LSE 网站上的声明

亲爱的 Danny，

恭喜您成为媒体关系和传播部门的主管！

将声明放在 LSE 网站上是个好主意。感谢您草拟这份声明，看起来很好。

但是，如果伦敦大学的总图书馆在图书馆收藏品数位化之前，是否仍保留其原始的"书籍搜寻索引卡"的纸本版本？如果是这样，当论文提交时，总图书馆是否为原始纸本论文分配了目录编号？

人们相信，如果可以找到分配给原始论文的目录编号，这就是蔡总统完成流程的确切证据。人们将不再有任何进一步的怀疑。至于提交的纸本发生了什么（甚至丢失），那是另一个故事。

您认为您可以协助找到并添加这个目录编号吗？非常感谢！我目前在西雅图，将在 4 小时后飞往台湾参加一个密集的国际课程，直到 10 月 17 日，然后将在捷克的马萨里克大学教课，并于 10 月 28 日回到伦敦。如果我在这里可以帮忙做些什么，请不要犹豫告诉我。

祝一切顺利，

施芳珑

RE_ Status of Media Relations request

From: O'Connor,D
To: GLPD.Info.Rights; Winterstein,J
Cc: Metcalfe,F
Subject: RE: Status of Media Relations request
Date: 10 October 2019 10:44:00

Hi Rachael,

I understand the reasoning but I really don't want to add anything more to the statement.

Every time we give a bit more info, they just come back with more questions.

We have to draw the line somewhere.

Thanks,
Danny

(Fiona, FYI)

From: GLPD.Info.Rights
Sent: 10 October 2019 10:38
To: O'Connor,D <D.O'Connor@lse.ac.uk>; Winterstein,J <J.Winterstein@lse.ac.uk>
Subject: RE: Status of Media Relations request

Hello Danny,

A common thread to the questions are the names and dates. Can we add these to the statement please?

I was hoping we'd had a request through What Do They Know we could link to but no luck there.

Regards,
Rachael

From: O'Connor,D
Sent: 10 October 2019 10:34
To: GLPD.Info.Rights <GLPD.Info.Rights@lse.ac.uk>; Winterstein,J <J.Winterstein@lse.ac.uk>
Subject: RE: Status of Media Relations request

Hi Rachael,

It's on the website now.

http://www.lse.ac.uk/News/Latest-news-from-LSE/2019/j-October-2019/LSE-statement-on-PhD-of-Dr-Tsai-Ing-wen

Though it doesn't address his specific questions.

Best wishes,

Danny

From: GLPD.Info.Rights
Sent: 10 October 2019 10:32
To: Winterstein,J <J.Winterstein@lse.ac.uk>
Cc: O'Connor,D <D.O'Connor@lse.ac.uk>

寄件者：O"Connor，D
收件者：GLPD.Info.Rights； Winterstein，J
副本：Metcalfe，F
主旨：RE： 媒体关系请求的状态　日期：2019年10月10日10：44：00

嗨 Rachael，

我理解这个理由，但我真的不想在声明中添加更多的资讯。每次我们提供一点更多的资讯，他们就会回来提出更多的问题。我们必须在某个地方划一条界线。

谢谢， Danny

（Fiona， FYI）

寄件者：GLPD.Info.Rights　日期：2019年10月10日10：38
收件者：O'Connor，D D.O'Connor@lse.ac.uk； Winterstein，J J.Winterstein@lse.ac.uk
主旨：RE： 媒体关系请求的状态

你好 Danny，

这些问题的一个共同点是名称和日期。我们可以在声明中添加这些内容吗？我希望我们能透过"WhatDoTheyKnow 网站"请求我们可以连结到那里，但没运气。

问候， Rachael

寄件者：O'Connor，D　日期：2019年10月10日10：34
收件者：GLPD.Info.Rights GLPD.Info.Rights@lse.ac.uk； Winterstein，J J.Winterstein@lse.ac.uk
主旨：RE： 媒体关系请求的状态

嗨 Rachael，

它现在在网站上了。

https://www.lse.ac.uk/News/Latest-news-from-LSE/2019/j-October-2019/LSE-statement-on-PhD-of-Dr-Tsai-Ing-wen

尽管它没有解答他的具体问题。

最好的祝愿，Danny

寄件者：GLPD.Info.Rights
日期：2019年10月10日10：32
收件者：Winterstein，J J.Winterstein@lse.ac.uk
副本：O'Connor，D D.O'Connor@lse.ac.uk

Subject: FW: Status of Media Relations request

Hello Jess,

Do we know when the statement will be on the School's website yet?

Regards,
Rachael

From: ▮▮▮▮▮▮▮▮▮▮▮▮▮▮▮▮▮▮▮▮▮
Sent: 10 October 2019 03:18
To: GLPD.Info.Rights <GLPD.Info.Rights@lse.ac.uk>
Cc: Winterstein,J <J.Winterstein@lse.ac.uk>
Subject: Status of Media Relations request

To Whom It May Conern:

Jessica Winterstein, Deputy Head of Media Relations, forwarded my request for information to your office. Below is my request to Ms. Winterstein. Please advise on when I will receive a response. Thank you.

▮▮▮▮▮▮▮▮▮▮▮▮

****

I am working on an article about the controversy surrounding Republic of China in-exile President Tsai Ing-wen's LSE graduate thesis. Ms. Tsai filed her 1984 theis with the LSE Library in 2019 and that has generated much public interest in Taiwan. The name of the thesis is "Unfair Trade Practices and Safeguard Actions."

My questions, for publication, are:

1) What is the name and degree of Tsai Ing-wen's LSE Advisor?
2) What are the names of the thesis Examiners?
3) What is the date of the thesis oral review?
4) What is the date of the Examiner's signatures of approval?

If you are not the correct person to handle this information request please forward to the appropriate individual.

Thank you for your attention to this request.

主旨：转发：媒体关系请求的状态

你好 Jess，

我们知道声明何时会在学校的网站上吗？

祝好，

Rachael

寄件者：▇▇▇▇▇▇▇▇
日期：2019 年 10 月 10 日 03：18
收件者：GLPD.Info.Rights GLPD.Info.Rights@lse.ac.uk
副本：Winterstein，J J.Winterstein@lse.ac.uk
主旨：媒体关系请求的状态

敬启者：

Jessica Winterstein，媒体关系副主管，已将我的资讯请求转发给您的办公室。以下是我对 Winterstein 女士的请求。请告知我何时会收到回应。

谢谢。

▇▇▇▇▇▇▇▇

****

我正在撰写一篇关于中华民国流亡政府总统蔡英文在 LSE 的研究生论文的争议文章。蔡女士于 2019 年将她 1984 年的论文提交给 LSE 图书馆，这在台湾引起了很大的公众兴趣。论文的名称是《不公平贸易和防卫机制》。

我的问题，供发表，是：

1. 蔡英文在 LSE 的指导教授的名字和学位是什么？
2. 口试委员的名字是什么？
3. 论文口试的日期是什么？
4. 审查员的批准签名的日期是什么？

如果您不是处理此资讯请求的正确人员，请转发给适当的人员。

感谢您对此请求的关注。

RE_-Tsai-Ing-Wen

From: Fisher,RW
To: Metcalfe,F; O'Connor,D; Smith,DAA
Subject: RE: Tsai Ing-Wen
Date: 09 October 2019 12:32:43
Attachments: image002.png
image003.png
image005.png

Thanks Fiona, I'll take that approach in future.

All the best,
Ross

From: Metcalfe,F
Sent: 09 October 2019 12:14
To: O'Connor,D <D.O'Connor@lse.ac.uk>; Fisher,RW <R.W.Fisher@lse.ac.uk>; Smith,DAA <D.A.A.Smith@lse.ac.uk>
Subject: Re: Tsai Ing-Wen

I agree with ignore and delete. Otherwise we keep feeding this.

From: O'Connor,D <D.O'Connor@lse.ac.uk>
Sent: Wednesday, October 9, 2019 9:54:22 AM
To: Fisher,RW <R.W.Fisher@lse.ac.uk>; Smith,DAA <D.A.A.Smith@lse.ac.uk>; Metcalfe,F <F.Metcalfe@lse.ac.uk>
Subject: Re: Tsai Ing-Wen

Thanks Ross.

I wonder if saying 'we consider this case closed' or 'final word' etc might be provocative to the trolls.

Probably worth deleting, I don't think many serious messages would go via the website.

From: Fisher,RW <R.W.Fisher@lse.ac.uk>
Sent: 09 October 2019 09:49
To: O'Connor,D <D.O'Connor@lse.ac.uk>; Smith,DAA <D.A.A.Smith@lse.ac.uk>; Metcalfe,F <F.Metcalfe@lse.ac.uk>
Subject: RE: Tsai Ing-Wen

Thanks Danny,

I agree that we shouldn't feed the trolls. Based on this feedback is there anything that you want to add to that statement? Even just to say this is our final word on this subject?

In future should we just delete these emails?

All the best,
Ross

寄件者：Fisher，RW
收件者：Metcalfe，F； O"Connor，D； Smith，DAA
主旨： 回复：蔡英文
日期：2019 年 10 月 9 日 12：32：43
感谢 Fiona，我未来会采取这种方法。祝一切顺利，Ross

寄件者：Metcalfe，F
日期：2019 年 10 月 9 日 12：14
收件者：O'Connor，D D.O'Connor@lse.ac.uk； Fisher，RW R.W.Fisher@lse.ac.uk；Smith，DAA
D.A.A.Smith@lse.ac.uk
主旨： 回复：蔡英文
我同意忽略并删除。否则我们会一直回应这些。

寄件者：O'Connor，D D.O'Connor@lse.ac.uk
日期：2019 年 10 月 9 日 9：54：22
收件者：Fisher，RW R.W.Fisher@lse.ac.uk； Smith，DAA D.A.A.Smith@lse.ac.uk； Metcalfe，F.Metcalfe@lse.ac.uk
主旨： 回复：蔡英文
谢谢 Ross。

我想说"我们认为这件事已经结束"或"最后的说法"等可能会激怒这些网路酸民。

可能值得删除，我不认为许多正经的讯息会通过网站发送。

寄件者：Fisher，RW R.W.Fisher@lse.ac.uk
日期：2019 年 10 月 9 日 09：49
收件者：O'Connor，D D.O'Connor@lse.ac.uk； Smith，DAA D.A.A.Smith@lse.ac.uk； Metcalfe，F
F.Metcalfe@lse.ac.uk
主旨： 回复：蔡英文
谢谢 Danny，

我同意我们不应该回应这些酸民。基于这个反馈，您想在该声明中添加什么内容吗？即使只是说这是我们对此主题的最后说法？

未来我们应该直接删除这些电子邮件吗？祝一切顺利，

Ross

From: O'Connor,D
Sent: 09 October 2019 09:41
To: Fisher,RW <R.W.Fisher@lse.ac.uk>; Smith,DAA <D.A.A.Smith@lse.ac.uk>; Metcalfe,F <F.Metcalfe@lse.ac.uk>
Subject: Re: Tsai Ing-Wen

I suppose this is the argument against putting up the statement online.

I don't think we should engage with any of this. The online statement is what we have to say about this. We haven't got anything else to say.

Danny

From: Fisher,RW <R.W.Fisher@lse.ac.uk>
Sent: 09 October 2019 09:35
To: O'Connor,D <D.O'Connor@lse.ac.uk>; Smith,DAA <D.A.A.Smith@lse.ac.uk>; Metcalfe,F <F.Metcalfe@lse.ac.uk>
Subject: Tsai Ing-Wen

Hi guys,

I guess someone put out another article about everyone's favourite alumna yesterday, because our inbox is suddenly full of complaints. What should the process be for these?

All the best
Ross

Ross Fisher
Digital Content Manager | Communications Division
The London School of Economics and Political Science
Houghton Street, London WC2A 2AE
t: +44 (0)20 7955 4658
e: r.w.fisher@lse.ac.uk
lse.ac.uk

LSE is ranked #1 in Europe for social sciences (QS World University Ranking 2019)

寄件者：O'Connor，D

日期：2019年10月9日 09：41

收件者：Fisher，RW R.W.Fisher@lse.ac.uk； Smith，DAA D.A.A.Smith@lse.ac.uk； Metcalfe，F F.Metcalfe@lse.ac.uk

主旨：回复：蔡英文

我想这是反对在线上发布声明的论点。

我认为我们不应该参与其中。线上的声明就是我们对此要说的。我们没有其他要说的。

Danny

寄件者：Fisher，RW R.W.Fisher@lse.ac.uk

日期：2019年10月9日 09：35

收件者：O'Connor，D D.O'Connor@lse.ac.uk； Smith，DAA D.A.A.Smith@lse.ac.uk； Metcalfe，F F.Metcalfe@lse.ac.uk

主旨：蔡英文

嗨各位，

我猜昨天有人发表了另一篇关于每个人最喜欢的校友文章，因为我们的收件夹突然充满了投诉。这些应该如何处理？

祝一切顺利

Ross

Ross Fisher

数位内容经理 | 传播部门

伦敦政经学院

Houghton Street， 伦敦 WC2A 2AE

电话：+44（0）20 7955 4658

电子邮件：r.w.fisher@lse.ac.uk

网站：lse.ac.uk

Statement on the LSE website

From:	O"Connor,D
To:	Shih,F
Subject:	Statement on the LSE website
Date:	08 October 2019 13:09:00
Attachments:	image002.png
	image003.png
	image005.png

Dear Fang-long

To let you know, we are planning to put up a statement on our website later today where we can direct enquiries about Dr Tsai's PhD (as below)

It doesn't go into all the details being requested but provides an overview.

Best wishes,

Danny

LSE statement on PhD of Dr Tsai Ing-wen

LSE has received a number of queries regarding the academic status of our alumna, Dr Tsai Ing-wen, President of Taiwan.

We can be clear the records of LSE and of the University of London - the degree awarding body at the time - confirm that Dr Tsai was correctly awarded a PhD in Law in 1984.

All degrees from that period were awarded via the University of London and the thesis would have been sent first to their Senate House Library. However, it has recently been discovered that the University of London Senate House Library are unable to find the hard copy of the thesis.

The Senate House Library records confirm that a copy was received and sent by them to the Institute for Advanced Legal Studies (IALS). There is a listing of Dr Tsai's thesis 'Unfair trade practices and safeguard actions' in the IALS index document "Legal Research in the United Kingdom 1905-1984", which was published in 1985.

Dr Tsai recently provided the LSE Library with a facsimile of a personal copy of the thesis, *Unfair trade practices and safeguard actions* which is available to view in the Library's Reading Room. We understand Dr Tsai has also provided a digital version of her personal copy to the National Central Library of Taiwan.

寄件者：O"Connor，D
收件者：Shih，F
主旨：伦敦政治经济学院网站上的声明
日期：2019年10月8日 13：09：00
附件：image002.png image003.png image005.png

亲爱的芳珑，

为了让您知道，我们计划今天稍后在我们的网站上发布一份声明，以回应有关蔡博士的博士学位的询问（如下）。

它没有详细回答所有的问题，但提供了一个概览。

祝好，

Danny

LSE 关于蔡英文博士的博士学位的声明

LSE 收到了许多关于我们的校友，台湾总统蔡英文的学术地位的查询。

我们可以清楚地说，LSE 和当时的学位授予机构 - 伦敦大学的记录确认蔡博士在 1984 年正确地获得了法学博士学位。

那段时期的所有学位都是通过伦敦大学授予的，论文首先会被发送到他们的总图书馆。

总图书馆的记录确认他们收到了一份副本，并将其发送到高等法律研究所（IALS）。蔡博士的论文"不公平贸易和防卫机制"在 IALS 的索引文件 "1905-1984 年英国的法律研究" 中有列出，该文件于 1985 年出版。

蔡博士最近向 LSE 图书馆提供了论文"不公平贸易和防卫机制"的个人纸本的复制品，该复制品可以在图书馆阅览室查看。我们了解蔡博士还向台湾的国家中央图书馆提供了她个人纸本的数位版本。

Daniel O'Connor
Head of Media Relations | Communications Division
The London School of Economics and Political Science
Houghton Street, London WC2A 2AE
t: +44 (0)20 7955 7417
e: oconnord@lse.ac.uk
lse.ac.uk

LSE is ranked #1 in Europe for social sciences
(QS World University Ranking 2019)

Daniel O'Connor

媒体关系主管 | 传播部门

伦敦政经学院

霍顿街，伦敦 WC2A 2AE

电话：+44（0）20 7955 7417

电邮：oconnord@lse.ac.uk

网站：lse.ac.uk

LSE 在社会科学领域中在欧洲排名第一
（QS 世界大学排名 2019）

《恶官Ⅰ》收藏于世界各大图书馆

美国国会图书馆

← Refine Your Search   1 of 1

BOOK
E guan

Full Record   MARC Tags

Personal name
Zhang, Jing (Lawyer) author.
張靜 (Lawyer) author.

Main title
E guan / Zhang Jing, Li Zhenhua, Lin Bingsong he zhu ; Peng Wenzheng zhu bian.
惡官 / 張靜, 李震華, 林秉松合著 ; 彭文正主編.

Edition
Chu ban.
初版.

Published/Produced
United States : Thesis7ting LLC, 2022.

[Request this Item]   [LC Find It]

LCCN Permalink	https://lccn.loc.gov/2022400496
Description	480 pages : illustrations, facsimiles ; 24 cm
ISBN	9798986219301
LC classification	DS799.849.C353 Z42 2022+
Related names	Peng, Dennis, editor.
Summary	This book chronicles the event behind Taiwan President Tsai Ing-wen's academic fraud and how she obtained a fake PH. D. from the London School of Economics and Political Science. Author Dr. Dennis Peng, in his quest for truth, has been politically persecuted for his thorough investigation into the matter.
LC Subjects	Tsai, Ing-wen.
Other Subjects	蔡英文.
Browse by shelf order	DS799.849.C353
LCCN	2022400496

大英图书馆

 THESIS7TING LLC <thesis7ting.llc@gmail.com>

Donation 2804: RE: Book donation to British Library

2022年12月22日 晚上7:17

Just to let you know that we have received your book. I will send it to be added to our collection.

This process can often take a few months. The only way to check when it becomes available is to search our public catalogue 'Explore' on a regular basis. http://explore.bl.uk

Thank you for donating to the British Library.

Kind regards

Brian

Brian Elvidge

Donation Coordinators

Content Development Implementation

Building 2, Room 2.07

The British Library,

Boston Spa,

Wetherby,

West Yorkshire.

LS23 7BQ

donations@bl.uk

澳洲国家图书馆

 **Gmail** THESIS7TING LLC <thesis7ting.llc@gmail.com>

NLAacq85761 National Library of Australia - collection offer update
2 封邮件

2022年12月2日 上午11:58

Update on offer #: NLAacq85761

National Library of Australia

Update on offer #: NLAacq85761

Our update is:

Dear Sandy Lin

Thank you for offering "Evils" to the National Library of Australia. The Library would be delighted to accept this material. From your description, I can see that the material would be a valuable addition to the Library's collections and a useful resource for researchers. Your generosity in donating this material is greatly appreciated.

In terms of transferring the material to the Library, we prefer that donors send items in a padded bag or small box, via Australia Post, to the address below. Please reference this letter and quote NLAacq85761.

Could you please fill in our NLA donation slip (please see attached) and send it with the materials to:

Collection Donations, Collect & Acquire
National Library of Australia
Parkes Place
Canberra ACT 2600

Please feel free to contact me if you have any questions or concerns.

Yours sincerely

Jie Chen
Senior Library Officer
Curatorial & Collection Research
National Library of Australia
Number of documents attached to this message:1
Attached documents may be listed at the beginning or end of this email

哈佛大学图书馆

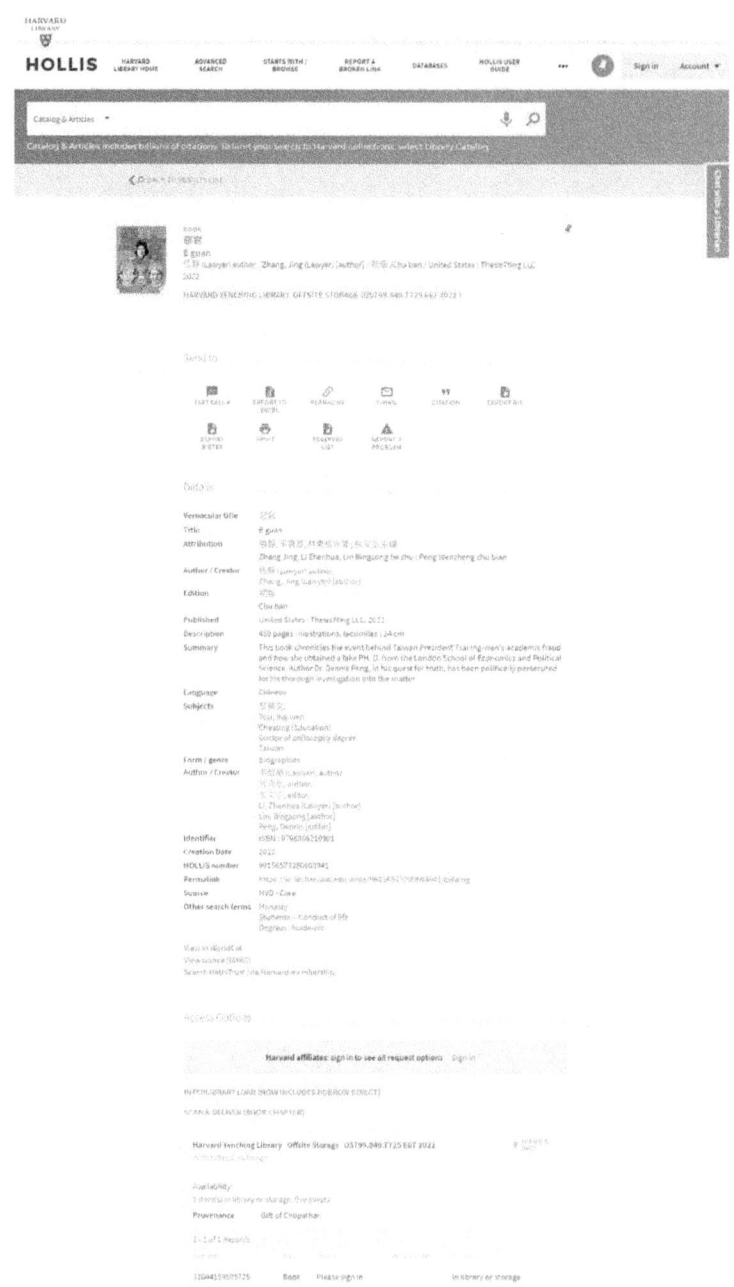

人类史上最大学位诈骗案

普林斯顿大学图书馆

PRINCETON UNIVERSITY LIBRARY
PRINCETON, NEW JERSEY 08544
TEL: (609) 258-3182 FAX: (609) 258-4573

Nov. 14, 2022

On behalf of the Trustees of Princeton University, I am pleased to acknowledge the receipt of

張靜，李震華，林秉松合著， 惡官 (Thesis7ting, 2022)

which you have presented to the University Library. In compliance with Internal Revenue Service Code, we must state that we provided neither goods nor services in return for this kind gift.

Please accept our most cordial thanks.

Sincerely,

[signature]

Joshua Seufert
Chinese Studies Librarian
The East Asian Library and
The Gest Collection

辱蒙厚贈 嘉惠學林 隆情銘感 謹函布謝

史丹佛大学图书馆

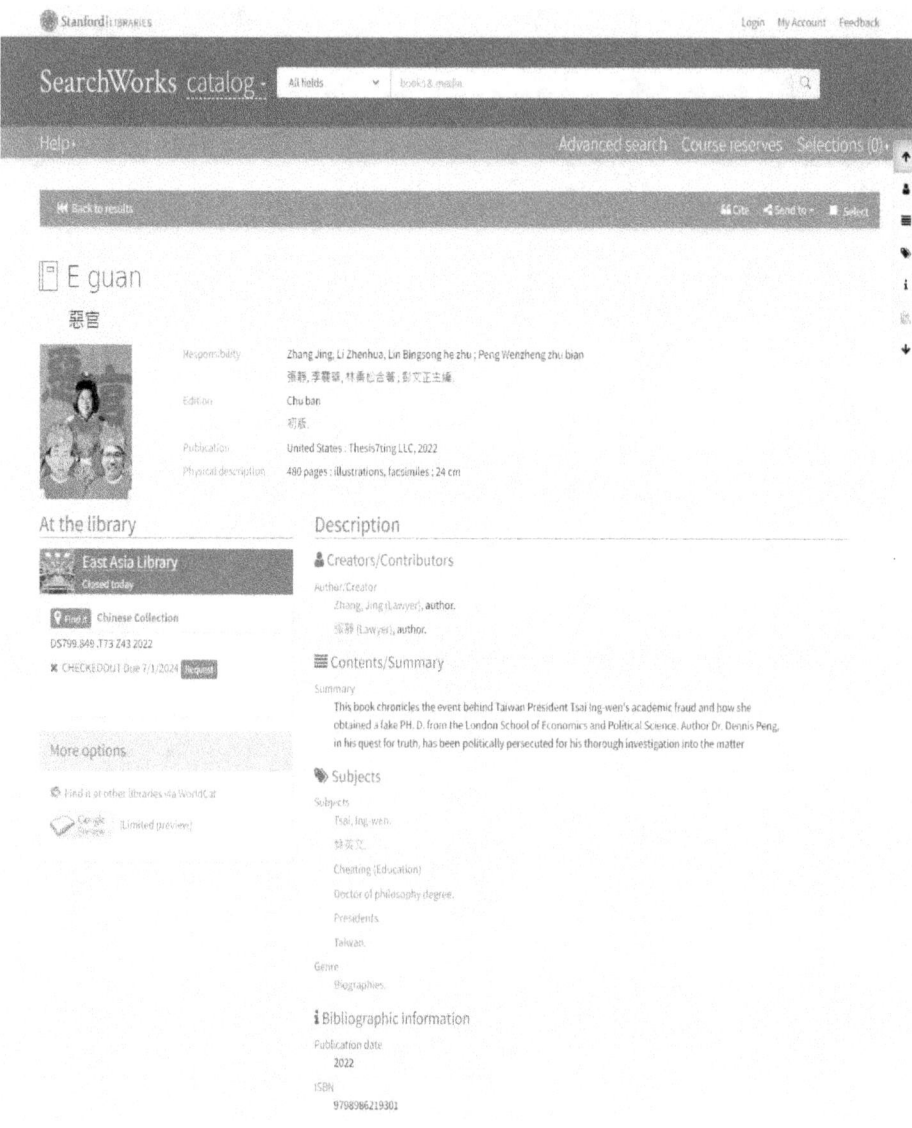

耶鲁大学图书馆

Yale UNIVERSITY LIBRARY

October 3, 2022

We gratefully acknowledge receipt of the gift mentioned below and extend to you our sincere appreciation.

For the Chinese Collection

感言

Sincerely,

Michael Meng
Head, East Asia Library and Librarian for Chinese Studies
212 Sterling Memorial Library
Yale University Library
Phone: 203-432-4438
michael.meng@yale.edu

宾夕法尼亚大学图书馆

UNIVERSITY of PENNSYLVANIA

I write to thank you for your gift of 《恶官》 to the University of Pennsylvania Library. We very much appreciate your interest in our collection and your generosity in supporting us.

Sincerely,

Brian Vivier
Chinese Studies Librarian

PENN

哥伦比亚大学图书馆

COLUMBIA UNIVERSITY
Weatherhead East Asian Institute

November 16, 2022

I received Mr. Peng's book, 《惡官》. Thank you so much for sending it. I'm writing you by mail because I have lost your email address. The book arrived last week. It is very kind of you to send it.

Best,

Andy

Andrew J. Nathan
Class of 1919 Professor of Political Science

加州大学洛杉矶分校图书馆

UCLA Library
Richard C. Rudolph East Asian Library

January 5, 2023

Thank you very much for donating the following publication to the UCLA East Asian Library.

惡官 / 張靜, 李震華, 林秉松合著; 彭文正主編

We have included this book in our collection, and made it available to our faculty, students, researchers and general library users. Please accept my sincere appreciation.

Truly yours,

Hong Cheng

Hong Cheng, Ph.D.
Chinese Studies Librarian

加州大学圣地牙哥分校图书馆

UC San Diego

December 15, 2022

Thank you for your donation of the following title to the UC San Diego Library's collection.

恶官

As you may know, we have for many years been building and shaping a Chinese-language collection in the humanities and social sciences covering China, Hong Kong, and Taiwan. This collection is a regional and national resource for Chinese Studies researchers and students throughout San Diego County, the state of California, and the U.S.

Your donation will most likely be used by students in UC San Diego's classes on politics and legal studies and faculty and graduate students who research the same topics.

Thank you again for your donation to the Library at UC San Diego.

Xi Chen
Sally T. WongAvery Librarian of Chinese Studies and East Asia Collection Strategist

密西根大学图书馆

THE UNIVERSITY OF MICHIGAN
THE ASIA LIBRARY

920 N. UNIVERSITY
ANN ARBOR, MICHIGAN 48109-1205 U.S.A.
734 764-0406   FAX 734 647-2885
http://asia.lib.umich.edu

October 10, 2022

  On behalf of the Regents of the University of Michigan, we have the honor to acknowledge with gratitude receipt of 惡官 at the Asia Library. This book will be accessible from the University Library catalogue. We believe your generous gift will benefit not only academic community at our university, but also scholars outside the University of Michigan.

With thanks and kind regards,

Liangyu Fu, Ph.D.

威斯康辛大学麦迪逊分校图书馆

November 16, 2022

Thank you for your gift to the libraries at the University of Wisconsin-Madison. We appreciate your generosity and thoughtfulness in donating this material to the General Library System. It is with your help that we continue to build useful and distinctive collections for the University community.

We gratefully acknowledge your contribution:

    Peng, Dennis, author.
    惡官 /張靜、李震華、林秉松合著 ; 彭文正主編.
    E guan / Zhang Jing, Li Zhenhua, Lin Bingsong he zhu ; Peng Wenzheng zhu bian.
    初版.
    Chu ban.

With appreciation,

Lisa R Carter
Lisa R. Carter
Vice Provost for Libraries

cc: Nancy Graff Schultz
    Elizabeth Lightfoot
    Anlin Yang

This gift is made unconditionally and is free from any restrictions, obligations, or arrangements.

The IRS further requires us to state that you have received no goods or services in exchange for this contribution, or the value of any items received in exchange for this contribution falls within the definition of "low cost articles" under section 513(h)(2) of the Internal Revenue Service Code.

General Library System

康乃尔大学图书馆

Wason Collection on East Asia
Cornell University
171 Kroch Library
Ithaca, NY 14853

Telephone: 607 255-4357
Fax: 607 255-8438
E-mail: wason.collection@cornell.edu

January 5, 2023

This letter is to acknowledge that the Wason Collection on East Asia at Cornell University Library has received the following title

《恶官》第一卷，彭文正 主编，張靜 李震華 林秉松 合著，Thesis7ting LLC, USA 出版

We greatly appreciate your generosity and believe that our patrons will certainly benefit from your donations. We look forward to your continuing support for our library and wish you the best.

Sincerely yours,

Jing Carlson

华盛顿大学图书馆

UNIVERSITY LIBRARIES
UNIVERSITY of WASHINGTON
Gifts Program

6 November 2022

On behalf of the University of Washington Libraries, it is my privilege to express our appreciation for your gift to the Tateuchi East Asia Library. We gratefully acknowledge the 10 June 2022 receipt of 悉官.

The UW Libraries is the heart of our great university. Our facilities, services, and collections nurture the dynamic teaching, learning, and research that are the hallmark of the University of Washington. Students and scholars from around the world rely on our 9.5 million volumes and vast electronic resources for information and inspiration. Our mission to advance intellectual discovery and enrich the quality of life by connecting people with knowledge is not just an idea, it is what we do. But we cannot do it without the support of people like you. Together we are fostering research and engagement that transform lives and create a better world.

Thank you again for your generosity.

Sincerely yours,

Carolyn H. Aamot
Head, Gifts Program / Content Manager

牛津大学图书馆

Book donation to The Bodleian Libraries.

UAS Development Bodleian <development@bodleian.ox.ac.uk> 2022年12月21日 下午6:14
收件者：THESIS7TING LLC <thesis7ting.llc@gmail.com>, UAS Development Bodleian <development@bodleian.ox.ac.uk>

Dear Sandy

Thank you very much for your intention of donating the book you mention below, we will be delighted to receive it!

At the moment the only way to donate books is by post.

Please send it to this address with a brief accompanying message explaining it is a gift from you:

Acquisitions Services
Collections & Resource Description (C & RD)
Bodleian Libraries
Osney One Building
Osney Mead
Oxford
OX2 0EW
UK

The Acquisitions Team will acknowledge receipt and thank you personally.

Many thanks once again.
Best wishes,
Emanuele

Emanuele Faccenda
Development Coordinator – Gardens, Libraries and Museums

Bodleian Libraries, Clarendon Building

Broad street, Oxford, OX1 3BG United Kingdom
E emanuele.faccenda@devoff.ox.ac.uk

https://www.development.ox.ac.uk/bodleian-libraries
Twitter: twitter.com/OxfordGiving

Facebook: www.facebook.com/OxfordGiving

To find out more about how we collect, store and process your data, including your rights and choices, please read our privacy notice. If you no longer wish to hear from us, please let us know at database@devoff.ox.ac.uk

[隱藏引用文字]

伦敦大学亚非学院图书馆

 Gmail

THESIS7TING LLC <thesis7ting.llc@gmail.com>

Book donation to SOAS Library.

2022年12月13日 晚上9:35

Dear Sandy,

Thank you for your kind offer.

We would be happy to take on this book.

Please could you post to:

Ludi Price
SOAS Library
Thornhaugh St,
Russell Square,
London WC1H 0XG

Before sending, please read our donation policy and make sure you are happy with it. We would also be grateful if you could fill out our donation form, and send it with your donation.

Please do let me know if you have any further questions.

Best wishes,
Ludi

附录

- In 2011, Tsai Ing-wen, then the chairperson of the Democratic Progressive Party, planned to run for the 2012 Taiwan presidential election. On June 7th, she led a delegation to LSE, meeting with then British Lord, former LSE director Anthony Giddens, and David Held, who was the supervising professor for Muammar Gaddafi's son in a "degree scandal". Subsequently, in July 2011, LSE initiated its first arrangement regarding the non-existence of Tsai Ing-wen's thesis.

- 2011 年，时任民进党主席蔡英文计画参选 2012 年台湾总统。6 月 7 日，她率团去了一趟 LSE，与时任英国上议员、前伦敦政经学院院长安东尼·纪登斯（Anthony Giddens）与利比亚前独裁强人格达费（Muammar Gaddafi）儿子"学位丑闻"的指导教授大卫·海尔德（DavidHeld）会面。随后 2011 年 7 月，LSE 展开第一次有关蔡英文不存在论文的布局。

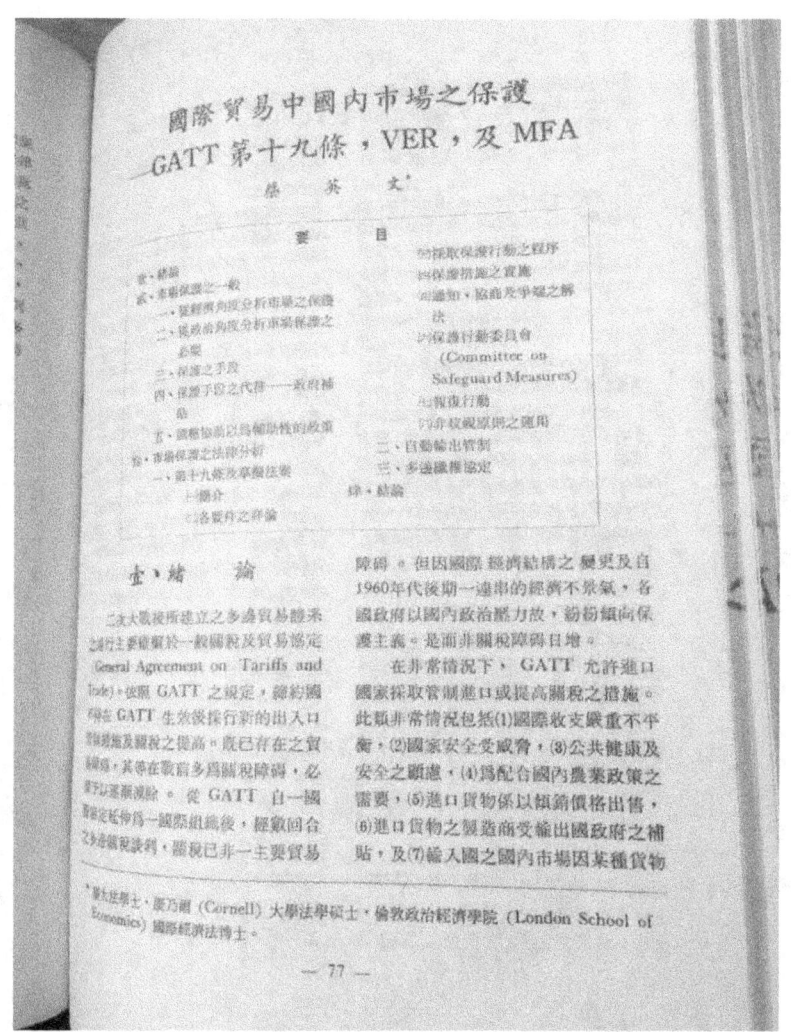

- In June 1983, Tsai Ing-wen published an article in the Law Journal of National Chengchi University in Taiwan. At that time, she hadn't even submitted her claimed doctoral thesis to the London School of Economics and Political Science (LSE) yet, but she identified herself as a Doctor of International Economic Law from LSE in the journal. This entire article was translated verbatim into a chapter of her so-called doctoral thesis.

- 蔡英文在 1983 年 6 月发表一篇文章在台湾国立政治大学法学期刊上，当时她甚至连其声称在伦敦政经学院的博士论文都还没提交，就在国立政治大学法学期刊上自称为伦敦政经学院国际经济法博士，这整篇文章一字不漏地原文翻译成她所谓博士论文中的一个章节。

- On October 20, 1983, Tsai Ing-wen submitted an article titled "On the Anti-Dumping Tax for Our Color TVs Exported to the US" to the United Daily News in Taiwan, identifying herself as a Doctor of International Economic Law from the London School of Economics and Political Science (LSE). However, this was just four days after LSE claimed she had attended her doctoral Viva examination on October 16, 1983.
- 1983年10月20日，蔡英文在台湾以"从我彩视机输美谈反倾销税"为题投稿《联合报》自称伦敦政经学院国际经济法博士，但这个时刻距离伦敦政经学院称她参加博士Viva口试的1983年10月16日仅过四天。

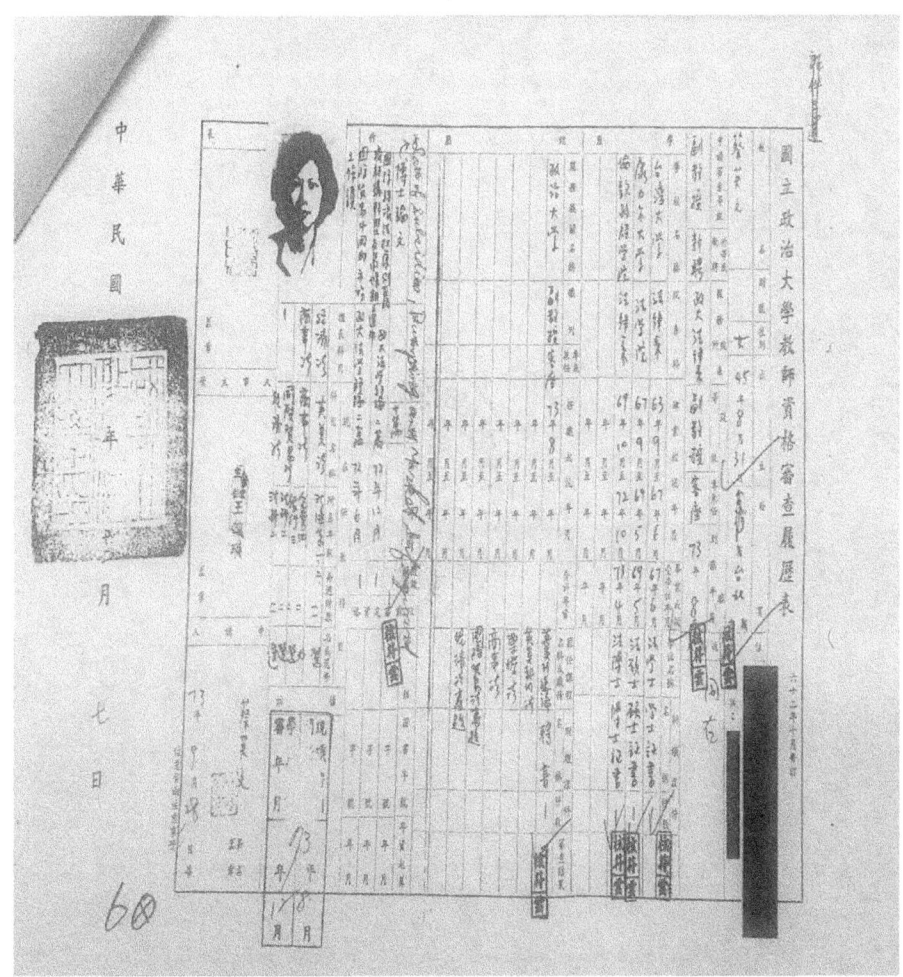

- Due to Tsai Ing-wen's sealing of her curriculum vitae and promotion materials from National Chengchi University, Professor Emeritus He Defen of the College of Law at National Taiwan University filed an administrative lawsuit against the Ministry of Education. As a result, she obtained Tsai Ing-wen's teacher qualification review CV from September 1984. At that time, the doctoral thesis title filled out by Tsai Ing-wen herself was "Law of Subsidies, Dumping, and Market Safeguards," not "Unfair Trade Practices and Safeguard Actions."

- 因蔡英文封存自己的国立政治大学履历表与升等资料，国立台湾大学法学院名誉教授贺德芬对教育部进行行政诉讼，取得蔡英文 1984 年 9 月的教师资格审查履历表，当时蔡英文自己填的博士论文题目为《Law of Subsidies, Dumping, and Market Safeguards》，而非《Unfair Trade Practices and Safeguard Actions》

- In her book "洋葱炒蛋与小英便当," published on October 25, 2011, Tsai Ing-wen wrote that the title of her doctoral thesis was: "Unfair Trade Practices and Safeguard for Domestic Market."

- 蔡英文于 2011 年 10 月 25 日出版的《洋葱炒蛋与小英便当》书中写的自己的博士论文题目为《Unfair Trade Practices and Safeguard for Domestic Market》

- In Tsai Ing-wen's autobiography 〞洋葱炒蛋与小英便当 ,〞there is a photo of her with her elder sister, Tsai Ying-ling. The caption reads: "For my doctoral thesis defense, my sister specially flew to the UK to accompany me." However, in 2019, netizens identified the background of the photo, including the streetlights and vehicles, and accurately determined that the location was St. Paul's Cathedral in Boston, USA. Tsai Ing-wen promptly changed the caption in the e-book version of her autobiography to: "A photo with my elder sister, Tsai Ying-ling."
- 蔡英文的自传《洋葱炒蛋与小英便当》有一张与姊姊蔡英玲的合照，图说上写着："博士论文口试，姊姊特地飞来英国陪我"。结果 2019 年，网友靠着照片背景中的路灯与车辆，正确的搜寻出拍摄地点为美国波士顿圣保罗大教堂，蔡英文立刻将自己自传的电子书图说改为："我与大姊蔡英玲合照"。

- In June 2019, Tsai Ing-wen placed her so-called "thesis" in the Women's Library of the London School of Economics (LSE) for public viewing. However, there were strict restrictions on accessing it. When interviewed by the media, Tsai Ing-wen expressed surprise, saying, "Is that so?" indicating she was unaware of the situation. Yet, the tummy band on Tsai Ing-wen's "thesis" at LSE clearly stated that the restrictions were imposed by the author herself.
- 2019 年 6 月蔡英文将自己的所谓"论文"放到伦敦政经学院妇女图书馆供大众阅览,但借阅却有十分严格的限制,蔡英文在接受媒体访问时惊讶表示:"不会是吧。"说明自己并不知情,但伦敦政经学院的蔡英文"论文"书腰却明确的表示这是来自作者的限制。

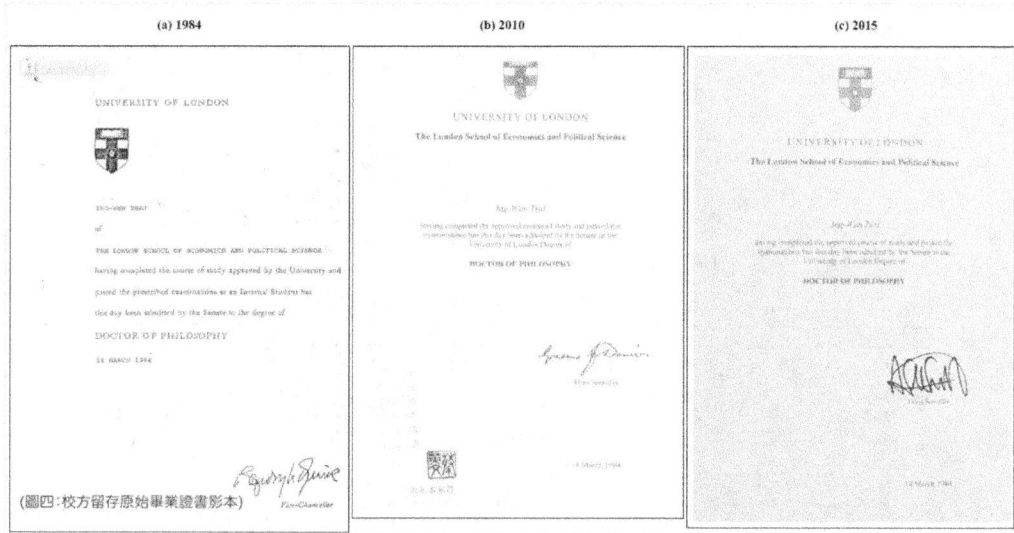

- Despite the clear regulations of the University of London that a doctoral degree certificate can only be reissued once in a lifetime and that an application requires a notarized statement of loss, Tsai Ing-wen has had her degree certificate reissued twice, resulting in three certificates in total.
- 尽管伦敦大学有明确的规定，博士毕业证书一生只能补发一次，而且申请时必须先去公证遗失。但蔡英文却出现三张毕业证书补发两次的情况。

(圖二：LSE學生紀錄)

- On September 4, 2019, the Taiwan Presidential Office Spokesperson's Office posted Tsai Ing-wen's student record on Facebook. The remarks clearly indicated that Tsai Ing-wen "withdrew from the course" on November 10, 1982. Additionally, there were no records of fees paid or a Supervisor for her in 1983.

- 总统府发言人室于 2019 年 9 月 4 日脸书上丢出蔡英文的学生记录表，备注明确表示蔡英文于 1982 年 11 月 10 日 withdraw from course，1983 年也没有缴费记录与指导老师。

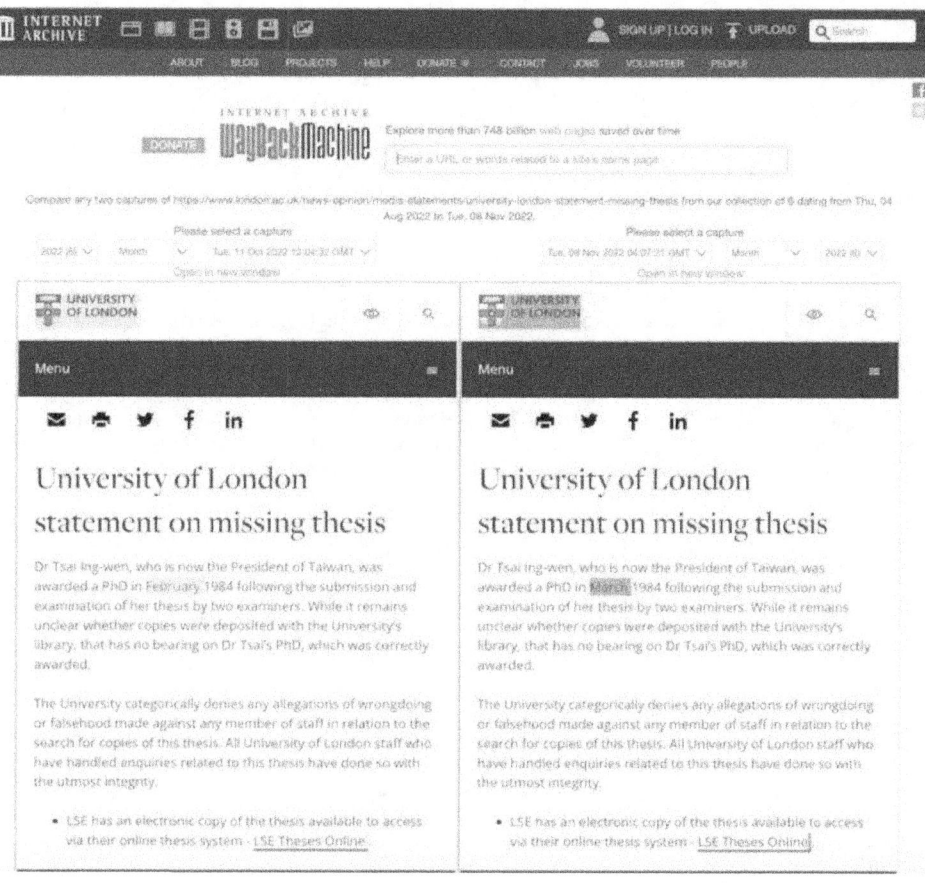

- In February 2022, the University of London issued a statement regarding Tsai Ing-wen's missing thesis. Initially, they claimed that Tsai Ing-wen obtained her degree in February 1984. However, it was later discovered that the webpage was discreetly altered to state March 1984.
- 伦敦大学于 2022 年 2 月曾经替蔡英文消失的论文发出一篇声明，第一时间指称蔡英文于 1984 年 2 月取得学位，但随后被发现网页偷偷更改为 1984 年 3 月。

In considering this balancing test, I have taken into account the following factors:

- the potential harm or distress that disclosure may cause
- whether the information is already in the public domain
- whether the information is already known to some individuals
- whether the individual expressed concern to the disclosure; and
- the reasonable expectations of the individual.

In my view, a key issue is whether the individual concerned has a reasonable expectation that their information will not be disclosed. These expectations can be shaped by factors such as an individual's general expectation of privacy, whether the information relates to an employee in their professional role or to them as individuals, and the purpose for which they provided their personal data.

The requested information is associated with an individual in a private/personal capacity. I am satisfied that the individual concerned (the student) would have the reasonable expectation that their personal data – that is, specific information about their thesis – who examined it and when - would not be disclosed to world at large in response to a FOI request.

I consider it likely that disclosing this information would cause that individual a degree of damage or distress.

You have not presented an argument for the information's disclosure that is sufficiently compelling to override the data subject's rights and freedoms.

You have also noted that UL did not discuss the matter of the examiners' personal data. However, as the regulator whose role is to safeguard personal data, the Commissioner will actively consider whether releasing information would disclose anyone's personal data – whether a public authority has considered it or not. In this case, releasing the information you have requested would disclose the examiners' personal data (their names). Again, I am satisfied that they would not expect this to be disclosed in response to a FOIA request and that disclosure would not be lawful.

Having therefore considered all the circumstances, I consider that your legitimate interest in the information in question is insufficient to outweigh the data subjects' fundamental rights and freedoms. I therefore consider that there is no Article 6 basis for processing and so the disclosure of the information would not be lawful.

Given the above conclusion that disclosure would be unlawful, it is not necessary to separately consider whether disclosure would be fair or transparent.

- 2020.3.23 ICO 英国资讯办公室，回复 Michael Richardson 询问蔡英文口试委员 FOIA 询问，ICO 答复"公布口试委员会造成蔡英文的痛苦与伤害。"

> Records Management, 11 January 2022
>
> Dear Li Xing Chen
>
> Many thanks for your patience in waiting for an answer to your request during our University closure period.
>
> I am sorry but the University of London does not hold any information relating to information held by LSE about Ing-Wen Tsai. I am unable to give you any information in response to your questions about this.
>
> The primary record for PhD awards is held by the Member Institution, not the University of London.
>
> Kind regards
>
> Suzie Mereweather
> Head of Data Protection and Information Compliance
>
> University of London Senate House
> Malet Street London WC1E 7HU UK
> [email address]
> +44 (0)20 7862 5844 www.london.ac.uk
>
> show quoted sections

https://www.whatdotheyknow.com/request/did_rachael_maguire_of_lse_get_trincom   Link to this   Report

- 2022.1.11 伦敦大学资讯保护经理 Suzie Mereweather 在 WDTK 对外公开回应伦敦大学是否有蔡英文的博士口试相关资讯。伦敦大学否认并表示是由机构成员保存。

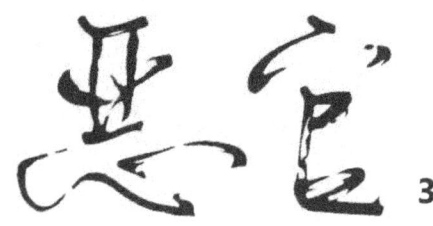

论文门关系人物列表

Daniel Gulliford 丹尼尔·古利福德

Admin Assistant | Directorate (Former)
ASCRU Administrator and NIHR SSCR Capacity-Building Officer | CPEC (Present)
The London School of Economics and Political Science
Houghton Street, London WC2A 2AE
t: +44 (0)20 7852 3601
e: D.J.Gulliford@lse.ac.uk
时任伦敦政经学院　董事会 | 行政助理
现任 LSE 成人社会关怀政策研究室管理员与社会关怀研究学院能力建构办事员
伦敦霍顿街 WC2A 2AE
电话：+44 (0)20 7852 3601
电子邮件：D.J.Gulliford@lse.ac.uk

Baroness Minouche Shafik 米努什·莎菲克男爵夫人

President of the London School
of Economics and Political Science
(Sep. 2017~June. 2023)
President of Columbia University (Jul. 2023~Present)
时任伦敦政经学院院长 (2017 年 9 月至 2023 年 6 月)
现任哥伦比亚大学校长 (2023 年 7 月至今)

Nicola Wright 妮可拉·莱特

Director of LSE Library (Jan. 2015 - Dec. 2022)
LSE Library
10 Portugal Street London WC2A 2HD
e: n.c.wright@lse.ac.uk
伦敦政经学院图书馆 | 图书馆馆长
（2015 年 1 月 - 2022 年 12 月）
伦敦葡萄牙街 10 号 WC2A 2HD
电子邮件：n.c.wright@lse.ac.uk

Fang-long Shih 施芳珑

Co-Director, Taiwan Research Programme
The London School of Economics and Political Science
Houghton Street, London WC2A 2AE
伦敦政经学院 | 台湾研究计画室共同主任
伦敦霍顿街 WC2A 2AE

Shuma Begum 苏玛·贝格姆

Research Degrees Officer | PhD Academy
The London School of Economics and Political Science
Houghton Street London WC2A 2AE
伦敦政经学院 博士生学院 | 研究学位办事员
伦敦霍顿街 WC2A 2AE

Sue Donnelly 苏·唐纳利

LSE Archivist | Secretary`s Division
The London School of Economics and Political Science
Houghton Street, London WC2A 2AE
t: +44 (0)20 7955 2840
e: s.donnelly@lse.ac.uk
伦敦政经学院 秘书部门 | 档案管理员
伦敦霍顿街 WC2A 2AE
电话： +44 (0)20 7955 2840
电子邮件：s.donnelly@lse.ac.uk

Liz Jaggs 利兹·贾格斯

Head of Executive Support (Feb. 2019 - Nov. 2022)
Head of Communications (Jun. 2022 - Present)
LSE Philanthropy and Global Engagement
Houghton Street, London WC2A 2AE
t: +44 (0)20 7955 7783
e: l.jaggs@lse.ac.uk
伦敦政经学院 慈善事业与全球交流部门 |
时任行政支援主管（2019 年 2 月 - 2022 年 11 月），
现任传讯主管（2022 年 6 月至今）
伦敦霍顿街 WC2A 2AE
电话： +44 (0)20 7955 7783
电子邮件：l.jaggs@lse.ac.uk

Simeon Underwood 西米恩·安德伍德

Academic Registrar and Director of Academic
(Retired in 2015)
The London School of Economics and Political Science
Houghton Street, London WC2A 2AE
时任伦敦政经学院 | 教务长（2015年退休）
伦敦霍顿街 WC2A 2AE

Ross Fisher 罗斯·费雪

Digital Content Manager | Communications Division
The London School of Economics and Political Science
(Aug. 2018~Oct. 2010)
Content Editor, Historic England Appointment (Present)
时任伦敦政经学院 通信部门 | 数位内容经理
（2018年8月-2020年10月）
英格兰历史遗产保护局 | 内容编辑(现职)

Simon Hix 赛门·希克斯

Academic Director of LSE (2017 - 2018)
Pro-Director for Research of LSE (2019 - 2021)
EUI Stein Rokkan Chair in Comparative Politics
(2021 - Present)
e: S.Hix@lse.ac.uk
时任伦敦政经学院 教务长（2017年-2018年），
伦敦政经学院 研究副院长（2019年-2021年）
现任欧洲大学学院史坦洛肯比较政治学主席(2021年至今)
电子邮件：S.Hix@lse.ac.uk

Louisa Green 路易莎·格林

Research Degrees Manager of LSE (Former)
Executive Director for Student Services of Kingston University (Present)
时任伦敦政经学院 | 学位研究经理
现任英国金斯顿大学学生服务执行总监

Daniel O'Connor 丹尼尔·奥康纳

Head of Media Relations | Communications Division
The London School of Economics and Political Science
Houghton Street, London WC2A 2AE
t: +44 (0)20 7955 7417
e: d.o'connor@lse.ac.uk
伦敦政经学院 通讯事业部 | 媒体关系部门负责人
伦敦霍顿街 WC2A 2AE
电话：+44 (0)20 7955 7417
电子邮件：d.o'connor@lse.ac.uk

Mark Thomson 马克·汤姆森

Academic Registrar | Academic Registrar's Division
The London School of Economics and Political Science
Houghton Street, London WC2A 2AE
e: m.t.thomson@lse.ac.uk
伦敦政经学院 学术注册部门 | 学术注册职员
伦敦霍顿街 WC2A 2AE
电子邮件： m.t.thomson@lse.ac.uk

Clive Wilson 克莱夫·威尔逊

Enquiry Services Manager | Academic Services
LSE Library
10 Portugal Street London WC2A 2HD
t: +44 (0)2079227475
e: clive.wilson@lse.ac.uk
伦敦政经学院 咨询服务经理（学术服务）
伦敦霍顿街 WC2A 2AE
电话：+44 (0)2079227475
电子邮件：clive.wilson@lse.ac.uk

Charlotte Kelloway 夏洛特·凯洛韦

Media Relations Manager | Communications Division
The London School of Economics and Political Science
Houghton Street, London WC2A 2AE
t: +44 (0)20 7955 6558
e: c.kelloway@lse.ac.uk
伦敦政经学院 通讯事业部 | 媒体关系经理
伦敦霍顿街 WC2A 2AE
电话：+44 (0)20 7955 6558
电子邮件：c.kelloway@lse.ac.uk

Fiona Metcalfe 费欧娜·梅特卡夫

Director of Communications | Communications Division
The London School of Economics and Political Science
Houghton Street, London WC2A 2AE
t: +44 (0)20 3486 2892
e: f.metcalfe@lse.ac.uk
伦敦政经学院 通讯事业部 | 传讯处长
伦敦霍顿街 WC2A 2AE
电话：+44 (0)20 3486 2892
电子邮件：f.metcalfe@lse.ac.uk,

Nancy Graham 南西·格林汉

Associate Director | Collections and Academic Services
LSE Library
10 Portugal Street, London WC2A 2HD
e: n.graham1@lse.ac.uk
伦敦政经学院图书馆 收藏和学术服务 | 副馆长
伦敦葡萄牙街 10 号 WC2A 2HD
电子邮件： n.graham1@lse.ac.uk

Alex Huang 黄重谚

Spokesperson of the President
Office of the President, ROC (Taiwan)
No.122, Sec.1, Chongqing S. Rd, Taipei City, Taiwan
中华民国（台湾）总统府 | 副秘书长（时任总统府发言人）
台湾台北市重庆南路一段 122 号

Remi Adeyemi 雷米·阿德耶米

Executive Assistant to the Academic Registrar | Academic Registrar's Division
The London School of Economics and Political Science
Houghton Street, London WC2A 2AE
t: +44 (0)20 7955 7121
e: r.adeyemi@lse.ac.uk
伦敦政经学院 学术注册处 | 学术注册官行政助理
伦敦霍顿街 WC2A 2AE
电话：+44 (0)20 7955 7121
电子邮件：r.adeyemi@lse.ac.uk

Marcus Cerny 马库斯·切尼

Deputy Director ｜ PhD Academy (Nov. 2016~Nov. 2021)
The London School of Economics and Political Science
Houghton Street London WC2A 2AE
e: m.w.cerny@lse.ac.uk
伦敦政经学院 博士生学院 ｜ 副院长
（2016 年 11 月至 2021 年 11 月）
伦敦霍顿街 WC2A 2AE
电子邮件：m.w.cerny@lse.ac.uk

Beth Clark 贝丝·克拉克

Associate Director ｜ Digital Scholarship and Innovation
LSE Library
10 Portugal Street London WC2A 2HD
e: b.clark1@lse.ac.uk
伦敦政经学院图书馆　数位学术与创新 ｜ 副馆长
伦敦葡萄牙街 10 号 WC2A 2HD
电子邮件；　b.clark1@lse.ac.uk

Ruth Orson 路得·奥森

Library Assistant, Research Support Services |
LSE Research Online
LSE Library
10 Portugal Street, London WC2A 2HD
t: +44 (0)020 7955 3528
e: R.Orson@lse.ac.uk
伦敦政经学院图书馆 研究支援处 | 图书馆助理
伦敦葡萄牙街 10 号 WC2A 2HD
电话：+44 (0)20 7955 3528
电子邮件：R.Orson@lse.ac.uk

Kevin Haynes 凯文·海恩斯

Head of Legal Team | Legal Team, Secretary's Division
The London School of Economics and Political Science
Houghton Street, London WC2A 2AE
t: +44 (0)20 79557823
e: K.J.Haynes@lse.ac.uk
伦敦政经学院 秘书部门法务团队 | 法律团队负责人
伦敦霍顿街 WC2A 2AE
电话：+44 (0)20 79557823
电子邮件：K.J.Haynes@lse.ac.uk

Refel Ismail 拉斐尔·伊斯迈尔

Senior Legal Counsel | Legal Team, Secretary`s Division
The London School of Economics and Political Science
Houghton Street, London WC2A 2AE
t: +44 (0)20 7955 6171
e: r.ismail@lse.ac.uk
伦敦政经学院 秘书部门法务团队 | 资深法律顾问
伦敦霍顿街 WC2A 2AE
电话：+44 (0)20 7955 6171
电子邮件：r.ismail@lse.ac.uk

Chris Kendrick 克里斯·肯卓克

Deputy Director of Alumni & Supporter Engagement |
LSE Philanthropy and Global Engagement
The London School of Economics and Political Science
Houghton Street, London WC2A 2AE
t:+44 (0)20 7107 5200
e: c.kendrick@lse.ac.uk
伦敦政经学院
慈善事业与全球交流部门 | 校方与赞助人交流副处长
伦敦霍顿街 WC2A 2AE
电话：+44 (0)20 7107 5200
电子邮件：c.kendrick@lse.ac.uk

Jessica Winterstein 洁西卡·温特斯坦

Deputy Head of Media Relations ｜ Media Relations team
The London School of Economics and Political Science
Houghton Street, London WC2A 2AE
t: +44 (0)20 7107 5025
e: j.winterstein@lse.ac.uk
伦敦政经学院 媒体关系团队｜媒体关系副主管
伦敦霍顿街 WC2A 2AE
电话：+44 (0)20 7107 5025
电子邮件：j.winterstein@lse.ac.uk

Sue Windebank 苏·温德班克

Senior Media Relations Manager ｜ Media Relations team
The London School of Economics and Political Science
Houghton Street, London WC2A 2AE
t: +44 (0)20 7849 4624
e: s.windebank@lse.ac.uk
伦敦政经学院 媒体关系团队｜资深媒体关系经理
伦敦霍顿街 WC2A 2AE
电话：+44 (0)20 7849 4624
电子邮件：s.windebank@lse.ac.uk

Joanna Bale 乔安纳·贝尔

Senior Media Relations Manager | Media Relations team
The London School of Economics and Political Science
Houghton Street, London WC2A 2AE
t: +44 (0)20 7955 7440
e: j.m.bale@lse.ac.uk
伦敦政经学院 媒体关系团队 | 资深媒体关系经理
伦敦霍顿街 WC2A 2AE
电话：+44 (0)20 7955 7440
电子邮件：j.m.bale@lse.ac.uk

Marta Gajewska 玛塔·盖耶斯卡

Executive Assistant to Baroness Minouche Shafik, LSE Director (Feb. 2019 - Oct. 2021)
Executive Manager CEO Office of The Association of Commonwealth Universities (Present)
时任伦敦政经学院校长执行助理
（2019 年 2 月至 2021 年 10 月）
现任大英国协大学协会执行长室高阶主管

Simeon Underwood 西米恩·安德伍德

Academic Registrar and Director of Academic
(Retired in 2015)
The London School of Economics and Political Science
Houghton Street, London WC2A 2AE
伦敦政经学院 | 教务长（2015 年退休）
伦敦霍顿街 WC2A 2AE

Rachael Maguire 蕾秋·马奎尔

Information and Records Manager | Secretary's Division
The London School of Economics and Political Science
t: +44(0)20 7849 4622
e: R.E.Maguire@lse.ac.uk
伦敦政经学院 秘书部门 | 资讯暨记录经理
伦敦霍顿街 WC2A 2AE
电话：+44(0)20 7849 4622
电子邮件：R.E.Maguire@lse.ac.uk

Mike Pearson 麦克·皮尔森

Head of Digital | Communications Division
(Sep. 2018 - Mar. 2022)
The London School of Economics and Political Science
Houghton Street, London WC2A 2AE
e: m.k.pearson@lse.ac.uk
时任伦敦政经学院通信部门数位主管
（2018 年 9 月 - 2022 年 3 月）
伦敦霍顿街 WC2A 2AE
电子邮件：m.k.pearson@lse.ac.uk

Inderbir Bhullar 因德尔比尔·布拉尔

Curator for Economics and Social Policy
LSE Library
10 Portugal Street London WC2A 2HD
e: i.bhullar@lse.ac.uk
伦敦政经学院图书馆 经济与社会政策馆长
伦敦葡萄牙街 10 号 WC2A 2HD
电子邮件：i.bhullar@lse.ac.uk

Louise Nadal 路易斯·纳达尔

School Secretary | Secretary's Division
The London School of Economics and Political Science
Houghton Street, London WC2A 2AE
t: +44(0)20 7849 4959
e: L.Nadal@lse.ac.uk
伦敦政经学院 秘书部门 | 学校秘书
伦敦霍顿街 WC2A 2AE
电话：+44(0)20 7849 4959
电子邮件：L.Nadal@lse.ac.uk

Maria Bell 玛丽亚·贝尔

Learning Support Services Manager
LSE Library
10 Portugal Street London WC2A 2HD
e: m.bell@lse.ac.uk
伦敦政经学院图书馆 学习支援服务经理
伦敦葡萄牙街 10 号 WC2A 2HD
电子邮件：m.bell@lse.ac.uk

Heather Dawson 海瑟·道森

Librarian
LSE Library
10 Portugal Street London WC2A 2HD
e: h.dawson@lse.ac.uk
伦敦政经学院图书馆 | 图书管理员
伦敦葡萄牙街 10 号 WC2A 2HD
电子邮件：h.dawson@lse.ac.uk

Andra Fry 安卓雅·福莱

Information Specialist
LSE Library
10 Portugal Street London WC2A 2HD
e: a.e.fry@lse.ac.uk
伦敦政经学院图书馆 | 资讯专员
伦敦葡萄牙街 10 号 WC2A 2HD
电子邮件：a.e.fry@lse.ac.uk

Sonia Gomes 索尼亚·葛姆斯

Librarian
LSE Library
10 Portugal Street London WC2A 2HD
e: s.gomes@lse.ac.uk
伦敦政经学院图书馆 | 图书管理员
伦敦葡萄牙街 10 号 WC2A 2HD
电子邮件：s.gomes@lse.ac.uk

Anna Towlson 安娜·托尔森

Archives and Special Collections Manager
LSE Library
10 Portugal Street London WC2A 2HD
伦敦政经学院图书馆 | 档案与特藏经理
伦敦葡萄牙街 10 号 WC2A 2HD

Dr Paul Horsler 保罗·霍斯勒博士

Librarian LSE Library
10 Portugal Street London WC2A 2HD
e: p.n.horsler@lse.ac.uk
伦敦政经学院图书馆 | 图书管理员
伦敦葡萄牙街 10 号 WC2A 2HD
电子邮件：p.n.horsler@lse.ac.uk

Ridhwaan Hussain 里德万·胡笙

Financial Planning Analyst ǀ Financial Division
The London School of Economics and Political Science
Houghton Street, London WC2A 2AE
e: R.Hussain2@lse.ac.uk
伦敦政经学院 财务部门 ǀ 财务规划分析师
伦敦霍顿街 WC2A 2AE
电子邮件：R.Hussain2@lse.ac.uk

Dr Gillian Murphy 吉莲·墨菲博士

Curator for Equality, Rights and Citizenship
LSE Library
10 Portugal Street London WC2A 2HD
e: g.e.murphy@lse.ac.uk
伦敦政经学院图书馆 ǀ 平等、人权与公民权馆长
伦敦葡萄牙街 10 号 WC2A 2HD
电子邮件：g.e.murphy@lse.ac.uk

Ellen Wilkinson 艾伦·威尔金森

Librarian
LSE Library
10 Portugal Street London WC2A 2HD
e: e.wilkinson@lse.ac.uk
伦敦政经学院图书馆 ǀ 图书管理员
伦敦葡萄牙街 10 号 WC2A 2HD
电子邮件：e.wilkinson@lse.ac.uk

Professor Rita Astuti 丽塔·阿斯图蒂教授

Professor of Social Anthropology |
Department of Anthropology
The London School of Economics and Political Science
Houghton Street, London WC2A 2AE
e: r.astuti@lse.ac.uk
伦敦政经学院　人类学系 | 社会人类学教授
伦敦霍顿街 WC2A 2AE
电子邮件：r.astuti@lse.ac.uk

Professor Max Schulze 马克思·舒兹教授

Professor of Economic History |
Department of Economic History
The London School of Economics and Political Science
Houghton Street, London WC2A 2AE
t: +44 (0)2 7955 6784
e: m.s.schulze@lse.ac.uk
伦敦政经学院 经济史系 | 经济史教授
伦敦霍顿街 WC2A 2AE
电话：+44 (0)2 7955 6784
电子邮件：m.s.schulze@lse.ac.uk

Nicola Foster 妮可拉·佛斯特

Department Manager (interim) |
School of Public Policy
The London School of Economics and Political Science
Houghton Street, London WC2A 2AE
e: N.K.Foster@lse.ac.uk
伦敦政经学院 公共政策学院 | 部门经理（暂代）
伦敦霍顿街 WC2A 2AE
电子邮件：N.K.Foster@lse.ac.uk

Matthew Brack 马修·布拉克

PhD Academy | Assistant Director
The London School of Economics and Political Science
Houghton Street, London WC2A 2AE
e: m.brack@lse.ac.uk
伦敦政经学院 博士生学院 | 助理院长
伦敦霍顿街 WC2A 2AE
电子邮件：m.brack@lse.ac.uk

结语

在这《恶官 III》出版的同时（2023 年 11 月），蔡英文仍然在台湾担任她任期最后半年的总统，伦敦政经学院院长莎菲克（Nemat "Minouche" Shafik）去了美国哥伦比亚大学担任校长，其他在这个台湾英国联合学术诈骗丑闻中，扮演装聋作哑、制造伪证、欺骗说谎和湮灭证据的人，现在都还在台北和伦敦，穿着 Burberry 的风衣，过着他们岁月静好，平庸而且邪恶的日子……

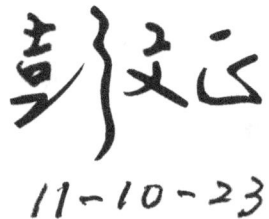

11-10-23

www.ingramcontent.com/pod-product-compliance
Lightning Source LLC
Chambersburg PA
CBHW081226080526
44587CB00022B/3845